STAGE PLAYS FROM THE CLASSICS

Stage Plays
from
the Classics

*One-act adaptations from
famous short stories, novels,
and plays*

by JOELLEN BLAND

Boston   PLAYS, INC.   *Publishers*

Library of Congress Cataloging-in-Publication Data

Bland, Joellen.
  Stage plays from the classics.

    One-act stage adaptations of famous short stories, novels, and plays. Includes "The Prince and the Pauper," "Nicholas Nickleby," and "Frankenstein."
    1. Children's plays, American. 2. Stage adaptations. 3. Plays. 3. Stage adaptations. I. Title.
  PS3552.L36543 1987   812'.54   87-14669
          ISBN 0-8238-0281-7

Manufactured in the United States of America

CONTENTS

STAGE PLAYS FROM THE CLASSICS

The Prince and the Pauper

by Mark Twain

Characters

EDWARD, PRINCE OF WALES
TOM CANTY, *the Pauper*
LORD HERTFORD
LORD ST. JOHN
KING HENRY VIII
HERALD
MILES HENDON
JOHN CANTY, *Tom's father*
HUGO, *a young thief*
TWO WOMEN
JUSTICE
CONSTABLE
JAILER
SIR HUGH HENDON
TWO PRISONERS
TWO GUARDS
THREE PAGES
LORDS AND LADIES
VILLAGERS

SCENE 1

TIME: *1547.*

SETTING: *Westminster Palace, England. Gates leading to courtyard are at right. Slightly to the left, off courtyard and inside
gates, interior of palace anteroom is visible. There is a couch
with a rich robe draped on it, screen at rear, bellcord, mirror,
chairs, and a table with bowl of nuts, and a large golden seal
on it. Piece of armor hangs on one wall. Exits are rear and
downstage.*

AT RISE: TWO GUARDS—*one at right, one at left—stand in front
of gates, and several* VILLAGERS *hover nearby, straining to
see into courtyard where* PRINCE *may be seen through fence,
playing.* TWO WOMEN *enter right.*

1ST WOMAN: I have walked all morning just to have a glimpse of
Westminster Palace.

2ND WOMAN: Maybe if we can get near enough to the gates, we
can have a glimpse of the young prince. (TOM CANTY, *dirty
and ragged, comes out of crowd and steps close to gates.*) I
have always dreamed of seeing a real prince! *(Excited, he
presses his nose against gates.)*

1ST GUARD: Mind your manners, you young beggar! *(Seizes* TOM
by collar and sends him sprawling into crowd. VILLAGERS
laugh, as TOM *slowly gets to his feet.)*

PRINCE *(Rushing to gates):* How dare you treat a poor subject of
the King in such a manner! Open the gates and let him in! *(As*
VILLAGERS *see* PRINCE, *they take off their hats and bow low.)*

VILLAGERS *(Shouting together):* Long live the Prince of Wales!
(GUARDS *open gates and* TOM *slowly passes through, as if in a
dream.*)

PRINCE *(To* TOM): You look tired, and you have been treated
cruelly. I am Edward, Prince of Wales. What is your name?

TOM *(Looking around in awe):* Tom Canty, Your Highness.

PRINCE: Come into the palace with me, Tom. (PRINCE *leads* TOM
into anteroom. VILLAGERS *pantomime conversation, and all
but a few exit.*) Where do you live, Tom?

TOM: In the city, Your Highness, in Offal Court.

PRINCE: Offal Court? That is an odd name. Do you have parents?

TOM: Yes, Your Highness.

PRINCE: How does your father treat you?

TOM: If it please you, Your Highness, when I am not able to beg a penny for our supper, he treats me to beatings.

PRINCE *(Shocked)*: What! Beatings? My father is not a calm man, but he does not beat me. *(Looks at* TOM *thoughtfully)* You speak well and have an easy grace. Have you been schooled?

TOM: Very little, Your Highness. A good priest who shares our house in Offal Court has taught me from his books.

PRINCE: Do you have a pleasant life in Offal Court?

TOM: Pleasant enough, Your Highness, save when I am hungry. We have Punch and Judy shows, and sometimes we lads have fights in the street.

PRINCE *(Eagerly)*: I should like that. Tell me more.

TOM: In summer, we run races and swim in the river, and we love to wallow in the mud.

PRINCE *(Sighing, wistfully)*: If I could wear your clothes and play in the mud just once, with no one to forbid me, I think I could give up the crown!

TOM *(Shaking his head)*: And if I could wear your fine clothes just once, Your Highness. . .

PRINCE: Would you like that? Come, then. We shall change places. You can take off your rags and put on my clothes—and I will put on yours. *(He leads* TOM *behind screen, and they return shortly, each wearing the other's clothes.)* Let's look at ourselves in this mirror. *(Leads* TOM *to mirror)*

TOM: Oh, Your Highness, it is not proper for me to wear such clothes.

PRINCE *(Excitedly, as he looks in mirror)*: Heavens, do you not see it? We look like brothers! We have the same features and bearing. If we went about together, dressed alike, there is no one who could say which is the Prince of Wales and which Tom Canty!

TOM (*Drawing back and rubbing his hand*): Your Highness, I am frightened . . . .

PRINCE: Do not worry. (*Seeing* TOM *rub his hand*) Is that a bruise on your hand?

TOM: Yes, but it is a slight thing, Your Highness.

PRINCE (*Angrily*): It was shameful and cruel of that guard to strike you. Do not stir a step until I come back. I command you! (*He picks up golden Seal of England and carefully puts it into piece of armor. He then dashes out to gates.*) Open! Unbar the gates at once! (2ND GUARD *opens gates, and as* PRINCE *runs out, in rags,* 1ST GUARD *seizes him, boxes him on the ear, and knocks him to the ground.*)

1ST GUARD: Take that, you little beggar, for the trouble you have made for me with the Prince. (VILLAGERS *roar with laughter.*)

PRINCE (*Picking himself up, turning on* GUARD *furiously*): I am Prince of Wales! You shall hang for laying your hand on me!

1ST GUARD (*Presenting arms; mockingly*): I salute Your Gracious Highness! (*Then, angrily,* 1ST GUARD *shoves* PRINCE *roughly aside.*) Be off, you mad bag of rags! (PRINCE *is surrounded by* VILLAGERS, *who hustle him off.*)

VILLAGERS (*Ad lib, as they exit, shouting*): Make way for His Royal Highness! Make way for the Prince of Wales! Hail to the Prince! (*Etc.*)

TOM (*Admiring himself in mirror*): If only the boys in Offal Court could see me! They will not believe me when I tell them about this. (*Looks around anxiously*) But where is the Prince? (*Looks cautiously into courtyard.* TWO GUARDS *immediately snap to attention and salute. He quickly ducks back into anteroom as* HERTFORD *and* ST. JOHN *enter at rear.*)

HERTFORD (*Going toward* TOM, *then stopping and bowing low*): My Lord, you look distressed. What is wrong?

TOM (*Trembling*): Oh, I beg of you, be merciful. I am no Prince, but poor Tom Canty of Offal Court. Please let me see the Prince, and he will give my rags back to me and let me go unhurt. (*Kneeling*) Please, be merciful and spare me!

HERTFORD *(Puzzled and disturbed):* Your Highness, on your knees? To me? *(Bows quickly, then, aside to* ST. JOHN*)* The Prince has gone mad! We must inform the King. *(To* TOM*)* A moment, Your Highness. (HERTFORD *and* ST. JOHN *exit rear.)*

TOM: Oh, there is no hope for me now. They will hang me for certain! (HERTFORD *and* ST. JOHN *re-enter, supporting* KING. TOM *watches in awe as they help him to couch, where he sinks down wearily.)*

KING *(Beckoning* TOM *close to him):* Now, my son, Edward, my prince. What is this? Do you mean to deceive me, the King, your father, who loves you and treats you so kindly?

TOM *(Dropping to his knees):* You are the King? Then I have no hope!

KING *(Stunned):* My child, you are not well. Do not break your father's old heart. Say you know me.

TOM: Yes, you are my lord the King, whom God preserve.

KING: True, that is right. Now, you will not deny that you are Prince of Wales, as they say you did just a while ago?

TOM: I beg you, Your Grace, believe me. I am the lowest of your subjects, being born a pauper, and it is by a great mistake that I am here. I am too young to die. Oh, please, spare me, sire!

KING *(Amazed):* Die? Do not talk so, my child. You shall not die.

TOM *(Gratefully):* God save you, my king! And now, may I go?

KING: Go? Where would you go?

TOM: Back to the alley where I was born and bred to misery.

KING: My poor child, rest your head here. *(He holds* TOM'S *head and pats his shoulder, then turns to* HERTFORD *and* ST. JOHN.*)* Alas, I am old and ill, and my son is mad. But this shall pass. Mad or sane, he is my heir and shall rule England. Tomorrow he shall be installed and confirmed in his princely dignity! Bring the Great Seal!

HERTFORD *(Bowing low):* Please, Your Majesty, you took the Great Seal from the Chancellor two days ago to give to His Highness the Prince.

KING: So I did. *(To* TOM*)* My child, tell me, where is the Great Seal?

TOM *(Trembling):* Indeed, my lord, I do not know.

KING: Ah, your affliction hangs heavily upon you. 'Tis no matter. You will remember later. Listen, carefully! *(Gently, but firmly)* I command you to hide your affliction in all ways that be within your power. You shall deny to no one that you are the true prince, and if your memory should fail you upon any occasion of state, you shall be advised by your uncle, the Lord Hertford.

TOM *(Resigned):* The King has spoken. The King shall be obeyed.

KING: And now, my child, I go to rest. *(He stands weakly, and* HERTFORD *leads him off, rear.)*

TOM *(Wearily, to* ST. JOHN): May it please your lordship to let me rest now?

ST. JOHN: So it please Your Highness, it is for you to command and us to obey. But it is wise that you rest, for this evening you must attend the Lord Mayor's banquet in your honor. *(He pulls bellcord, and* THREE PAGES *enter and kneel before* TOM.)

TOM: Banquet? *(Terrified, he sits on couch and reaches for cup of water, but* 1ST PAGE *instantly seizes cup, drops on one knee, and serves it to him.* TOM *starts to take off his boots, but* 2ND PAGE *stops him and does it for him. He tries to remove his cape and gloves, and* 3RD PAGE *does it for him.)* I wonder that you do not try to breathe for me also! *(Lies down cautiously.* PAGES *cover him with robe, then back away and exit.)*

ST. JOHN *(To* HERTFORD, *as he enters):* Plainly, what do you think?

HERTFORD: Plainly, this. The King is near death, my nephew the Prince of Wales is clearly mad and will mount the throne mad. God protect England, for she will need it!

ST. JOHN: Does it not seem strange that madness could so change his manner from what it used to be? It troubles me, his saying he is not the Prince.

HERTFORD: Peace, my lord! If he were an impostor and called himself Prince, that would be natural. But was there ever an impostor, who being called Prince by the King and court, denied it? Never! This is the true Prince gone mad. And tonight all London shall honor him. (HERTFORD *and* ST. JOHN *exit.* TOM *sits up, looks around helplessly, then gets up.*)

TOM: I should have thought to order something to eat. *(Sees bowl of nuts on table)* Ah! Here are some nuts! *(Looks around, sees Great Seal in armor, takes it out, looks at it curiously.)* This will make a good nutcracker. *(He takes bowl of nuts, sits on couch and begins to crack nuts with Great Seal and eat them, as curtain falls.)*

*   *   *   *   *

SCENE 2

TIME: *Later that night.*

SETTING: *A street in London, near Offal Court. Played before the curtain.*

AT RISE: PRINCE *limps in, dirty and tousled. He looks around wearily. Several* VILLAGERS *pass by, pushing against him.*

PRINCE: I have never seen this poor section of London. I must be near Offal Court. If I can only find it before I drop! (JOHN CANTY *steps out of crowd, seizes* PRINCE *roughly.*)

CANTY: Out at this time of night, and I warrant you haven't brought a farthing home! If that is the case and I do not break all the bones in your miserable body, then I am not John Canty!

PRINCE *(Eagerly):* Oh, are you his father?

CANTY: *His* father? I am *your* father, and—

PRINCE: Take me to the palace at once, and your son will be returned to you. The King, my father, will make you rich beyond your wildest dreams. Oh, save me, for I am indeed the Prince of Wales.

CANTY *(Staring in amazement):* Gone stark mad! But mad or not, I'll soon find where the soft places lie in your bones. Come home! *(Starts to drag* PRINCE *off)*

PRINCE *(Struggling):* Let me go! I am the Prince of Wales, and the King shall have your life for this!

CANTY *(Angrily):* I'll take no more of your madness! *(Raises stick to strike, but* PRINCE *struggles free and runs off, and* CANTY *runs after him)*

* * * * *

SCENE 3

SETTING: *Same as Scene 1, with addition of dining table, set with dishes and goblets, on raised platform. Throne-like chair is at head of table.*

AT RISE: *A banquet is in progress.* TOM, *in royal robes, sits at head of table, with* HERTFORD *at his right and* ST. JOHN *at his left.* LORDS *and* LADIES *sit around table eating and talking softly.*

TOM *(To* HERTFORD): What is this, my Lord? *(Holds up a plate)*

HERTFORD: Lettuce and turnips, Your Highness.

TOM: Lettuce and turnips? I have never seen them before. Am I to eat them?

HERTFORD *(Discreetly):* Yes, Your Highness, if you so desire. *(*TOM *begins to eat food with his fingers. Fanfare of trumpets is heard, and* HERALD *enters, carrying scroll. All turn to look.)*

HERALD *(Reading from scroll):* His Majesty, King Henry VIII, is dead! The King is dead! *(All rise and turn to* TOM, *who sits, stunned.)*

ALL *(Together):* The King is dead. Long live the King! Long live Edward, King of England! *(All bow to* TOM. HERALD *bows and exits.)*

HERTFORD *(To* TOM): Your Majesty, we must call the council. Come, St. John. *(*HERTFORD *and* ST. JOHN *lead* TOM *off at rear.* LORDS *and* LADIES *follow, talking among themselves. At gates, down right,* VILLAGERS *enter and mill about.* PRINCE *enters right, pounds on gates and shouts.)*

PRINCE: Open the gates! I am the Prince of Wales! Open, I say! And though I am friendless with no one to help me, I will not be driven from my ground.

MILES HENDON *(Entering through crowd)*: Though you be Prince or not, you are indeed a gallant lad and not friendless. Here I stand to prove it, and you might have a worse friend than Miles Hendon.

1ST VILLAGER: 'Tis another prince in disguise. Take the lad and dunk him in the pond! *(He seizes* PRINCE, *but* MILES *strikes him with flat of his sword. Crowd, now angry, presses forward threateningly, when fanfare of trumpets is heard offstage.* HERALD, *carrying scroll, enters up left at gates.)*

HERALD: Make way for the King's messenger! *(Reading from scroll)* His Majesty, King Henry VIII is dead! The King is dead! *(He exits right, repeating message, and* VILLAGERS *stand in stunned silence.)*

PRINCE *(Stunned)*: The King is dead!

1ST VILLAGER *(Shouting)*: Long live Edward, King of England!

VILLAGERS *(Together)*: Long live the King! *(Shouting, ad lib)* Long live King Edward! Heaven protect Edward, King of England! *(Etc.)*

MILES *(Taking* PRINCE *by the arm)*: Come, lad, before the crowd remembers us. I have a room at the inn, and you can stay there. *(He hurries off with stunned* PRINCE. TOM, *led by* HERTFORD, *enters courtyard up rear.* VILLAGERS *see them.)*

VILLAGERS *(Together)*: Long live the King! *(They fall to their knees as curtains close.)*

* * * * *

SCENE 4

SETTING: *Miles' room at the inn. At right is table set with dishes and bowls of food, a chair at each side. At left is bed, with table and chair next to it, and a window. Candle is on table.*

AT RISE: MILES *and* PRINCE *approach table.*

MILES: I have had a hot supper prepared. I'll bet you're hungry, lad.

PRINCE: Yes, I am. It's kind of you to let me stay with you, Miles. I am truly Edward, King of England, and you shall not go unrewarded. *(Sits at table)*

MILES *(To himself):* First he called himself Prince, and now he is King. Well, I will humor him. *(Starts to sit)*

PRINCE *(Angrily):* Stop! Would you sit in the presence of the King?

MILES *(Surprised, standing up quickly):* I beg your pardon, Your Majesty. I was not thinking. *(Stares uncertainly at* PRINCE, *who sits at table, expectantly.* MILES *starts to uncover dishes of food, serves* PRINCE *and fills glasses.)*

PRINCE: Miles, you have a gallant way about you. Are you nobly born?

MILES: My father is a baronet, Your Majesty.

PRINCE: Then you must also be a baronet.

MILES *(Shaking his head):* My father banished me from home seven years ago, so I fought in the wars. I was taken prisoner, and I have spent the past seven years in prison. Now I am free, and I am returning home.

PRINCE: You have been shamefully wronged! But I will make things right for you. You have saved me from injury and possible death. Name your reward and if it be within the compass of my royal power, it is yours.

MILES *(Pausing briefly, then dropping to his knee):* Since Your Majesty is pleased to hold my simple duty worthy of reward, I ask that I and my successors may hold the privilege of sitting in the presence of the King.

PRINCE *(Taking* MILES' *sword, tapping him lightly on each shoulder):* Rise and seat yourself. *(Returns sword to* MILES, *then rises and goes over to bed)*

MILES *(Rising):* He should have been born a king. He plays the part to a marvel! If I had not thought of this favor, I might have had to stand for weeks. *(Sits down and begins to eat)*

PRINCE: Sir Miles, you will stand guard while I sleep. *(Lies down and instantly falls asleep)*

MILES: Yes, Your Majesty. *(With a rueful look at his uneaten supper, he stands up.)* Poor little chap. I suppose his mind has been disordered with ill usage. *(Covers PRINCE with his cape)* Well, I will be his friend and watch over him. *(Blows out candle, then yawns, sits on chair next to bed, and falls asleep. JOHN CANTY and HUGO appear at window, peer around room, then enter cautiously through window. They lift the sleeping PRINCE, staring nervously at MILES.)*

CANTY *(In loud whisper):* I swore the day he was born he would be a thief and a beggar, and I won't lose him now. Lead the way to the camp, Hugo! (CANTY *and* HUGO *carry* PRINCE *off right, as* MILES *sleeps on and curtain falls.)*

* * * * *

SCENE 5

TIME: *Two weeks later.*

SETTING: *Country village street.*

BEFORE RISE: VILLAGERS *walk about.* CANTY, HUGO, *and* PRINCE *enter.*

CANTY: I will go in this direction. Hugo, keep my mad son with you, and see that he doesn't escape again! *(Exits)*

HUGO *(Seizing PRINCE by the arm):* He won't escape! I'll see that he earns his bread today, or else!

PRINCE *(Pulling away):* I will not beg with you, and I will not steal! I have suffered enough in this miserable company of thieves!

HUGO: You shall suffer more if you do not do as I tell you! *(Raises clenched fist at PRINCE)* Refuse if you dare! (WOMAN *enters, carrying wrapped bundle in a basket on her arm.)* Wait here until I come back. (HUGO *sneaks along after* WOMAN, *then snatches her bundle, runs back to* PRINCE, *and*

thrusts it into his arms.) Run after me and call, "Stop, thief!"
But be sure you lead her astray! (*Runs off.* PRINCE *throws
down bundle in disgust.*)

WOMAN: Help! Thief! Stop, thief! (*Rushes at* PRINCE *and seizes
him, just as several* VILLAGERS *enter)* You little thief! What
do you mean by robbing a poor woman? Somebody bring the
constable! (MILES *enters and watches.*)

1ST VILLAGER (*Grabbing* PRINCE): I'll teach him a lesson, the
little villain!

PRINCE (*Struggling):* Take your hands off me! I did not rob this
woman!

MILES (*Stepping out of crowd and pushing man back with the
flat of his sword):* Let us proceed gently, my friends. This is a
matter for the law.

PRINCE (*Springing to* MILES' *side):* You have come just in time,
Sir Miles. Carve this rabble to rags!

MILES: Speak softly. Trust in me and all shall go well.

CONSTABLE (*Entering and reaching for* PRINCE): Come along,
young rascal!

MILES: Gently, good friend. He shall go peaceably to the Justice.

PRINCE: I will not go before a Justice! I did not do this thing!

MILES (*Taking him aside):* Sire, will you reject the laws of the
realm, yet demand that your subjects respect them?

PRINCE (*Calmer):* You are right, Sir Miles. Whatever the King
requires a subject to suffer under the law, he will suffer
himself while he holds the station of a subject. (CONSTABLE
leads them off right. VILLAGERS *follow. Curtain*)

*   *   *   *   *

SETTING: *Office of the Justice. A high bench is at center.*

AT RISE: JUSTICE *sits behind bench.* CONSTABLE *enters with*
MILES *and* PRINCE, *followed by* VILLAGERS. WOMAN *carries
wrapped bundle.*

CONSTABLE (*To* JUSTICE): A young thief, your worship, is accused of stealing a dressed pig from this poor woman.

JUSTICE *(Looking down at* PRINCE, *then* WOMAN): My good woman, are you absolutely certain this lad stole your pig?

WOMAN: It was none other than he, your worship.

JUSTICE: Are there no witnesses to the contrary? *(All shake their heads.)* Then the lad stands convicted. *(To* WOMAN) What do you hold this property to be worth?

WOMAN: Three shillings and eight pence, your worship.

JUSTICE *(Leaning down to* WOMAN): Good woman, do you know that when one steals a thing above the value of thirteen pence, the law says he shall hang for it?

WOMAN *(Upset):* Oh, what have I done? I would not hang the poor boy for the whole world! Save me from this, your worship. What can I do?

JUSTICE *(Gravely):* You may revise the value, since it is not yet written in the record.

WOMAN: Then call the pig eight pence, your worship.

JUSTICE: So be it. You may take your property and go. (WOMAN *starts off, and is followed by* CONSTABLE. MILES *follows them cautiously down right.)*

CONSTABLE *(Stopping* WOMAN): Good woman, I will buy your pig from you. *(Takes coins from pocket)* Here is eight pence.

WOMAN: Eight pence! It cost me three shillings and eight pence!

CONSTABLE: Indeed! Then come back before his worship and answer for this. The lad must hang!

WOMAN: No! No! Say no more. Give me the eight pence and hold your peace. (CONSTABLE *hands her coins and takes pig.* WOMAN *exits, angrily.* MILES *returns to bench.)*

JUSTICE: The boy is sentenced to a fortnight in the common jail. Take him away, Constable! (JUSTICE *exits.* PRINCE *gives* MILES *a nervous glance.)*

MILES *(Following* CONSTABLE): Good sir, turn your back a moment and let the poor lad escape. He is innocent.

CONSTABLE *(Outraged):* What? You say this to me? Sir, I arrest you in—

MILES: Do not be so hasty! *(Slyly)* The pig you have purchased for eight pence may cost you your neck, man.

CONSTABLE *(Laughing nervously):* Ah, but I was merely jesting with the woman, sir.

MILES: Would the Justice think it a jest?

CONSTABLE: Good sir! The Justice has no more sympathy with a jest than a dead corpse! *(Perplexed)* Very well, I will turn my back and see nothing! But go quickly! *(Exits)*

MILES *(To* PRINCE*):* Come, my liege. We are free to go. And that band of thieves shall not set hands on you again, I swear it!

PRINCE *(Wearily):* Can you believe, Sir Miles, that in the last fortnight, I, the King of England, have escaped from thieves and begged for food on the road? I have slept in a barn with a calf! I have washed dishes in a peasant's kitchen, and narrowly escaped death. And not once in all my wanderings did I see a courier searching for me! Is it no matter for commotion and distress that the head of state is gone?

MILES *(Sadly, aside):* Still busy with his pathetic dream. *(To* PRINCE*)* It is strange indeed, my liege. But come, I will take you to my father's home in Kent. We are not far away. There you may rest in a house with seventy rooms! Come, I am all impatience to be home again! *(They exit,* MILES *in cheerful spirits,* PRINCE *looking puzzled, as curtains close.)*

* * * * *

SCENE 6

SETTING: *Village jail. Bare stage, with barred window on one wall.*

AT RISE: TWO PRISONERS, *in chains, are onstage.* JAILER *shoves* MILES *and* PRINCE, *in chains, onstage. They struggle and protest.*

MILES: But I tell you I *am* Miles Hendon! My brother, Sir Hugh, has stolen my bride and my estate!

JAILER: Be silent! Impostor! Sir Hugh will see that you pay well for claiming to be his dead brother and for assaulting him in his own house! *(Exits)*

MILES *(Sitting, with head in hands):* Oh, my dear Edith . . .
now wife to my brother Hugh, against her will, and my poor
father . . . dead!

1ST PRISONER: At least you have your life, sir. I am sentenced to
be hanged for killing a deer in the King's park.

2ND PRISONER: And I must hang for stealing a yard of cloth to
dress my children.

PRINCE *(Moved; to* PRISONERS*):* When I mount my throne, you
shall all be free. And the laws that have dishonored you shall
be swept from the books. *(Turning away)* Kings should go to
school to learn their own laws and be merciful.

1ST PRISONER: What does the lad mean? I have heard that the
King is mad, but merciful.

2ND PRISONER: He is to be crowned at Westminster tomorrow.

PRINCE *(Violently):* King? What King, good sir?

1ST PRISONER: Why, we have only one, his most sacred majesty,
King Edward the Sixth.

2ND PRISONER: And whether he be mad or not, his praises are
on all men's lips. He has saved many innocent lives, and now
he means to destroy the cruelest laws that oppress the people.

PRINCE *(Turning away, shaking his head):* How can this be?
Surely it is not that little beggar boy! (SIR HUGH *enters with*
JAILER.)

SIR HUGH: Seize the impostor!

MILES *(As* JAILER *pulls him to his feet):* Hugh, this has gone far
enough!

SIR HUGH: You will sit in the public stocks for two hours, and
the boy would join you if he were not so young. See to it, jailer,
and after two hours, you may release them. Meanwhile, I ride
to London for the coronation! (SIR HUGH *exits and* MILES *is
hustled out by* JAILER.)

PRINCE: Coronation! What does he mean? There can be no
coronation without me! *(Curtain falls.)*

*   *   *   *   *

SCENE 7

TIME: *Coronation Day.*

SETTING: *Outside gates of Westminster Abbey, played before curtain. Painted screen or flat at rear represents Abbey. Throne is center. Bench is near it.*

AT RISE: LORDS *and* LADIES *crowd Abbey. Outside gates,* GUARDS *drive back cheering* VILLAGERS, *among them* MILES.

MILES *(Distraught):* I've lost him! Poor little chap! He has been swallowed up in the crowd! *(Fanfare of trumpets is heard, then silence.* HERTFORD, ST. JOHN, LORDS *and* LADIES *enter slowly, in a procession, followed by* PAGES, *one of whom carries crown on small cushion.* TOM *follows procession, looking about nervously. Suddenly,* PRINCE, *in rags, steps out from crowd, his hand raised.)*

PRINCE: I forbid you to set the crown of England upon that head. I am the King!

HERTFORD: Seize the little vagabond!

TOM: I forbid it! He *is* the King! *(Kneels before* PRINCE) Oh, my lord the King, let poor Tom Canty be the first to say, "Put on your crown and enter into your own right again." (HERTFORD *and several* LORDS *look closely at both boys.)*

HERTFORD: This is strange indeed. *(To* TOM) By your favor, sir, I wish to ask certain questons of this lad.

PRINCE: I will answer truly whatever you may ask, my lord.

HERTFORD: But if you have been well trained, you may answer my questions as well as our lord the King. I need a definite proof. *(Thinks a moment)* Ah! Where lies the Great Seal of England? It has been missing for weeks, and only the true Prince of Wales can say where it lies.

TOM: Wait! Was the seal round and thick, with letters engraved on it? (HERTFORD *nods.)* I know where it is, but it was not I who put it there. The rightful King shall tell you. *(To* PRINCE) Think, my King, it was the very last thing you did that day before you rushed out of the palace wearing my rags.

PRINCE *(Pausing):* I recall how we exchanged clothes, but have no recollection of hiding the Great Seal.

TOM *(Eagerly):* Remember when you saw the bruise on my hand, you ran to the door, but first you hid this thing you call the Seal.

PRINCE *(Suddenly):* Ah! I remember! *(To* ST. JOHN*)* Go, my good St. John, and you shall find the Great Seal in the armor that hangs on the wall in my chamber. (ST. JOHN *hesitates, but at a nod from* TOM, *hurries off.)*

TOM *(Pleased):* Right, my King! Now the scepter of England is yours again. (ST. JOHN *returns in a moment with Great Seal.)*

ALL *(Shouting):* Long live Edward, King of England! (TOM *takes off his cape and throws it over* PRINCE's *rags. Trumpet fanfare is heard.* ST. JOHN *takes crown and places it on* PRINCE. *All kneel.)*

HERTFORD: Let the small imposter be flung into the Tower!

PRINCE *(Firmly):* I will not have it so. But for him, I would not have my crown. *(To* TOM*)* My poor boy, how was it that you could remember where I hid the Seal, when I could not?

TOM *(Embarrassed):* I did not know what it was, my King, and I used it to . . . to crack nuts. *(All laugh, and* TOM *steps back.* MILES *steps forward, staring in amazement.)*

MILES: Is he really the King? Is he indeed the sovereign of England, and not the poor and friendless Tom o' Bedlam I thought he was? *(He sinks down on bench.)* I wish I had a bag to hide my head in!

1ST GUARD *(Rushing up to him):* Stand up, you mannerless clown! How dare you sit in the presence of the King!

PRINCE: Do not touch him! He is my trusty servant, Miles Hendon, who saved me from shame and possible death. For his service, he owns the right to sit in my presence.

MILES *(Bowing, then kneeling):* Your Majesty!

PRINCE: Rise, Sir Miles. I command that Sir Hugh Hendon, who sits within this hall, be seized and put under lock and key until I have need of him. *(Beckons to* TOM*)* From what I have heard,

Tom Canty, you have governed the realm with royal gentleness and mercy in my absence. Henceforth, you shall hold the honorable title of King's Ward! (TOM *kneels and kisses* PRINCE's *hand.*) And because I have suffered with the poorest of my subjects and felt the cruel force of unjust laws, I pledge myself to a reign of mercy for all! *(All bow low, then rise.)*

ALL *(Shouting):* Long live the King! Long live Edward, King of England! *(Curtain)*

THE END

PRODUCTION NOTES

THE PRINCE AND THE PAUPER

Characters: 9 male; 2 female; 11 male or female for Herald, Justice, Constable, Jailer, Prisoners, Guards, and Pages; as many male and female extras as desired for Villagers, Lords and Ladies. Actors playing Tom and Prince should resemble each other, if possible.

Playing Time: 30 minutes.

Costumes: Appropriate 16th-century English costume. All court members wear royal robes or rich costumes. Villagers wear ragged or very simple dress. Miles Hendon's cavalier clothes are worn and faded.

Properties: Swords; scroll; basket with wrapped bundle in it; coins; chains; crown on pillow.

Setting: Scene 1: Westminster Palace. Gates are visible at left, and at right, a palace anteroom furnished with a couch and rich robe, screen at rear, bellcord, table, mirror, and chairs. On table are cup, bowl of nuts, and large golden seal. A piece of armor hangs on one wall. Exits are rear and downstage. Scene 2: London street. Played before curtain. Scene 3: Same as Scene 1. Dining table set with dishes and goblets is center, with throne-like chair at head. Scene 4: Miles' room in an inn. Rough table and chairs are center; table is set with covered dishes and mugs. At left is couch or bed with heavy blanket on it; next to it is table with candle on it. There is window in one wall. Scene 5: Justice's office. High bench is at center. Scene 6: Village jail. Bare stage, with barred window on one wall. Scene 7: Outside gates of Westminster Abbey. Painted screen or flat at rear represents the Abbey. Note: Furnishings should be kept to a minimum, and screens used to indicate partitions.

Lighting: If possible, lights should be used to highlight action.

Sound: Trumpet fanfare, as indicated.

Dr. Jekyll and Mr. Hyde

by Robert Louis Stevenson

Characters

MR. UTTERSON, *lawyer*
MR. ENFIELD, *his friend*
DR. HASTIE LANYON
DR. HENRY JEKYLL
MR. EDWARD HYDE
POOLE, *butler*

SCENE 1

TIME: *Mid-nineteenth century.*

SETTING: *London. Divided stage. At far downstage right is a street—with street lamp and park bench—extending across downstage to left. At center right are door and adjoining outside wall of Dr. Jekyll's laboratory. Slightly upstage center and left is laboratory interior, with long counter cluttered with bottles, tubes, and other laboratory apparatus at center, bookshelves along walls, two chairs and small desk down center. Door to rest of house is at left. Other exits are down left and down right.*

AT RISE: MR. EDWARD HYDE, *a stooped, small figure wearing hat low over his eyes and carrying cane, enters left door, crosses laboratory to street door, opens it, looks out cautiously. He steps into street, closing door behind him. With a*

nasty chuckle, he darts off, toward right, just as MR. UTTER-
SON *and* MR. ENFIELD *enter.* HYDE *brushes roughly past
them, knocking them aside.*

ENFIELD (*Seizing* HYDE'*s arm*): I say, sir! Can't you watch
where you are going?

HYDE *(Angrily):* I know where I'm going, and you are in my
way! *(Pulls away)* Take your hands off me!

UTTERSON: Just one moment, sir! You can't go knocking respectable gentlemen about. You owe us an apology.

HYDE: I don't owe you a thing! *(Shaking cane in their faces)*
Now, leave me alone or I'm likely to give you something you
won't like! *(Rushes off right)*

ENFIELD: Here! Come back!

UTTERSON: Nasty fellow! Oh, let him go, Enfield.

ENFIELD *(Thoughtfully):* Utterson, I think I've seen him before. His voice . . . *(Suddenly)* Yes, of course! It must be he.
This is the very door. *(Points to door at center)*

UTTERSON: This door? This is the rear entrance to the laboratory of my good friend and client, Dr. Henry Jekyll.

ENFIELD: So it is, and it is connected with a very odd story.

UTTERSON *(Sitting on bench):* Indeed! Do tell me!

ENFIELD *(Sitting beside him):* I assure you this is unusual, but
true. I was coming home late one night along a street near
here, when I saw two figures approaching from opposite direc-
tions. One was a rather small man, hunched over and walking
briskly with the aid of a cane, and the other a girl of maybe ten
years. Neither saw the other until they ran into each other,
and then, to my horror, the man knocked the child down and
went on his way as calmly as you please!

UTTERSON: Good heavens! You went after him, I'm sure?

ENFIELD: Of course! I collared him and brought him back to
where a crowd had gathered around the screaming child.

UTTERSON: Was she hurt?

ENFIELD: No, but terribly frightened, and her family meant to
make her attacker pay for his deed. They threatened to make
a scandal of the event, and all the while the man stood there

sneering. But he agreed to settle the matter with a hundred pounds. *(After a pause)* Where do you think he went for the money?

UTTERSON: I have no idea.

ENFIELD: Here! To this door. He had a key to it, went inside, and came back with a check signed by Dr. Henry Jekyll.

UTTERSON *(Astounded):* What?

ENFIELD: We all thought it was a forgery and stayed with the fellow until the bank opened the next morning. But the check was genuine. This disgusting, hateful man was in the clear.

UTTERSON: Did you get his name?

ENFIELD: Hyde. Edward Hyde.

UTTERSON *(Startled):* Hyde!

ENFIELD: Do you know him?

UTTERSON: I've heard of him, though today was the first time I've seen him. You see—and I tell you this in the strictest confidence—Jekyll has changed his will and made Edward Hyde his sole heir! Ever since, I've been suspicious. I've known Jekyll for thirty years, but I never heard of Edward Hyde until three months ago.

ENFIELD: I would say you have good grounds for suspicion. (DR. LANYON *enters left.*)

LANYON *(Cheerfully):* Utterson! Enfield! How are you? It's been weeks since I've seen you!

UTTERSON *(Rising; warmly):* Lanyon! Old friends should keep in closer touch. *(Shakes* LANYON's *hand)*

ENFIELD *(Shaking hands):* How are you, Doctor?

UTTERSON: We must all get together over dinner soon, with Henry Jekyll, too.

LANYON: Jekyll? I haven't seen much of him lately.

UTTERSON *(Surprised):* Why, I thought you two often had your heads together.

LANYON: We used to share common medical and scientific interests, but about a year ago, Jekyll began to go wrong.

UTTERSON: What do you mean?

LANYON: As a young man, Jekyll often dabbled in wild and

bizarre experiments, but as he grew older, he started taking his work seriously. Then, suddenly, he started in again on this unscientific balderdash! He came out with a lot of ridiculous gibberish about man having two inner selves, two identities, one good and one bad. *(Sputters)* Utter nonsense!

UTTERSON: Did you ever meet an acquaintance of his named Hyde?

LANYON: Hyde? No. Never heard of him. *(Quickly)* I'm sorry, but I'm late for an appointment. I'll see you again soon, I hope. Good day!

UTTERSON *and* ENFIELD: Good day! (LANYON *exits right.)*

ENFIELD *(Looking at pocket watch):* I must also be on my way. I'll see you on Tuesday.

UTTERSON: Tuesday it is, Enfield. (ENFIELD *exits left.* UTTERSON *sits on bench; looks off right.)* Well, now, look at this! He's coming back. This time *I* will accost *him. (Rises and steps down left as* HYDE *enters furtively right, goes to door, takes out a key and is about to unlock door when* UTTERSON *quickly steps in front of him.)* Mr. Hyde?

HYDE *(Shrinking back; hissing):* That is my name. What do you want?

UTTERSON: I am Gabriel Utterson, an old friend of Dr. Jekyll's, and also his lawyer.

HYDE: Dr. Jekyll is not at home now. *(Suddenly)* How did you know me?

UTTERSON: Before I answer that, will you do me a favor?

HYDE *(Roughly):* What is it?

UTTERSON: Will you let me see your face? (HYDE *hesitates, then defiantly pulls off hat and looks up. Both men stare at each other.)*

HYDE: And now, Mr. Utterson, how did you know me?

UTTERSON: We have common friends. Dr. Jekyll, for one.

HYDE *(With savage laugh):* Jekyll! Hah! *He* never told you about me! Not Jekyll! *(He turns key and rushes into laboratory, slamming door behind him. He hurries across laboratory and exits through left door.)*

UTTERSON: What a thoroughly disagreeable fellow! Ah, Jekyll, there is Satan's signature upon the face of this man Hyde. (POOLE *enters down left, holding a letter.*)

POOLE: Oh, good evening, Mr. Utterson.

UTTERSON: Good evening, Poole. I was thinking of calling on Dr. Jekyll. Is he home now?

POOLE: No, sir. He went out early this afternoon and isn't expected back until late tonight. I was just going on an errand for him.

UTTERSON: Poole, I just saw Mr. Hyde enter the house through this laboratory door. Is that all right, when Dr. Jekyll is not home?

POOLE: Quite all right, sir. Dr. Jekyll has given him a key.

UTTERSON: Your master places a great deal of trust in Mr. Hyde, then.

POOLE: Yes, sir. I have orders to obey Mr. Hyde in everything.

UTTERSON: I don't recall seeing him before now.

POOLE: No, sir. He never dines here. I see very little of him in the house. He usually comes and goes by this rear door.

UTTERSON: I see. Well, don't let me detain you.

POOLE: Thank you, sir. *(Exits right)*

UTTERSON: Poor Jekyll! Can Hyde's game be blackmail? Or perhaps he knows about Jekyll's will and is impatient to inherit. Things cannot continue this way. I must see Jekyll soon, but first I will see what I can learn about Edward Hyde. *(Glances at door, then exits down left. Curtain)*

*   *   *   *   *

SCENE 2

TIME: *A week later.*

SETTING: *The same.*

AT RISE: DR. JEKYLL, *dignified and gracious, and* UTTERSON *sit in chairs near desk in laboratory.*

UTTERSON: I'm so glad to find you at home this morning, Henry. It's been too long since I've had the pleasure of seeing you.

JEKYLL: My dear Utterson, I'm equally happy to see you.

UTTERSON *(With concern):* I'm afraid you've been working too hard. You don't look at all well.

JEKYLL: I'm deeply engaged in a very important experiment requiring all my energy.

UTTERSON: Yes. Lanyon mentioned your work to me last week.

JEKYLL *(Surprised):* Did he? Well, I'm sure he added his usual scorn and disapproval to the report. He criticizes me continually because my studies are focused on mystical propositions, while he cannot see beyond the purely medical point of view.

UTTERSON: Your theory is interesting, Henry. One man really being two.

JEKYLL *(Excitedly):* It's true, Utterson! Two natures contend within a person's consciousness, one just, and one unjust. I've made a special study to learn how they might be housed in separate identities, and I've—oh, well, I'm sure you haven't come to me for a scientific lecture. Forgive me.

UTTERSON: Someday you will explain it all to me, Henry. But for now, I want to speak to you about your will. You know I do not approve of it.

JEKYLL: You have told me so more than once.

UTTERSON: And I tell you again, because I've learned something about this Edward Hyde.

JEKYLL *(Sharply):* What have you learned?

UTTERSON: That he bludgeons anyone who chances to get in his way, that he mixes with the worst possible company, and behaves in public like a madman! I'm sorry, Henry, but I've made it my business to find out all I can about him.

JEKYLL *(Rising; nervously):* It makes no difference what you know. You do not understand, Utterson. I am in a very difficult situation.

UTTERSON: Henry, you can trust me. Confide in me, and I have no doubt that I can help you.

JEKYLL: This is very good of you, Utterson. I would trust you before any other man, but I have nothing to confide. You see, I can be rid of Hyde whenever I wish.

UTTERSON: Then why do you keep him on? What possible use can he be to you?

JEKYLL *(Fervently):* He helps me in my experiments! He is of tremendous value to me. If anything should happen to me, you *must* see that he gets his rights!

UTTERSON *(With a sigh):* That is my duty, Henry. I will do it. *(Rises)*

JEKYLL: Thank you. And now, if you'll excuse me, I have much to do today.

UTTERSON: Of course. I'll call again soon.

JEKYLL: Please do. It was good of you to come. *(Shakes his hand)* Good day, Utterson. (UTTERSON *exits left.* JEKYLL *follows and locks door.)* Oh, Utterson, you have aroused the evil within me. I have tried to stifle it, but you have unknowingly awakened it with your questions! *(He crosses to counter, and with shaking hands, empties a white powder into a vial of red liquid.)* I am afraid of what may happen if I surrender again. It is horrible! But the temptation is too great. *(He stares at vial.)* I cannot resist! *(He swallows liquid as curtain falls.)*

* * * * *

SCENE 3

TIME: *The next morning.*
SETTING: *The same as Scene 2.*
AT RISE: JEKYLL, *looking ill and upset, sits near desk. Knock at left door is heard.*
JEKYLL *(In trembling voice):* Who is it?
POOLE *(Opening door and entering):* Mr. Utterson to see you, sir.

JEKYLL: Tell him I can't see anyone. *(Hesitating)* I . . . no, no, show him in, Poole. Show him in.

POOLE: Yes, sir. *(Steps to doorway)* You may come in, Mr. Utterson. (UTTERSON *enters as* POOLE *exits, closing door.*)

UTTERSON: Henry, I have dreadful news! Sir Danvers Carew was murdered last night!

JEKYLL *(Dully):* Yes . . . I've heard.

UTTERSON: Have you also heard that a young woman witnessed the deed from her window? Sir Danvers was beaten to death with a cane, and the woman recognized the murderer as Edward Hyde!

JEKYLL *(Jumping up; wildly):* Yes! Yes! I know! *(He paces restlessly, head in hands.)*

UTTESON: The police have been unable to track down Hyde. He has vanished! No one, other than you, seems to know anything of his family or connections. The police want to question you, but I persuaded them to let me see you first.

JEKYLL *(Miserably):* I can tell you nothing, Utterson. Nothing!

UTTERSON *(Firmly):* Tell me the truth, Henry. You have not been foolish enough to conceal Hyde, have you?

JEKYLL: No! I swear I will never see him again!

UTTERSON: If the police find him, there will be a trial, of course, and you would certainly be involved.

JEKYLL: The police will never find him! He is . . . gone! Gone! Do you understand?

UTTERSON *(Gently):* No, I don't understand, but for the sake of our friendship, I will take you at your word. However, I must ask one question. Did Hyde dictate the terms when you changed your will and made him sole heir?

JEKYLL *(Hesitantly):* Yes.

UTTERSON: Then he surely meant to murder you! By chance another man was his victim last night. You have had a narrow escape.

JEKYLL *(Sitting by desk):* I have had a lesson! A tragic lesson!

UTTERSON: Jekyll, you need rest. Leave this laboratory and get away from your papers and experiments! *(As he grabs some papers from desk, he notices one and examines it closely.)* Is this a sample of Hyde's handwriting? *(Shows paper to* JEKYLL)

JEKYLL *(Looking up):* What? Oh, yes, I suppose it is.

UTTERSON: Are you aware that his writing bears a decided resemblance to yours? There is a different slant, but at many points it is identical. How do you account for that?

JEKYLL: Hyde is very clever, very quick. *(Snatches paper)* Please leave me now, Utterson. I need to be alone.

UTTERSON: Very well. Do get some rest, Henry. Call me if you need me. *(Shaking his head worriedly, he exits slowly left.)*

JEKYLL: Yes. Thank you. *(Rises slowly, goes to counter and takes up another vial of red liquid. He stares at it for a moment, his hand trembling violently, then suddenly hurls it to the floor, smashing it.)* Never again! Never! *(Curtain)*

* * * * *

SCENE 4

TIME: *A month later.*

SETTING: *Same. A small package, wrapped in brown paper, is placed beside outside laboratory door.*

AT RISE: JEKYLL *sits on stool by counter, bent over some vials and small white paper packets. He works desperately, pouring and mixing, growing more and more hurried. Throughout following dialogue, he is unaware of* UTTERSON *and* ENFIELD, *who enter slowly down right.*

UTTERSON: The reward for Hyde's capture is now in the thousands of pounds. I wonder if he'll ever be found.

ENFIELD: It's only been a month since he disappeared. He'll show up somewhere, and get exactly what he deserves! How is Jekyll these days?

UTTERSON: I'm worried about him, Enfield. He was ill and distraught when he first learned of Sir Danvers' murder, but then he seemed to recover. He got some rest and began to visit with his old friends again. I saw him every day for nearly a month, and it was almost like old times. Then, suddenly, and for the last three days, he has refused to see me. When I call, Poole always tells me his master is in the laboratory and will see no one.

ENFIELD: He must be resuming his experiments.

UTTERSON: Apparently. One of them must have upset poor Lanyon.

ENFIELD (*Shaking his head*): I still can't believe Lanyon is dead! He changed for the worse almost overnight.

UTTERSON: Yes, he came to see me two days before he died. He looked terrible . . . said he had witnessed a shocking event at Jekyll's from which he would never recover. He left a sealed envelope with me, with express instructions not to open it until after Jekyll's death. (JEKYLL *suddenly rises and hurries to street door. He opens it and looks out anxiously.*)

ENFIELD (*Seeing* JEKYLL): Utterson, look! (*Points*)

UTTERSON: Henry! (*Crosses center*)

JEKYLL (*Startled*): Oh! (*He grabs package and starts back inside, but* UTTERSON *stops him.*)

UTTERSON: Henry! How good to see you! I hope you are better.

JEKYLL (*Nervously*): No. I am very much worse, Utterson. Much worse.

ENFIELD (*Cheerfully*): You've been staying indoors too much. Why not come for a walk with us? It would do you good.

JEKYLL (*Smiling faintly*): I would like to very much . . . it would be very pleasant, but I . . . I . . . (*He suddenly looks terrified, gasps, clutches his throat.*) Not now! Not now! No! No! (*Gasping, he dashes in, slamming and locking door behind him, then staggers to counter, dropping package.*)

UTTERSON (*Shocked*): Henry! (*Tries door, then pounds on it*) Henry! What is it? What's the matter?

ENFIELD: He was terrified!

UTTERSON (*Pounding on door*): Henry! Are you all right?

JEKYLL (*In a choked voice*): Please, go away!

UTTERSON: Can we help you?

JEKYLL: No! No one can help me! No one! *(He sinks to his knees, gasping and writhing.* UTTERSON *and* ENFIELD *look at each other helplessly as curtain falls.)*

*   *   *   *   *

SCENE 5

TIME: *A week later.*

SETTING: *Same. Envelope is on desk.*

AT RISE: HYDE, *wearing a suit too large for him, huddles near counter, looking into large book.* JEKYLL *is concealed behind counter.* UTTERSON *and* POOLE *enter hurriedly right, unnoticed by* HYDE.

POOLE: Forgive me for bringing you here at this time of night, Mr. Utterson, but I had to so something! My master has been shut up in the laboratory all this past week, sir, and . . . I'm afraid.

UTTERSON: Afraid? Of what?

POOLE: I . . . I think there has been foul play.

UTTERSON: Poole, whatever do you mean?

POOLE: Listen carefully, sir. *(Leads* UTTERSON *to door, where he knocks.* HYDE *leaps to his feet in alarm.)* Dr. Jekyll, sir, Mr. Utterson is here to see you.

HYDE *(Hoarsely):* Tell him I cannot see him!

POOLE: Yes, sir. Thank you, sir. *(Draws* UTTERSON *down right)* Sir, I have been Dr. Jekyll's butler for twenty years. That voice we just heard is not his voice! But that is the voice I have heard the past seven days. Now, I ask you, sir, where is my master? Who is in there in my master's place, and why does he stay? (HYDE *anxiously sits by counter, staring fixedly at street door.)*

UTTERSON: I can't say, Poole.

POOLE: All this week, whoever is in there has been crying night and day for some sort of medicine. Notes with orders and complaints have been thrown into the hall. I've been sent rushing to all the wholesale chemists in town, and every time I've brought something back, there's been another note telling me to return it because it isn't pure. The man sounds desperate!

UTTERSON: I can't understand it.

POOLE: But that's not all, sir. I've seen him. The other day I came suddenly into the hall where he was rummaging in some boxes. When he saw me, he gave a horrible cry and dashed into the laboratory, slamming and locking the door!

UTTERSON: Perhaps . . . perhaps your master has been seized with an illness that tortures and deforms. That would explain the change in his voice, and why he has secluded himself. He is desperately seeking some medicine.

POOLE *(Shaking his head):* Sir, that person I saw was not Dr. Jekyll, ill or not. My master is a tall, fine-looking man. The thing I saw was hunched over, an ugly, creeping form. Oh, sir, I truly believe that my master has been murdered.

UTTERSON *(Shocked):* Murdered! *(After a pause)* Poole, was this crouching figure at all familiar to you?

POOLE: Well, yes, sir. . . . He did look like Mr. Hyde.

UTTERSON: Then let's waste no time! *(Goes to door; shouting)* Henry! I demand to see you! You must open the door, or Poole and I shall break it down!

HYDE *(Jumping up and backing away to left):* No! No, Utterson! Have mercy! Stay away!

UTTERSON: That is Hyde's voice! Down with the door, Poole!

HYDE *(Seizing small brown bottle from shelf):* No! Stay back! Spare me, I beg of you! *(*UTTERSON *and* POOLE *run at door with their shoulders, but fail to open it.* HYDE *cowers beside counter and opens brown bottle.)* Don't come in, Utterson, please! *(*HYDE *swallows contents of bottle and staggers behind counter, when he lets out a strangled cry and falls.* UTTERSON *and* POOLE *run at door again and it bursts open. They rush into laboratory, looking about.)*

POOLE: There's no one here, sir! *(Looks behind counter)* Wait! *(Points)* There, sir! It's Hyde!

UTTERSON *(Rushing behind counter):* It's Hyde, all right . . . but we're too late. *(Picks up brown bottle and sniffs it)* He has taken poison! *(During following dialogue,* HYDE, *unseen by audience, exits through concealed door, rear.)*

POOLE: There is no sign of Dr. Jekyll. *(Crosses to desk)* But look, sir, here on the desk is an envelope bearing your name, in my master's writing.

UTTERSON *(Taking envelope, opening it, taking out three documents):* Dr. Jekyll's will. *(He puts down other documents and opens will, scans it.)* It is just as I have it in my office . . . but, no! Here is a change! Instead of Edward Hyde's name as beneficiary, there is my name!

POOLE: Ah! My master made a wise decision in the end, sir.

UTTERSON: How strange! He had this copy of the will here. Hyde must have seen it and been enraged to see himself displaced by me, and yet he did not destroy the document. *(Shaking his head, he opens second letter.)* Poole! This letter is in Dr. Jekyll's handwriting, and it is dated today! He must still be alive. *(Reading)* "My dear Utterson, when this falls into your hands, I shall have disappeared." *(Looks up, puzzled)* Disappeared? *(Reading)* "I beg of you to read the narrative that Lanyon promised me he would place in your hands. Then, if you care to hear the tragic details, turn to the confession of your unworthy and unhappy friend, Henry Jekyll."

POOLE *(Handing him third letter):* This must be his confession, sir. But where can he be? I don't understand.

UTTERSON: Lock the street door, Poole. I have Dr. Lanyon's document with me. We shall read it together and hope for an answer to this bizarre mystery.

POOLE: Yes, sir. *(Crosses to street door and locks it)*

UTTERSON *(Sitting at desk):* We won't send for the police just yet. Please, sit down, Poole. (POOLE *sits opposite* UTTERSON, *who takes envelope from inside pocket)* Well, Lanyon, my old friend, I wish you could have lived to tell me what I must know, but at least you saw fit to write it. *(Opens document and reads)* "On the ninth of January, I, Dr. Hastie Lanyon, went to Henry Jekyll's laboratory at his urgent request."

POOLE: Yes, I remember that night. Dr. Lanyon went alone to the laboratory.

UTTERSON *(Reading):* "Jekyll had told me that another person would meet me there, and that he would join me later, but I was not prepared for the creature who opened the door for me. I can only describe him as a disgusting curiosity." *(Behind* UTTERSON *and* POOLE, HYDE, *in suit that is too large, enters left, followed by* DR. LANYON. *Throughout following dialogue,* UTTERSON *and* POOLE *remain seated, as if reading letter, while action goes on behind them.)*

HYDE: This way, Dr. Lanyon. *(Closes left door and locks it)* At Dr. Jekyll's insistence, I am to show you an experiment.

LANYON: I am not interested in any of Jekyll's experiments!

HYDE: I assure you this experiment will sustain your closest attention. Now observe, if you will, this red tincture. *(Lifts vial of red liquid)* And this white powder. *(Shows packet of power)* See how I mix them together in this glass. *(He mixes the two in a glass.)*

LANYON *(Impatiently):* What is the purpose of this?

HYDE: What you are about to see is for your eyes alone. You, Dr. Lanyon, who have always held to the most narrow and materialistic views of man's nature, you who have always harshly denounced your fellow scientist, Henry Jekyll, behold! *(He drinks contents of glass. There is a pause, while* LANYON *watches him uneasily. Then* HYDE *gasps, utters a choking cry, drops glass, clutches his throat, then staggers blindly behind counter, where he suddenly falls to floor.)*

LANYON *(Rushing to counter):* What is this? What have you done? Sir! I demand an explanation! *(He stops abruptly, staring behind counter. Slowly, he backs away in horror)* What . . . what is this? What am I seeing? (HYDE *struggles behind counter, his hands waving above it. Then they disappear and slowly,* JEKYLL's *hands are seen. Gasping and groping his way to his feet,* JEKYLL, *wearing an identical suit, which fits*

him, rises from behind counter.) Jekyll! No! This can't be! My
eyes play tricks on me! It can't be you.

JEKYLL *(Weakly):* Yes, Lanyon, it is Jekyll, but I don't know for
how long.

LANYON *(Backing away):* A hideous transformation before my
very eyes! A nightmare come to life!

JEKYLL: Get a hold of yourself and listen to me, Lanyon! Sit
down! (LANYON *stumbles onto stool, staring at* JEKYLL.) You
know I have always believed that man has two natures, that he
is really two different personalities.

LANYON *(Weakly):* Yes.

JEKYLL: I believed that if each element of man could be placed in
a separate identity, life could be relieved of everything evil!
The good and bad could be separated and never bother the
other! If somehow man's solid flesh might change from one
appearance to another, from good to evil . . .

LANYON *(Terrified):* Jekyll, you speak of things I never dared to
think of!

JEKYLL: But this was my life's work! And one day I compounded
a formula that I was sure could effect this change. I knew I
risked death if I tested it on myself, but the temptation of a
discovery so unique and profound was too great to deny. One
accursed night I combined my elements, watched them boil
and smoke, and with a burst of courage, I drank!

LANYON: Jekyll, you could have been a brilliant scientist! Why
did you waste your time on this?

JEKYLL: I had to know the result! The pain of the transformation
was terrible, but when it subsided, I was a changed being! I
not only felt but looked younger! Reckless! Wicked! I could
say and do things that Henry Jekyll would never do, for you
see, I wasn't Jekyll anymore. I was Edward Hyde!

LANYON: Edward Hyde! *(Shrinking back)* Edward Hyde is a
murderer!

JEKYLL: Yes. Even though Jekyll was good, Hyde was thoroughly evil and repulsive in mind and body. But strange as it

may seem, I welcomed this change. As Jekyll, I was growing old. My studies were boring, my life dull and dreary. I took the potion again—several times. Through Hyde a whole new life opened up for me.

LANYON: I can't believe what I'm hearing. Do you realize what you've done?

JEKYLL: Oh, yes, Lanyon! Heaven help me, it wasn't long before I knew and feared what Hyde was—a villain, totally wicked and unscrupulous. His crimes horrified me, but then, he and I were two separate persons—until one morning, when I awakened not as Jekyll, but as Hyde. Without drinking the potion, I had become Hyde again! I was terror-stricken! The balance between my two natures was upset. I was slowly losing hold of my better self and becoming totally immersed in my worse!

LANYON: Surely, you must have thought of this in advance!

JEKYLL: How could I have known? But in the face of this calamity I knew I had to choose between the two. To stay with Jekyll was to give up the wild freedom, however wicked. But to become Hyde was to be despised and friendless, hunted and pursued until death. I wanted to remain with Jekyll, but I couldn't!

LANYON: What do you mean?

JEKYLL: My unconscious desire for Hyde's energy and freedom was too strong. In a moment of moral weakness I again mixed the formula and swallowed it. But Hyde had been caged too long. He came out mad with fury and before the night was gone, he had murdered the innocent Sir Danvers. Later, as Jekyll, I swore never to release Hyde again. I resolved that my future conduct would redeem the past, and for a month I succeeded in remaining the respected doctor. But then the animal in me stirred again, and although I did not take the potion, Hyde escaped!

LANYON: Why have you made me witness to this? I shall never be the same man!

JEKYLL: Someone had to see it, Lanyon! Someone had to know the reason for my madness. At any hour I may feel the shuddering pangs that transform me into Hyde. The only way I can become Jekyll again is by taking the drug, and my supply of one of the necessary chemicals is nearly gone, and cannot be replaced. I cannot allow Hyde to wreak his evil any longer. Death is my only salvation. I just pray I have the courage to carry it out.

LANYON *(Rising):* Jekyll, you have shaken me to the core! Sickened my soul! *(Rushes to left door)* Let me out of here!

JEKYLL *(Going to door and unlocking it):* Wait, Lanyon. You must write down what I have said and give the document to Utterson. Then he will believe my own confession, which I shall leave for him to read after my death. Please! I beg of you!

LANYON: Yes, Yes, I will do it. Now, let me go! *(He rushes out. JEKYLL closes door, turns slowly into room, then suddenly gasps.)*

JEKYLL: No, not yet! I've not had one hour of peace! No, Hyde! Leave me alone! Leave me alone! *(He clutches his throat and sinks to his knees, then falls behind counter. Lights slowly dim in laboratory.)*

UTTERSON *(Shaking head; in disbelief):* Jekyll knew he could never remain himself, so he took his life, and Hyde's, to end the terror forever.

POOLE *(Overwhelmed):* Sir . . . I'm not sure I understand. Does this mean that my master and Mr. Hyde were . . . the same person?

UTTERSON: Yes, Poole. Two opposite natures within one body. Hyde fought and overpowered your master, and when the necessary chemical was used up, your master knew there was nothing left but death!

POOLE *(Rising and slowly going to counter):* I always wondered why I never saw my master and Mr. Hyde together. *(Looks down)* Oh, sir! Look!

UTTERSON: What, Poole?

POOLE *(Horrified):* It is my master! He . . . he is dead . . . but it is my master lying here—and not that wicked murderer!

UTTERSON *(Crossing to look, then gently leading* POOLE *away):* Your master has found peace at last, Poole. Both Dr. Jekyll and Mr. Hyde have found peace at last. *(Curtain)*

THE END

PRODUCTION NOTES

DR. JEKYLL AND MR. HYDE

Characters: 6 male.

Playing Time: 30 minutes.

Costumes: Dark gentlemen's suits, hats and overcoats of the mid-nineteenth century period for Utterson, Enfield, Jekyll and Lanyon. Poole wears a plainer suit and overcoat. Jekyll appears tall while Hyde is stooped. Hyde wears black suit, well fitting in the first scene; in Scene 5 his suit is too large, and is identical to Jekyll's suit in Scene 5.

Properties: Cane; door key; letters; vial with red liquid; small paper packets of white powder; a small glass; a small brown bottle; a small package wrapped in brown paper; a large envelope with a will and two letters inside; document in an envelope.

Setting: A London street and Dr. Jekyll's laboratory. A street lamp and wooden park bench are right. Center right, a workable door in a frame, with adjoining wall. The door flat should be well braced to withstand slamming and breaking in. Slightly up center and left is the laboratory, with a long counter holding laboratory apparatus, center; bookshelves on the walls, a small desk and two chairs, down center. The counter must be large enough to conceal two men behind it. There should be concealed opening in the back wall or curtain where Hyde can exit, unseen by audience, in Scene 5.

Lighting: Lighting may be used to highlight various areas of the stage. When the action is in the street, lighting on the laboratory may be dim, and vice versa. In Scene 5, lighting on Poole and Utterson may dim during action with Hyde, Jekyll and Lanyon, then highlight Poole and Utterson again. A blackout may be used after every scene instead of a curtain.

Oliver Twist

by Charles Dickens

Characters

OLIVER TWIST, *orphan boy*
MR. BUMBLE, *parish officer*
MRS. CORNEY, *matron of the workhouse*
OLD SALLY, *pauper*
THE ARTFUL DODGER ⎫ *young*
CHARLEY BATES ⎭ *pickpockets*
FAGIN, *leader of a gang of thieves*
BILL SIKES, *robber*
NANCY, *member of Fagin's gang*
MR. BROWNLOW, *gentleman*
BOOKSELLER
MAN AT BOOKSTALL
MR. GRIMWIG, *friend of Brownlow's*
ROSE MAYLIE, *young lady*
MRS. BEDWIN, *Mr. Brownlow's housekeeper*
WORKHOUSE BOYS
FAGIN'S BOYS
TOWNSPEOPLE
TWO POLICE OFFICERS

Scene 1

TIME: *The 1830's.*

SETTING: *The dirty dining hall of the parish workhouse in an English country village. Long table with benches around it is center.*

AT RISE: *Ragged* WORKHOUSE BOYS, *including* OLIVER TWIST, *huddle together, eating from wooden bowls, watching anxiously as* MR. BUMBLE *marches about pompously, carrying a cane, with haughty* MRS. CORNEY *following.* OLD SALLY *stands holding a pot of gruel.*

MRS. CORNEY *(Sternly):* All right! Eat up and be quick about it! Mr. Bumble and I haven't got all night to be standing here while you orphans gorge yourselves! (MRS. CORNEY *examines* BOYS' *necks and ears, and* MR. BUMBLE *thumps them on the back with his cane as they eat.)*

BUMBLE *(Removing hat and attempting to look pious):* For this bountiful meal before you, and for all the blessings given to penniless workhouse orphans, may you ever be humble, grateful, and obedient! (BOYS *finish eating and all turn anxiously to* OLIVER.)

1ST BOY: Go on, Oliver. We drew straws, and you got the short one. (OLIVER *takes his bowl and walks timidly up to* BUMBLE.)

BUMBLE *(Fiercely):* Well?

OLIVER *(In a shaking voice):* Please, sir, I want some more.

BUMBLE: *What?*

OLIVER: Please, sir, I . . . I want some more.

BUMBLE *(Enraged):* More? (*Snatches* OLIVER *by collar*) Mrs. Corney, do my ears deceive me? Did Oliver Twist ask for more?

MRS. CORNEY: Indeed he did, sir!

BUMBLE: Well, he won't do it again! (*Pushes* OLIVER *to* MRS. CORNEY) Lock him up! Tomorrow I shall see if someone . . . perhaps the undertaker . . . will take this ungrateful young sinner off our hands! (*Leers at* OLIVER) You'd like to be a coffin maker's apprentice, wouldn't you, Oliver?

OLIVER (*Frightened*): No, sir.

BUMBLE: But you *will* like it! Yes, the undertaker can surely be persuaded to take you for, shall we say, five pounds? Take him away, Mrs. Corney. I shall be along directly to honor him with a sound thrashing!

OLD SALLY: Wait, mistress! Don't be hard with the boy. I know something about him that—

MRS. CORNEY: Be quiet, old Sally! Get back to your work! (*Starts to hustle* OLIVER *off*)

OLD SALLY: But, mistress, I was at the bedside of this boy when he was born. And before his poor young mother died, she gave me something to keep for—

OLIVER (*Turning eagerly to* OLD SALLY): My mother? Did you know my mother?

MRS. CORNEY (*Scornfully*): Your mother was a pauper and a regular, downright bad one she was, if I ever saw one! We found her in the street!

OLIVER (*Angrily*): That's not true! Don't talk about my mother like that!

MRS. CORNEY (*Outraged*): Mr. Bumble! Did you hear how he spoke to me?

BUMBLE (*Approaching* OLIVER, *with cane upraised*): I did, ma'am, and I shall make certain he doesn't do it again. (OLIVER *struggles free of* MRS. CORNEY *and starts to run.*)

OLD SALLY: Run, boy! Run for your life! (BOYS *jump up and shout encouragement as* OLIVER *runs and dodges* MR. BUMBLE *and* MRS. CORNEY, *who chase him. He is almost cornered when* OLD SALLY *steps in front of* MRS. CORNEY, *allowing* OLIVER *a chance to run offstage.*)

MRS. CORNEY: Stop him! He's running away! Stop him! (BUMBLE *starts after* OLIVER, *but* OLD SALLY *and* BOYS, *cheering, crowd in his way, preventing him from following* OLIVER. *Curtain falls.*)

*   *   *   *   *

Scene 2

BEFORE RISE: *A London street. A few* TOWNSPEOPLE *pass back and forth.* OLIVER *limps in, very tired, but looks about in amazement.*

OLIVER: What a big city London is! And so far away from the workhouse. Mr. Bumble will never find me here, and maybe I can make my fortune. (THE ARTFUL DODGER *enters, passes* OLIVER, *stops to look at him curiously, then strikes a jaunty pose.)*

DODGER: Hello, my covey! What's the matter?

OLIVER: I've been walking for seven days, and I'm very tired and hungry.

DODGER: Walking for seven days! Running away from home?

OLIVER: I don't have a home.

DODGER *(Thoughtfully):* I see. First time in London?

OLIVER: Yes.

DODGER: Parents living?

OLIVER: No.

DODGER: Got any relations?

OLIVER: None that I know of.

DODGER: Money?

OLIVER: Not a farthing.

DODGER: That's *un*-fortunate! I suppose you want some grub and a place to sleep tonight.

OLIVER: I haven't slept under a roof since I left the country.

DODGER: Well, don't fret your eyelids on that score. I happen to know a respectable old gentleman who'll give you lodgings for nothing and never ask for change.

OLIVER: You do? Are you sure he won't mind?

DODGER: Not if any gentleman he knows introduces you. What's your name?

OLIVER: Oliver Twist.

DODGER: Mine's Jack Dawkins, although among my intimate acquaintances I'm better known as the *Art*-ful *Dodg*-er. (*They shake hands.*) It's dark enough now. Let's be off! (OLIVER *eagerly follows* DODGER *offstage. Curtains open.)*

*   *   *   *   *

SETTING: *Fagin's Den. There are a few pallets on floor at one side, and boxes, old clothes and dirty dishes scattered about. At rear is fireplace cluttered with clothes and pans. Above it, handkerchiefs hang in a row on a line.*

AT RISE: FAGIN *and his* BOYS, *including* CHARLEY BATES, *are toasting sausages over fire.* DODGER *and* OLIVER *enter, and* BOYS *look up curiously.* DODGER *whispers a few words in* FAGIN's *ear, then points to* OLIVER.

DODGER: Fagin, here's my new friend, Oliver Twist.

FAGIN *(Bowing low):* Well, Oliver, I hope I may have the honor of your intimate acquaintance.

OLIVER *(Bowing in return):* Thank you, sir. (BOYS *crowd around* OLIVER, *shaking his hand, snatching off his cap and jacket.*)

CHARLEY: I'm Charley Bates, Oliver. Allow me to empty your pockets for you before you sit down to supper!

FAGIN *(Waving* BOYS *back with his toasting fork):* That's enough for now, boys. We are very glad to see you Oliver. Dodger, take off the sausages. (*Leads* OLIVER *to fireplace.* OLIVER *looks about curiously.*) Ah, you're staring at the pocket hand-kerchiefs, eh? We've just washed and hung 'em out, haven't we, boys? Ha! Ha! (BOYS *laugh loudly as they sit down and pass the sausages.*) I hope you've all been hard at work today!

CHARLEY: Hard as can be, Fagin.

FAGIN: What have you got, Dodger?

DODGER: A couple of pocketbooks. (*Hands* FAGIN *two pocketbooks*)

FAGIN: Not so heavy as they might be, but very neat and nicely made. Ingenious workman, isn't he, Oliver?

OLIVER: Yes, sir. (BOYS *burst out laughing, nudging each other.*)

FAGIN: And what do you have, Charley?

CHARLEY: Wipes! (*Hands* FAGIN *several handkerchiefs, which he pulls out of his jacket*)

FAGIN: They're very good ones, but the monograms will have to be picked out with a needle. We'll show Oliver how to do it. Would you like that, Oliver?

OLIVER *(Eagerly):* Oh, yes! Will you teach me, sir?

FAGIN: Of course! You'll be one of us in no time! I'll tell you what—we'll show you a little game we play. Come, boys! *(He takes a locked chest from cupboard, opens it, takes out jewelry, watches, etc., and puts them all into his pockets.)* Now, Oliver, I'm going to pretend that I'm one of those absent-minded old gentlemen who wander about Clerkenwell Square. *(He trots around room, humming and slapping his pockets. BOYS bump into him, distract him, slyly take things from his pockets.)*

DODGER: You're a poor man, Fagin.

FAGIN *(Checking his pockets):* Ah, so I am. Good boys! There, you see what a jolly time we have at this game, Oliver?

OLIVER *(Laughing):* Yes, sir.

FAGIN: You shall learn to play it, too. Just make the Dodger your model. (NANCY *enters, followed by* BILL SIKES.)

DODGER: Hello, Nancy!

NANCY *(Cheerfully):* Hello, boys! *(Sees* OLIVER*)* Why, what's this, Fagin? You've got a new boy.

FAGIN: Yes, my dear. Oliver, I want you to meet Miss Nancy. (OLIVER *bows politely, and she drops a curtsy.)*

NANCY: He's not like the others. He has manners. I'm pleased to meet you, Oliver.

FAGIN: And this is Mr. Bill Sikes. (SIKES *scowls darkly at* OLIVER, *and takes some jewelry out of his coat, which he hands to* FAGIN. FAGIN *hastily slips jewelry into his pockets.)* You see, I have quite a thoughtful and generous family, Oliver. Now! Is my handkerchief hanging out of my pocket?

OLIVER *(Looking):* Yes, sir.

FAGIN: See if you can take it away without my feeling it. (OLIVER *makes several unsuccessful tries, then pulls out handkerchief.)* Is it gone?

OLIVER *(Delighted):* Yes, sir. Here it is.

FAGIN: Ah, you're a clever boy! In a few days you can go out to work with Charley and the Dodger. Now, go to bed over there with the boys. (BOYS *go to pallets.)* Goodnight.

OLIVER: Goodnight, sir. And thank you for being so kind to me. I think I'm going to feel right at home here. (OLIVER *lies on floor with* BOYS. NANCY *smiles at him kindly.* FAGIN *has a sly, thoughtful look on his face. Curtains close.*)

* * * * *

SCENE 3

TIME: *A few days later.*

BEFORE RISE: *Bookstall in Clerkenwell Square. Scene is played before curtain.* MR. BROWNLOW *is reading at bookstall center.* BOOKSELLER *is busy with* MAN *nearby.* TOWNSPEOPLE *pass back and forth.* DODGER, CHARLEY *and* OLIVER *enter, looking around idly. Suddenly* DODGER *stops and pulls* CHARLEY *and* OLIVER *to one side.*

DODGER: Do you see that old gentleman by the bookstall?

OLIVER: Yes, I see him.

CHARLEY: He'll do!

OLIVER: Do for what? Does he make handkerchiefs, too?

DODGER: Keep your eyes open, Oliver. You may learn a thing or two. (DODGER *and* CHARLEY *move cautiously toward* MR. BROWNLOW. OLIVER *starts to follow them, then stops, horror-stricken, as* DODGER *neatly takes handkerchief from* MR. BROWNLOW'*s back pocket and hands it to* CHARLEY. *Suddenly,* MR. BROWNLOW *looks up, and* DODGER *and* CHARLEY *slip out of sight behind bookstall.*)

MR. BROWNLOW: Here, what's this? *(Pats his pocket)* My handkerchief! *(Sees* OLIVER *backing away in fright)* Here, boy, give me my handkerchief! (OLIVER *turns in panic and starts to run.*) Stop! Thief! (TOWNSPEOPLE *rush to his aid.* OLIVER *is quickly captured by* MAN *and dragged back to* BROWNLOW.)

MAN: Here he is, sir. Took your handkerchief, did he?

1ST POLICE OFFICER *(Entering and coming through crowd)*:

Here, let me through! A young pickpocket, eh? (*Seizes* OLIVER) Don't try to escape, you little villain!

BROWNLOW: Oh, don't hurt him, Officer. He's quite frightened, poor fellow. And he doesn't seem to have my handkerchief after all.

1ST POLICE OFFICER: No matter, sir. He'll have to go before the magistrate. Come along!

OLIVER (*Struggling*): But I didn't take the handkerchief! It was another boy, sir.

BOOKSELLER (*Pushing through crowd*): Wait! That boy is innocent!

1ST POLICE OFFICER: Who are you?

BOOKSELLER: I keep the bookstall where the robbery took place, Officer. I saw what happened. An older boy took this gentleman's handkerchief, then disappeared into the crowd. (*Indicating* OLIVER) This boy watched it all in perfect amazement.

1ST POLICE OFFICER: Are you certain this boy is innocent?

BOOKSELLER: Absolutely, sir!

1ST POLICE OFFICER: Very well. There's no need to trouble the magistrate. (*Releases* OLIVER, *who falls to his knees, exhausted*)

BROWNLOW: Poor lad! (*Helps* OLIVER *to his feet*) Where do you live, my boy? (OLIVER *shakes his head, too frightened to speak.*)

BOOKSELLER: No doubt he's an orphan, sir, or he wouldn't be around the streets in such a sorry condition.

BROWNLOW (*Kindly; to* OLIVER): My name is Mr. Brownlow. I'll take you home with me, and my housekeeper will see that you get a warm supper and a clean bed. (*Puts his arm around* OLIVER *and turns to* BOOKSELLER) My thanks to you, sir. (BOOKSELLER *bows cordially.* BROWNLOW *leads* OLIVER *off and* TOWNSPEOPLE *gradually exit. In a moment,* DODGER *and* CHARLEY *peek out from behind bookstall, see that* BOOKSELLER *is not looking, and run downstage.*)

DODGER: We'd better go and tell Fagin. He won't like this! (DODGER *and* CHARLEY *hurry off.* BOOKSELLER *wheels book-stall away, offstage. Curtains open.*)

*   *   *   *   *

SETTING: *Same as Scene 2.*

AT RISE: NANCY *and* SIKES *sit at table.* FAGIN *and* BOYS *are by the fire.* DODGER *and* CHARLEY *enter.*

FAGIN *(Jumping up):* What? Only two of you? Where's Oliver? (*He grabs* DODGER *by the collar.*) Speak out, or I'll throttle you!

DODGER: A rich old gentleman took a liking to him, and that's all there is about it. He's gone! *(Pulls away)*

FAGIN *(Furiously):* Gone? I told you to look after him! (*Starts after* DODGER *and* CHARLEY, *swinging his toasting fork*) Oliver knows all about us! He could say something that will get us into trouble!

SIKES: Then somebody's got to find him and get him back. (*Turns to* NANCY) You can do it, Nancy. Nobody suspects you.

NANCY: The boy's better off out of this company. Let him be.

SIKES *(Roughly):* If he blabs to the police, it's the end for you as well as the rest of us! She'll go, Fagin. (*Grips* NANCY's *arm tightly*) Won't she?

NANCY *(Wincing):* All right, Bill. All right.

DODGER: Oliver can't be too far away. The old gentleman *walked* out of Clerkenwell Square.

FAGIN: You'd better start right away, my dear. *(Opens cupboard and takes out white apron and bonnet)* Wear a white apron and a bonnet, and you'll look like a perfectly respectable young woman when you walk into the better neighborhoods. (NANCY *puts on bonnet and apron.*) Just make some tearful inquiries about your lost little brother.

NANCY *(Reluctantly):* I'll see what I can do. But it may take time. *(Exits left)*

FAGIN: Ah, she's a clever girl, Bill.

SIKES: Aye! *(Lifts his cup)* Here's to Nancy! She'll find the boy! *(Curtain)*

* * * * *

SCENE 4

TIME: *A month later.*

SETTING: MR. BROWNLOW'*s parlor. There are chairs and tables placed around room, with lamps, vases of flowers, and a portrait of a young woman. There may also be a couch and a stool.*

AT RISE: OLIVER, *clean and neatly dressed, is seated on stool.* ROSE MAYLIE *stands near him, showing him a book.* MR. BROWNLOW *and* MR. GRIMWIG *sit together.*

GRIMWIG: So that's the boy you found in the street a month ago, eh, Brownlow? The boy who's had the fever?

BROWNLOW: That is the boy, Grimwig.

GRIMWIG *(To* OLIVER*)*: Boy! How are you feeling now?

OLIVER *(Standing and bowing; politely):* A great deal better, thank you, sir. Mr. Brownlow has been very good to me.

BROWNLOW *(Kindly):* And I promise I shall never desert you, my boy, unless you give me cause.

OLIVER *(Earnestly):* I never, never will, sir!

BROWNLOW: I'm sure you won't. Rose, will you step downstairs and tell Mrs. Bedwin we are ready for tea?

ROSE: Of course. Come and help me, Oliver. *(She leads* OLIVER *out right.)*

GRIMWIG: Do you know what you're doing, Brownlow? Where does that boy come from? Who is he?

BROWNLOW: I've made a number of inquiries, but I haven't yet received a satisfactory answer. I've even put an advertisement in the papers in hope of learning something about his past. *(Slowly)* I'm strangely drawn to him, Grimwig, and the thing that strikes me most about him is his remarkable likeness to that portrait of Rose's sister. *(Points to portrait)* He's quite fond of it.

GRIMWIG *(Harshly):* Nonsense! You found this boy in the street and that's where he'll end up! And have you no better occupation for Miss Rose Maylie than to set her fussing over that young guttersnipe?

BROWNLOW: You know that Rose is always welcome here for the sake of my old acquaintance with her family. She and Oliver have become close friends, and I'm certain her careful attention has helped him recover. (MRS. BEDWIN *enters with plate of muffins, followed by* ROSE *with tea tray and* OLIVER *with some books.*) Ah, here is our tea.

GRIMWIG *(Suddenly cheerful):* Ah, muffins! You always make the most excellent muffins, Mrs. Bedwin!

MRS. BEDWIN *(With a curtsy):* Thank you, sir.

OLIVER *(To* BROWNLOW): The boy from the bookstall has just brought these, sir.

BROWNLOW: Oh, but there are some books to go back.

ROSE: I'm afraid the boy has gone, sir. *(Pours tea for everyone)*

BROWNLOW: I'm sorry for that. I wanted to return these books tonight.

GRIMWIG *(With a sneer):* Why don't you send Oliver with them?

OLIVER *(Eagerly):* Oh, yes, do let me take them for you, sir.

MRS. BEDWIN: I don't think he's well enough to go into the streets, sir.

GRIMWIG: Nonsense! He looks perfectly well to me.

BROWNLOW: Well, I don't know . . . (As GRIMWIG *coughs loudly*) Very well, you may go, Oliver. It isn't far. *(Takes books from table and bill from wallet)* Here are the books and a five-pound note to pay my bill.

OLIVER: I won't be gone ten minutes, sir.

MRS. BEDWIN *(Following* OLIVER *out):* Let me tell you the quickest way to go, my dear. And you must button your jacket and put on your cap.

BROWNLOW *(Taking out his watch):* He should be back before dark.

GRIMWIG: Indeed! You really expect him to come back?

BROWNLOW: Why, of course. Why shouldn't he?

GRIMWIG: He has a new suit of clothes on his back, a set of valuable books under his arm, and a five-pound note in his pocket. He'll join his old friends in the streets and laugh at you all!

ROSE: Dear Mr. Grimwig, I've nursed Oliver these past weeks, and I assure you he is a gentle and grateful child.

GRIMWIG: Miss Maylie, I am sorry to say it, but if that boy ever returns to this house again, I'll eat my hat! *(Curtain)*

* * * * *

SCENE 5

SETTING: *Bookstall. Played before curtain.*

AT RISE: BOOKSELLER *enters, pushing bookstall into place, then exits.* OLIVER *enters with books, as* NANCY *enters from opposite side, wearing bonnet and apron, and looking about her. Seeing* OLIVER, *she rushes up to him and takes his hand.*

NANCY: Oliver! At last I've found you!

OLIVER *(Alarmed):* Let me go! Why are you stopping me? *(Recognizes her)* Why, it's you, Nancy.

NANCY: Yes, Oliver. Now, do be quiet and come along with me.

OLIVER: But I live with Mr. Brownlow now.

NANCY *(Nervously):* You must come with me, Oliver. I won't harm you.

OLIVER: No! You'll take me back to Fagin, ad he'll try to make me steal. Please, Nancy, let me go. Mr. Brownlow is waiting for me.

NANCY *(Reluctantly):* There's no help for it. Now, come along! *(Starts to lead him off left)*

OLIVER *(Struggling):* Help! Help!

SIKES (*Entering hurriedly from left, seizing* OLIVER *and clapping hand over his mouth*): Hold your noise, you young dog! (FAGIN, DODGER *and* CHARLEY *enter.*)

FAGIN: Ah! You've caught him!

CHARLEY *(With a shout of laughter):* Just look at him, Fagin!

FAGIN *(Bowing low):* Delighted to see you looking so well, Oliver.

CHARLEY: Fancy clothes, and books, too. Nothing but a gentleman!

OLIVER: Those books belong to Mr. Brownlow, who brought me into his house and took care of me. Please send them back to him. He'll think I stole them.

FAGIN *(Chuckling):* You're quite right, Oliver. He *will* think you've stolen them, and he won't ever want to see you again. It couldn't have happened better if we'd planned it! (*Suddenly,* OLIVER *breaks free and starts to run.*)

OLIVER: Police! Help! Help! (SIKES *runs after* OLIVER *and seizes him, as others quickly hide behind bookstall. After a moment,* DODGER *peeks out cautiously from one side,* CHARLEY *from the other side. When they see* SIKES *holding* OLIVER, *they step out, followed by* FAGIN *and* NANCY.)

FAGIN *(Furiously; to* OLIVER): So, you wanted to get away. Called for the police, did you? (SIKES *pushes* OLIVER *forward and* FAGIN *grabs him.*) I'll cure you of that, my young master! *(Raises his arm to strike)*

NANCY: No! *(Steps between* FAGIN *and* OLIVER) I won't stand by and see it done, Fagin! Let him be!

FAGIN *(Surprised):* Come, come, my dear. It's for our own good.

NANCY: You villain! I robbed for you when I was only half as old as he is, and see the good it's done me!

FAGIN: Well, my dear, it's been your living ever since.

NANCY: Yes, and the cold, dirty streets are my home, and the shadow of the gallows hangs over me every hour! You're the wretch that drove me to it, and you'll keep me there 'til I die!

FAGIN *(Fiercely):* I'll do you a mischief worse than that if you say much more.

SIKES: Keep quiet, Nancy! Who are you to be a friend to the boy? Go home and cool your temper!

NANCY: I wish I'd been struck dead before I lent a hand in bringing him back. He'll be a liar and a thief from this night on. *(Turns her back)*

FAGIN: Temper! Passion! It's the worst of having to do with women, but we can't get on in our line without them. Dodger, Charley! Hold the boy! (DODGER *and* CHARLEY *take a firm hold on* OLIVER. SIKES *and* FAGIN *start slowly off left,* NANCY *following closely.*) Are you set for the job next week, Bill?

SIKES: I need a small boy to get through the window and unlock the door of the house from inside.

FAGIN: A small boy? Use Oliver! He'll do everything you want, if you frighten him enough.

SIKES: Frighten him? Hah! If he makes one wrong turn, you won't see him again. Think of that before you send him on a job with me!

FAGIN: I have thought of it, Bill. I want to fill his mind with the idea that he's been a thief. Then he'll be ours forever, and he won't try to escape again. (*Beckons to* CHARLEY *and* DODGER *to follow, and all start off left, except* NANCY. OLIVER *looks back pleadingly at her before he is dragged off.*)

NANCY *(Moved):* Oh, Oliver, if I could help you, I would! But I haven't the power. I . . . *(Thinks a moment, wavers, then seems resolved)* Perhaps there is something . . . but the danger in it! If I am discovered *(Paces a moment)* . . . Mr. Brownlow is the boy's last hope. If only I can find him!

SIKES *(Roughly; offstage):* Nancy!

NANCY *(Hastily composing herself):* I'm coming, Bill. (*She hurries out. Lights dim for a moment to denote the passage of time.*)

*   *   *   *   *

TIME: *A few days later.*

SETTING: *The same.* ROSE *and* BROWNLOW *enter and stand at bookstall, browsing.* NANCY, *wearing shawl over her head, enters left. At sight of* BROWNLOW *and* ROSE, *she approaches eagerly, then stops, uncertain. Finally she moves forward and touches* ROSE *timidly on the arm.*

NANCY: Miss . . .

ROSE *(Kindly):* Yes? What is it?

NANCY: Forgive me, miss, but . . . is this gentleman Mr. Brownlow?

BROWNLOW *(Turning to* NANCY): Yes, I am Mr. Brownlow. What do you want, young woman?

NANCY: Sir, I'm risking my life to come here, but I must speak to you. *(Looks around nervously)* I am the girl who took Oliver away a few days ago, when you sent him here with your books.

ROSE *(Urgently):* What? Oh, where is he now? Is he safe?

NANCY: Yes, miss, as safe as he can be in a den of thieves.

ROSE: Thieves?

BROWNLOW *(Bitterly):* Then I'm sure the boy is quite at home!

NANCY: At home, sir? Why, the poor child is a prisoner, frightened and miserable!

ROSE: I knew he wouldn't leave us of his own will. *(To* BROWNLOW) I just can't believe what the gentleman told us this morning.

NANCY *(Nervously):* What gentleman?

BROWNLOW: A certain Mr. Bumble came to us from the parish workhouse where Oliver was born. He answered my newspaper advertisement about the boy. It seems that Oliver is an ungrateful child who ran away from the workhouse several weeks ago. He is also a young villain who has robbed me and run away, when I had thoughts of giving him a home. In short, I never want to hear of him again!

NANCY: Sir, please listen to me! Oliver was taken from you by force. He speaks of you and this young lady with the greatest affection, and his only wish is to be safe back with you again.

BROWNLOW *(Hesitantly):* I would like to believe you. I became very fond of the boy, but . . .

NANCY: If he isn't rescued soon, he'll be forced to steal and forever after keep company with villains and thieves. You are his only hope, sir!

ROSE: We must get him back, at once!

BROWNLOW *(Convinced):* Yes, yes, we must. *(To* NANCY*)* Can you help us?

NANCY: I'll try. But do not watch or follow me, now or any other time.

BROWNLOW: Very well.

NANCY: Sunday night at the stroke of twelve, meet me here. I'll bring Oliver if I can. But if I am discovered, you will never see either of us again.

BROWNLOW: We'll trust you to do what you can. And thank you!

NANCY: Until Sunday, then. *(Hurries off left, leaving* BROWNLOW *and* ROSE *looking anxiously after her. Lights dim to indicate passage of time.)*

*   *   *   *   *

TIME: *Sunday night.*

SETTING: *The same. As lights come up, a clock is heard chiming twelve.* MR. BROWNLOW *and* ROSE *enter and stand anxiously at bookstall.* NANCY *and* OLIVER *enter.*

ROSE: Oliver!

OLIVER *(Running to them):* Rose! Mr. Brownlow! I didn't think I would ever see you again.

BROWNLOW *(Hugging him):* My boy! *(Turns to* NANCY*)* Young woman, we shall always be grateful to you. Please tell me how I can help you.

NANCY *(Near tears):* I'm past all help. Take the boy and go quickly!

BROWNLOW: But you must let me do something for you. I can see you to a safe place. You don't have to return to your old haunts.

OLIVER: Yes, Nancy, please come with us. I'm afraid for you to go back.

NANCY *(Hesitating a moment):* No—I hate my life, but I cannot leave it. I must hurry back before I am missed. *(Hugs* OLIVER*)* Goodbye, Oliver. You'll have a home now, with these good people.

OLIVER: I shall never forget you, Nancy. Never! (NANCY *turns away quickly, sobbing.* BROWNLOW *and* ROSE *watch her anxiously for a moment, then lead* OLIVER *off right.* NANCY *watches them go, then starts off left. Suddenly,* SIKES *leaps out in front of her. He carries a club.)*

SIKES: Well, Nancy! It's a pretty piece of work you've been up to!

NANCY *(Frightened):* Bill! Bill, please, don't look at me like that!

SIKES: Keep quiet! You know what I have to do.

NANCY *(Struggling):* No! Bill, please! I haven't betrayed anyone! I only saved the boy, that's all.

SIKES *(Dragging her out of sight behind bookstall):* You put the mark on us! Betrayed us all to that meddling old man.

NANCY *(From behind bookstall):* No! *(She screams, and falls to floor. Her body is partially in view. She lies motionless.* SIKES *backs away from her, stunned and horrified.* FAGIN, DODGER, *and* CHARLEY *enter.)*

FAGIN: Bill! Did you find Nancy and the boy?

BROWNLOW *(Hurrying in from right):* Who's there? I heard a woman a scream. *(Seeing* NANCY's *body, he stops, then turns and runs off, shouting).* Murder! Help, police! *(Frantic,* SIKES *starts after* BROWNLOW, *and* FAGAN *darts a quick look at* NANCY. *Police whistles and shouts are heard off right.* SIKES *stops. All look around in a panic, then start off left, only to be met by* TWO POLICE OFFICERS *and* TOWNSPEOPLE, *who swarm in left and right.* CHARLEY *escapes up left, while* FAGIN *and* DODGER *are instantly seized and handcuffed.* SIKES *puts up a struggle, but is subdued and handcuffed by* POLICE OFFICERS.*)*

1ST POLICE OFFICER: All right! Let's go! (SIKES *is hustled off.)*

DODGER *(Cockily):* Watch how you handle me, my man. I'm an Englishman as much as you, and I've got my privileges.

2ND POLICE OFFICER: Hah! You're a young vagabond, and we've got you now. Your old master, too. Come along! (POLICE OFFICERS *lead* FAGIN *and* DODGER *off.* TOWNSPEOPLE *exit, pushing off bookstall.)*

* * * * *
SCENE 6

TIME: *A week later.*

SETTING: *Brownlow's parlor.*

AT RISE: BROWNLOW, GRIMWIG, OLIVER, ROSE *and* MRS. BEDWIN *are gathered, the women seated,* OLIVER *standing between the two men.* MR. GRIMWIG *holds a folded paper.*

BROWNLOW: Now, Oliver, my boy, you are going to hear some very astonishing things tonight. I have made some inquiries, and I've learned that my old friend, Edwin Leeford, was your father. He died ten years ago in Rome. But in his will, which my lawyer friend, Mr. Grimwig, has in his hands, your father left his property to you and your mother. Unfortunately, your mother did not know about it before she died.

GRIMWIG *(Referring to will):* Your father's will reads that you would inherit a sizable sum of money, on the condition that you did not stain your name with any public act of dishonor or wrong.

BROWNLOW: And since you have been an honest lad, Oliver, the money is yours.

GRIMWIG: We also learned that when your mother died, she left a gold locket with the old nurse who attended your birth.

OLIVER: Old Sally?

BROWNLOW: Yes. She has died, but she gave the locket to the workhouse matron, Mrs. Corney, who sold it for her own profit. Both she and Mr. Bumble are no longer in service at the workhouse. I saw to that!

GRIMWIG: The locket is gone forever, my boy, but we have learned that it contained your mother's wedding ring.

ROSE (*Leading* OLIVER *to portrait*): You see, Oliver, the sweet lady in this picture was your mother, Agnes. Your father had it painted and left it with Mr. Brownlow before he went to Rome. You look very much like her.

OLIVER: I have always loved her, and dreamed of seeing her face.

ROSE: Oliver, she was my older sister. And that means that I am your aunt! (*Hugs* OLIVER *joyfully*)

MRS. BEDWIN: Oliver, dear, you shall have a home here with us for as long as you like! (OLIVER *runs to her and hugs her happily.*)

GRIMWIG: Ahem! Now that everything has turned out well, and I'm truly glad of it, my boy, perhaps you could persuade Mrs. Bedwin to bring out a plate of those excellent muffins? Otherwise, I shall be forced to eat my hat!

MRS. BEDWIN (*Wiping her eyes and curtsying*): Oh, do come downstairs to tea, all of you! (*All rise, laughing, and start to exit as the curtain falls.*)

THE END

PRODUCTION NOTES

OLIVER TWIST

Characters: 12 male; 5 female; male extras for Workhouse Boys, Fagin's Boys, and male and female extras for Townspeople. Extra parts may be doubled.

Playing Time: 35 minutes.

Costumes: Appropriate dress for England in the 1830's. Oliver, Old Sally, and Workhouse Boys wear tattered, dirty clothes and are barefoot. Oliver later changes to a neat suit, shoes and stockings. Mr. Bumble and Mrs. Corney are better dressed; he carries a cane. Fagin wears a patched, grimy gown. The Artful Dodger wears a man's coat which hangs to his heels. Nancy wears a bright-colored dress, later adding a bonnet and apron, and a cloak and shawl. Mr. Brownlow, Bookseller and Mr. Grimwig wear trousers, waistcoats, hats, etc. Mrs. Bedwin wears white apron and cap, and Rose dresses as a proper young lady. Police Officers, uniforms.

Properties: Wooden bowls, a cooking pot, walking canes, toasting forks, sausages, handkerchiefs, two wallets, a strongbox, some jewelry and watches, a stout club, books and magazines, a plate of muffins, a tea service on a tray, a slip of paper, a paper representing will.

Setting: Scene 1: The dirty dining hall of the parish workhouse in an English country village. A long table with benches around it stands at center. Scene 2: Fagin's Den is cluttered with pallets on floor, a fireplace at rear (which may be painted on a flat) with pots and pans, and a line of handkerchiefs hanging over it. Other boxes, dishes, and old clothes are scattered about. Scene 3: A bookstall in Clerkenwell Square. The bookstall is a cart which can be wheeled on and off. A sign on the cart reads BOOKS. Scene 4: Mr. Brownlow's Parlor. The fireplace from Scene 2 is used, without the clutter, and chairs and tables are placed around the room, with lamps, vases of flowers, and a young woman's portrait. There may also be a couch and stool. Scene 5: The bookstall. Scene 6: Mr. Brownlow's parlor.

Lighting: Lights are dimmed in Scene 5.

Sound: Clock striking twelve.

Dracula

by Bram Stoker

Characters

JONATHAN HARKER
COUNT DRACULA
THREE VAMPIRES
MINA HARKER
LUCY WESTENRA
DR. JOHN SEWARD
PROFESSOR ABRAHAM VAN HELSING
RENFIELD, *a patient*
KARNES, *an attendant*

SCENE 1

TIME: *Early twentieth century.*
SETTING: *A gloomy room in Castle Dracula, in Transylvania. Torches over fireplace give flickering light. Table, center, is set with dishes of food, etc. Large open window is at left, and working door, at right.*
AT RISE: *After a moment of silence, a knock is heard.*
HARKER *(Calling from off right):* Hello? *(Pause; another knock)* Hello? *(Creaking sound is heard as* JONATHAN HARKER *opens door and looks in.)* Count Dracula? *(Steps in, carrying luggage)* It's Jonathan Harker . . . the lawyer you sent for from London! *(There is no answer.)* The coachman said I

should come in. *(Crosses center, sets down luggage. Suddenly, door slams behind him. He turns quickly.)* Count? *(Opens door, looks out)* No one there. *(Steps in, closing door)* That's odd. *(Looks around)* Gloomy old place . . . I know the Count is expecting me. *(Notices table)* Ah, see here, the table is set! *(Stands with back to window. As* HARKER *examines table,* COUNT DRACULA, *in black, with black cape, suddenly enters at window.)*

DRACULA: Welcome to Castle Dracula, Mr. Harker!

HARKER *(Startled; turning):* Oh! Count Dracula? (DRACULA bows.) Forgive me. *(Bows)* I didn't hear you come in. I apologize for arriving so late. It must be well after midnight.

DRACULA: I am often up at this hour of the night, Mr. Harker. You will need food and rest after your long journey. *(Crosses to table)* won't you sit down and eat? *(Pours wine while standing beside* HARKER)

HARKER: Thank you. I'm famished. Will you join me?

DRACULA: I have already dined, and I do not drink . . . wine, that is.

HARKER *(Sitting at table):* This is quite an honor. I've never eaten on gold tableware.

DRACULA: It has been in my family for many generations.

HARKER *(Holding up plate):* Extremely well polished! I can see my reflection in this piece. *(He starts, then looks quickly up at* DRACULA.) That's odd.

DRACULA *(Quickly stepping aside):* Is something the matter?

HARKER *(With a nervous laugh):* I didn't see your reflection in the plate, but I thought you were standing beside me.

DRACULA: The shadows in this room can be deceiving, Mr. Harker. Please—eat your meal. *(Sits in opposite chair)*

HARKER *(Staring at* DRACULA *a moment, then beginning to eat):* This is delicious. *(Sound of wolves howling is heard off left;* HARKER *looks up, alarmed.)* Wolves! They sound very close. *(Continues to eat)*

DRACULA *(Pleased):* Listen to them! The children of the night.

What music they make! *(With a sly smile)* But you are a city dweller, and perhaps you do not share my feelings about them.

HARKER: I'm afraid not. But you'll soon become a city dweller yourself, Count, once you move to London.

DRACULA *(Sighing):* Yes. I have read of your great city, and I long to go there, to share its life and *(Mysteriously)* its death. I want you to arrange my journey to England, Mr. Harker. I shall require your services for at least a month.

HARKER *(Startled):* A month! *(He cuts himself on knife; in pain)* Ah!

DRACULA: What is it?

HARKER: I've cut my finger.

DRACULA *(Rushing to* HARKER; *fiercely):* Your finger bleeds!

HARKER *(Drawing back, alarmed):* It's only a scratch. *(Pulls out handkerchief and wraps it around his finger)*

DRACULA *(Slowly turning away, breathing hard):* Take care, Mr. Harker. A cut . . . can be very dangerous.

HARKER: Yes, it was clumsy of me. *(Uncomfortably)* I had planned to stay only a day or two, Count.

DRACULA *(Icily):* You will stay as long as I need you! *(Fiercely gazes at* HARKER, *then turns and sits)*

HARKER *(Uneasily):* Very well. I will write to my wife and tell her my visit will be longer than I expected.

DRACULA: Good. *(Calmly)* Now, tell me about the house you have purchased for me.

HARKER *(Uneasily):* Yes, of course. It is called Carfax, and dates back to medieval times.

DRACULA: That will suit me perfectly. I am of an ancient family. *(Fiercely)* The blood of Attila the Hun flows in my veins! *(Quietly)* Shall I have any close neighbors at Carfax?

HARKER: Only Dr. John Seward, a most respectable gentleman who operates a private hospital there for the insane.

DRACULA: Very well. *(Sound of howling)* Ah! An hour until dawn. *(Rises)* I must leave you now. Sleep well, Mr. Harker. *(Smiles, baring his teeth)* And dream well! *(Bows and sweeps out right)*

HARKER: What a strange man! *(Sound of howling)* I'm beginning to wish I hadn't come! *(Goes to luggage)* I must write all this down in my journal, but first a letter to Mina. *(Takes paper from bag)* It's so dim in here. I'd better ask the Count for a candle. *(Crosses to door, tries to open it, finds it locked)* Locked! *(Pounds on door)* Count Dracula! *(No answer)* Count Dracula! *(No answer; he turns away.)* Why would he lock me in? Am I his guest, or his prisoner? *(Sound of howling; he crosses to window.)* This window must be a thousand feet above ground! How brightly the moon shines! *(Leans out window)* What's that! Something moving below me! *(Leans out window; astonished)* I . . . I can't believe my eyes! Count Dracula, crawling down the castle wall—head first!—with his cloak spread out behind him like the wings of a bat! *(Turns into room, overcome with fear)* What is this creature in the form of man? *(Stumbles to couch)* What's happening to me? *(Wipes brow)* There's a mist before me . . . something cloudy . . . I can't move! *(With effort)* I . . . I feel sleepy, but I can't close my eyes. . . . *(He lies motionless as* THREE VAMPIRES, *in flowing white gowns, enter right.)*

1ST VAMPIRE *(Urgently, to* 3RD): Go on. You are first tonight.

2ND VAMPIRE: Yes, go on. The master has brought him here for us.

1ST VAMPIRE: He is young and strong. He will have plenty for all.

3RD VAMPIRE: But the master said we must not touch him!

2ND VAMPIRE: We are hungry! This man's blood is warm and waiting. Go on! (3RD VAMPIRE *bends over* HARKER, *baring her teeth.* 1ST *and* 2ND VAMPIRES *hover expectantly. Suddenly,* DRACULA *swoops in from window, furious. He flings* 3RD VAMPIRE *aside and angrily gestures the other two away.)*

DRACULA: How dare you touch him when I have forbidden it! This man belongs to me! When I have finished with him, then you may have him. Now, go and seek your prey in the village! *(Laughing harshly,* VAMPIRES *exit right.* DRACULA *looks triumphantly at* HARKER.) You will remain here for as long as I command! (DRACULA *crosses to window, spreads his cape and swoops out. Lights slowly fade up as* HARKER *stirs and awakens from his trance.*)

HARKER: What horrid dream was this? Or was it a dream? *(Sits up)* Those creatures meant to suck my blood! *(Rushes to door, frantically shakes handle)* Still locked! *(Stumbles back to couch)* What is happening? I must get out of this place! *(Blackout. After a moment, lights come up on* HARKER, *looking tired, who is at table, writing.)* Today marks my fourth week here, and I have not left this room. I fear I shall never leave it! Count Dracula has always been very secretive, and he has destroyed every personal letter I have tried to send. His fierce, hypnotic eyes terrify me, and his hand, whenever it happens to brush against mine, is cold as death! Every night in his terrible presence I become more weak, helpless, unable to control my own will! Every night . . . *(He looks up, struck with a sudden thought.)* Every night! Why have I never seen him by day? He and those hideous, laughing women always vanish at dawn! *(Rises, putting notebook into pocket)* Tomorrow the Count leaves for England—he has also arranged to ship fifty large boxes—but he has said nothing about my departure. He must plan to leave me behind—a helpless prisoner. Those women . . . they must be waiting for my blood! *(Rushes to window)* I must get out of this room! If Dracula can find footholds along these walls, so can I! If what I suspect is true, I must find him before the sun sets! *(Climbs out window. Curtain)*

* * * * *

SCENE 2

SETTING: *A burial vault in Castle Dracula, played before the curtain. Two coffins with closed lids are center.*

AT RISE: HARKER *enters left, carrying a candle.*

HARKER: This underground crypt terrifies me. *(Sees coffins)*

What's this? *(Looks closer)* A shipping label directed to Carfax? Why would Count Dracula send coffins to England? *(Cautiously, he lifts lid of one box)* Dirt! A coffin full of dirt! *(Lifts lid of second coffin, then recoils in horror)* Count Dracula! Dead? *(Looks closer)* No, he can't be dead! His eyes are open . . . yet they are glassy. His lips are red . . . blood-red! *(Holds his hand before* DRACULA's *face)* No breath! *(Eagerly)* He is dead! *(Leans closer, then freezes in horror)* No! His eyes . . . his terrible red eyes . . . no! *(With a great effort he turns away, slams lid closed and staggers backward onto other coffin.)* Vampire! Count Dracula is a vampire! *(Suddenly realizing)* Tomorrow when those boxes are shipped to England, he will lie in one of them! Of course! It is the only way he can travel such a great distance without rays of sun. *(Jumps up)* I can't let him go to England. *(Looks around wildly, picks up loose board)* I must stop him! *(Hesitates)* Do I dare lift that lid again? I must! *(Flings up coffin lid and raises board to strike, but cries out and his arms stop in midair.)* No! His eyes—I can't look at him! *(Tries to lower board, but cannot)* I must break his spell! *(Suddenly)* I know—the cross. *(With tremendous effort, he moves one of his arms so that it forms a cross with the board. Sound of hissing is heard from inside coffin.* HARKER *falls backward.)* Yes! The cross repels vampires. The spell he held me in has been broken. *(Desperately)* I must escape to England before he does! *(Keeping cross before him, he backs off left. Blackout)*

* * * * *

SCENE 3

TIME: *Evening, six weeks later.*
SETTING: *Dr. Seward's Hospital, just outside London. Writing desk is at right. Scene is played before curtain.*
AT RISE: *Lights come up on* MINA HARKER, *writing at desk.*
MINA: August 19th. At last, after almost three months without

a word, I have a letter from my beloved Jonathan, in a hospital in Budapest. He has been dangerously ill, the result of some terrible shock. But he is nearly well and will soon be home. If only I could be equally happy for my poor friend Lucy! Her strange illness is much worse, and Dr. John Seward has brought her here to his private hospital. It is quiet except for one patient who escapes from his room every day. (MINA *looks up as* RENFIELD, *barefoot and wearing pajamas, dashes in left.*)

RENFIELD (*Calling over his shoulder*): You can't catch me, Karnes! I can run faster than you! (*He stumbles and falls beside desk.*)

MINA: Oh! (*Goes to him*) Have you hurt yourself? Let me help you. (*Helps him to his feet*)

RENFIELD: I'm all right. (*Anxiously*) Please, please, don't tell Karnes where I am.

KARNES (*Off left, closer*): Renfield!

RENFIELD: Please don't let him lock me up again. It's so lonely. Please! (*Huddles behind* MINA *as* KARNES *enters, followed by* DR. JOHN SEWARD.)

KARNES: Here he is, Dr. Seward. I'll get him.

MINA: Must you take him away?

KARNES: Yes, ma'am. He's under treatment, you see, and he shouldn't be out of his room. Come along, Renfield. (*Leads* RENFIELD *off right*)

MINA: The poor man.

SEWARD: He is a rather sad case. Has delusions, sees things no one else can see.

MINA: I hope you can help him.

SEWARD: I'm sure we can, Mrs. Harker. By the way, I understand your husband will arrive here in a few days.

MINA (*Smiling*): Yes. I'm so eager to see him. He's had a very hard time.

SEWARD: I'm sure you will be the right cure for him—just as your being here is helping your friend, Lucy.

MINA (*Concerned*): How is Lucy this evening, Dr. Seward?

SEWARD: No better, I'm afraid. But I've called in Professor Van Helsing, the best rare-disease specialist in Europe. He's examining Lucy now. If anyone can help her, he can.

PROF. VAN HELSING (*Entering left*): Ah, here you are, John!

SEWARD: Professor! Let me introduce Lucy's dearest friend, Mina Harker.

VAN HELSING (*Bowing*): Mrs. Harker.

MINA: Professor Van Helsing. Thank you for coming.

SEWARD: What is your opinion of Miss Lucy, Professor?

VAN HELSING: She has lost much blood, yet shows no signs of anemia. She complains of difficulty in breathing, heavy sleep, and dreams that frighten her. But the most serious symptom, and one she cannot explain, are the two small punctures in her throat! I am glad you sent for me, John.

SEWARD: Do you know what is wrong with her?

VAN HELSING: I have a suspicion, but I pray I am mistaken. Nevertheless, I must take precautions. Go back to her, John. She must not be left alone. Mrs. Harker, will you come with me to find the gardener?

MINA: Very well. (*Exits right with* VAN HELSING)

SEWARD (*Shaking his head*): Now, why does the Professor want to see the gardener? (*Exits left; blackout. Curtain*)

* * * * *

SCENE 4

TIME: *A few minutes later.*

SETTING: *Lucy's hospital room, with a bed near window at left, a small table and two chairs before fireplace at center. Mina's desk remains down right. There is a tray with coffeepot and cups on table; curtains at window.*

AT RISE: LUCY WESTENRA *lies in bed.* SEWARD *is drawing curtains closed.*

SEWARD: Try to sleep now, Lucy.

LUCY: But I am afraid to sleep, Dr. Seward. Every night, I have a dream, a horrible dream! I see two burning red eyes and a vicious face bending over me. It doesn't remain long, but it terrifies me! Afterwards, I awaken feeling so weak . . . so ill.

SEWARD (*In reassuring tone*): You may sleep tonight without fear. I'll keep watch, and if I see any evidence of bad dreams, I'll wake you at once.

LUCY: I want to sleep so much—peaceful, restful sleep. (*Gratefully*) Thank you, Dr. Seward. (VAN HELSING *and* MINA *enter with box containing flowers.*)

SEWARD: Well, Professor, what do you have there?

VAN HELSING: A cure, I hope!

MINA: It's the strangest medicine I've ever seen. Garlic flowers!

VAN HELSING: We must hang them around the window, door, and fireplace. (*He and* MINA *hang flowers.*) Ah, I see you turn up your nose, Miss Lucy, but these flowers are strong medicine.

LUCY (*Smiling*): Very strong! I believe you are playing a joke to cheer me up, Professor.

VAN HELSING: It is no joke! There is a purpose in all I do. You must also wear a wreath of these around your neck. (*Puts flowers around* LUCY's *neck*)

SEWARD: If I didn't know better, I'd say you were trying to keep out an evil spirit.

VAN HELSING (*Quietly*): Perhaps I am. Now, Miss Lucy, you must sleep. And take care not to disturb these flowers, no matter how disagreeable they may be.

LUCY: I won't, Professor. Thank you.

VAN HELSING: Good night. (*Exits*)

MINA: Good night, Lucy. Sleep well. (*Arranges covers over* LUCY, *kisses her on forehead, then exits.* SEWARD *pours cup of coffee. Sound of howling is heard off left.* LUCY *stirs restlessly.*)

SEWARD (*Startled*): What on earth is that? There are no wolves around here. Must be some stray dogs. (*Sounds of fluttering and banging are heard outside window.*) Now, what? Something at the window? (*Crosses to window, pulls curtains aside)* Why, it's a bat! The biggest one I've ever seen! *(Waves his arm)* Get away! Go on! Confounded creature! Never had bats attacking the windows before. There, it's gone. *(Closes curtains and looks at* LUCY, *who now lies quietly)* Good. She's asleep. (RENFIELD *suddenly bursts into room.)*

RENFIELD: Dr. Seward!

SEWARD *(Crossing to him; gently):* Now, Renfield, you know you mustn't be out of your room. Let me take you back.

RENFIELD: No! I don't want to go back. *(Playfully)* I'll run and you can chase me. We'll have a game! *(Runs out)*

SEWARD: No! Wait! Renfield! *(Runs out after him; howling sound again, then fluttering and banging sounds at window.* LUCY *tosses fitfully.* RENFIELD *re-enters, laughing, looking over his shoulder.)*

RENFIELD: I tricked you, Dr. Seward. You won't find me for a long time. *(Sound of thunder; he turns abruptly to window, transfixed; in an awed tone)* Yes, master, I obey your command. *(Crosses to window, opens curtains and removes garlic flowers)* I'll take the flowers away. I know you don't like them. *(Gently slips flowers from around* LUCY'S *neck, then turns to window)* It is done, master. Now reward me as you promised! *(Sound of thunder. Lightning is seen and* DRACULA *leaps into room at window. Frightened,* RENFIELD *backs toward door.)*

DRACULA: I will reward you, Renfield, but I have more important matters to attend to now.

RENFIELD: Yes, master. I will wait. But don't forget me! Don't forget Renfield! *(Runs out, closing door.* DRACULA *turns toward* LUCY, *who suddenly wakes, sits up, and stares, terrified, at him.)*

DRACULA: My nocturnal visits to you are almost over. Soon you shall be entirely mine . . . you shall be as I am! *(Moves toward her)* Do not resist! It is useless. No one can resist Dracula! *(He raises his cape; there is a flash of lightning, then thunder is heard. Blackout for a moment to indicate passage of time. When lights come up, it is the next morning.* LUCY *lies in bed.* SEWARD *sleeps in chair.* VAN HELSING *enters with* MINA.*)*

MINA *(Worried):* I hope Lucy is all right. *(Crosses to bed)*

VAN HELSING: Poor John. He looks exhausted. *(Shakes SEWARD)* John, wake up!

SEWARD *(Waking):* What? Oh . . . I must have nodded off. How is Miss Lucy?

MINA *(Screaming):* Professor!

VAN HELSING: What is it? *(Rushes to bed)* She has lost more blood! A great deal of blood!

MINA: The garlic flowers are gone!

SEWARD: What? But she has slept soundly all night.

VAN HELSING: Are you sure? Were you here every minute?

SEWARD: Yes! I only went to sleep after the sun came up. *(After a pause)* Wait. I was gone a little while when I went after Renfield.

VAN HELSING: Renfield?

SEWARD: Yes. He escaped from his room again last night. But I wasn't gone more than ten minutes.

VAN HELSING: Ah! That was long enough! *(Takes LUCY's pulse)*

MINA *(Frightened):* Professor, I've never seen her so pale.

VAN HELSING: Her heartbeat is very weak. She must have a transfusion.

SEWARD: I'm ready. *(Brings bag of instruments to bed and rolls up one of his sleeves. LUCY gasps for breath.)*

VAN HELSING: The two punctures in her throat are fresher, tinged with blood. I fear we are not in time! *(Raises LUCY's head. She gasps, looking wildly around.)*

MINA: Professor, what's happening to her? *(LUCY suddenly bares her teeth, and growling, lunges at SEWARD.)*

VAN HELSING *(Holding LUCY back):* Stay back, John! Don't let her touch you! This will pass in a moment. *(Lucy struggles frantically with VAN HELSING, then suddenly falls back, limp.)*

MINA: Lucy!

LUCY *(Weakly):* Mina, pray for me. Professor, I think you know what has happened to me. Give me peace, if you can.

VAN HELSING: I will, Miss Lucy. I swear it! *(LUCY smiles, closes her eyes and turns her head away.)*

MINA: Lucy! *(Kneels beside bed, sobbing)* Oh, Lucy!

VAN HELSING: She's dead, but her suffering is just beginning. I will do whatever I must to see that no one else suffers as she has! *(Blackout. Curtain. After a moment, lights come up on MINA, before curtain writing at her desk down right.)*

MINA: A week ago my poor Lucy was buried in the Hampstead Hill churchyard. How I miss my dearest friend! Thank heaven my Jonathan is here now, although it breaks my heart to see him so pale and worn, so nervous and agitated. Last night he gave me his journal to read. What a terrible ordeal he experienced! I thank heaven for his escape from Castle Dracula, and tremble when I think that he has sworn to find that monster here. Professor Van Helsing remains determined to find the cause of Lucy's death.

HARKER *(Running in with newspaper; anxiously)* Mina!

MINA: Jonathan, what is it?

HARKER: I saw him, just a moment ago!

MINA *(Frightened):* Do you mean—

HARKER: Dracula! Yes! He has arrived at Carfax. And look at this in today's paper! *(Hands her newspaper)*

MINA *(Reading):* A Hampstead Mystery. During the past week in the neighborhood of Hampstead, several young children have strayed from home. They often remain lost overnight, then are found the next morning, all wounded in the throat, as if attacked by an animal. The children tell of being led away by a beautiful lady in a long white dress. *(Looks up)* What does this mean, Jonathan?

HARKER: I believe Professor Van Helsing can explain it. He must read my journal. Come! *(Leads her off right. Blackout. Curtains open. Lights come up on LUCY's hospital room. VAN HELSING, SEWARD, HARKER and MINA are gathered around table; journal and newspaper are on table.)*

VAN HELSING: Jonathan, you were fortunate to escape with only a temporary breakdown of your sanity.

SEWARD *(Shaking his head):* This is incredible! Count Dracula—a vampire—at Carfax! I can't believe it! *(To VAN HELSING)* How can we be rid of this monster?

VAN HELSING: First, we must free Miss Lucy from his terrible bondage.

MINA: But Lucy is dead!

VAN HELSING *(Pointing to paper; soberly)* Not really. She is the beautiful lady of the Hampstead Mystery.

HARKER *(Nodding):* She has become like the vampires I saw at Castle Dracula.

SEWARD: But, how?

VAN HELSING: When the vampire sucked her blood, and she appeared to die, he made her like himself—undead.

MINA: What do you mean—undead?

VAN HELSING: Vampires are cursed with immortality. By night they feast on blood of the living, and so add new victims to their kind. Lucy has begun her undead existence on Hampstead Hill.

MINA *(Covering her face):* Oh, how horrible!

SEWARD: Professor, what can we do?

VAN HELSING: To free her from Dracula's power and give her eternal rest, we must seal her tomb after she leaves it at night. Then we will wait for her to return. She will not be able to enter, and if we keep her within a circle of crosses until sunrise, she will find her final peace.

MINA: Heaven help her! Let this be done!

VAN HELSING: We shall do it tonight. Then, we must track Count Dracula and destroy him! Jonathan, can you remember all of the places he sent his coffins filled with his native soil?

HARKER: Yes—to Carfax, Whitby, and Exeter. But there are fifty coffins!

VAN HELSING: We must locate each one and purify it with the cross so he cannot use it. Then we will arm ourselves with the things that repel him—garlic, and the cross—and when he seeks us out, as he most definitely will, we shall trap him! Come, we have much to do, and little time to accomplish it! *(Blackout. Curtain. A moment later, lights come up on* MINA *seated at her desk, writing. She wears a large cross on chain around her neck.)*

MINA: The task is done. At last, my dear Lucy's spirit is at peace. *(Sound of howling; she looks up a moment, then continues writing.)* Professor Van Hesling and Jonathan have found all but one of Count Dracula's coffins. Now we wait for this monster to seek his revenge upon us. Dr. Seward believes that Renfield was the means of Dracula's entrance here, for the vampire can enter only when invited by someone inside the house.

RENFIELD *(Rushing into room, very agitated):* Mrs. Harker!

MINA *(Jumping up):* Renfield!

RENFIELD: My master wants me to come to him, but I don't want to! You are my friend. *(Loud sound of howling; he turns to window, clutching his throat as if being strangled.)* No! No, master! *(Turns to* MINA; *anxiously)* I must warn you! (KARNES, SEWARD, HARKER *and* VAN HELSING *enter. All except* KARNES *wear crosses on chains around their necks.)*

KARNES: There he is!

SEWARD: Take him back to his room, Karnes, and stay with him.

RENFIELD: No! Wait! *(Dodges around* MINA's *desk)* Mrs. Harker, you must leave here at once! *(Sound of howling again;* RENFIELD *falls to his knees, clutching his throat, facing window.)* No, master! Leave me alone!

KARNES *(Puzzled):* What's the matter with him?

MINA *(Gently):* Renfield, why do you want me to leave? *(She puts her hand on his shoulder.)*

RENFIELD *(Urgently):* My master said he was coming for you. *(He winces and clutches his throat, struggling to speak)* He said I must let him in, just as I did before. *(He pulls his hands from his throat; angrily.)* But he promised to reward me, and he hasn't kept his promise! I'm very angry with him! Please go, while there is still time! *(Runs out)*

KARNES: I'll get him, Dr. Seward! *(Runs out)*

HARKER *(Excitedly):* There's no doubt that Dracula has power over Renfield, but he can't overpower us! We're ready for him. Each of us is wearing a cross. I've made sure there is garlic at every window, door, and fireplace in the hospital. And even if

Dracula should find a way in, the four of us can hold him here until dawn. *(Checks his watch)* It is less than an hour until sunrise.

SEWARD: It sounds simple, but what if we fail?

HARKER: We mustn't fail!

KARNES *(Running in; breathlessly):* Dr. Seward, Renfield's escaped onto the grounds. I'll need some help to catch him.

VAN HELSING: We mustn't lose sight of him. Come on! *(Runs out, followed by* KARNES *and* SEWARD*)*

HARKER: Mina, you stay here. This room is sealed.

MINA: I'll be all right. Be careful, Jonathan! (HARKER *exits;* MINA *closes door. Sound of howling off left;* MINA *folds her arms tightly together.)*

RENFIELD *(Off left):* Help! Somebody help me! He's following me! I can't get away from him!

MINA: That's Renfield!

RENFIELD *(Wildly; off left):* Help! Please, help me!

MINA: Poor Renfield! *(Runs to window, pulls curtains aside and looks out)* I can't see him. What's that? Something in the air . . . a bat, flying right toward the window! *(She backs away.)* No . . . no . . . *(She reaches for her cross, but her hands stop in midair; she stops, staring fixedly out window)* The eyes . . . the burning red eyes . . . no! *(She backs away a step, then stops, transfixed; sound of thunder)* Yes . . . I will do as you command. *(Slowly, she takes cross from around her neck and drops it on floor. Then she removes garlic flowers from window and opens pane.)* It is done. Come in. *(She backs slowly to center as* DRACULA *sweeps in through window.)*

DRACULA: You have a strong will, but I am stronger! You seek to destroy me, but you will submit to my power! You will become mine forever! *(Raises his cape and moves toward her.* MINA *remains at center, transfixed.)*

RENFIELD *(Bursting through door; breathlessly):* No, master! Do not touch her!

DRACULA: Fool! You betrayed me! *(Moves toward* RENFIELD*)*

RENFIELD: No! I'm not your slave anymore! *(Leaps at* DRAC-

ULA; DRACULA *seizes him by the throat.* RENFIELD *struggles for a moment, then slowly collapses and falls lifeless to the floor.)*

DRACULA *(Turning to* MINA): Now, I must drink . . . and fly to my resting place. I haven't much time! *(Raises his cape and moves toward* MINA. SEWARD, HARKER *and* VAN HELSING *rush in, each holding cross out in front of him.)*

HARKER: Mina! Mina! (DRACULA *whirls around, enraged.* MINA, *startled out of her trance, screams and recoils, but* DRACULA *seizes her.)*

VAN HELSING: Surround him with your crosses!

DRACULA *(Backing away):* Foolish mortals! You dare try to destroy me? Just as I have conquered my enemies for hundreds of years, I shall conquer you! This woman shall become as I am, and then each of you in turn shall become her victims!

HARKER *(Desperately):* You'll never have her, you devil! *(Leaps at* DRACULA, *dropping his cross)*

MINA: Jonathan, no! (DRACULA *releases* MINA *and seizes* HARKER *by throat.* VAN HELSING *thrusts his cross into* DRACULA'S *face.* DRACULA *recoils, hissing, releasing* HARKER. MINA *pulls* HARKER *away.)*

VAN HELSING: Remember our plan. Surround him! (VAN HELSING *guards door,* SEWARD, *the fireplace,* HARKER *and* MINA, *the window.)*

DRACULA *(Furiously):* You are clever, Van Helsing, but you cannot win! *(He hurls himself at window, but* HARKER *springs forward with his cross;* DRACULA *yells and cringes, as if in pain.)*

HARKER: We must hold him off only a little longer! It is almost sunrise! (DRACULA *rushes at door.)*

MINA: Watch out, Professor! (VAN HELSING *holds out cross and* DRACULA *turns back.)*

VAN HELSING: You cannot escape, monster! *(Sound of cock crowing is heard off left.* DRACULA, *frantic, hurls himself at window. Rays of sunlight shine in, and he falls back with a cry of rage.)*

HARKER: Move in! Keep him in the sunlight! (VAN HELSING *and* SEWARD *move behind* DRACULA.)

DRACULA: My curse upon you, Jonathan Harker! My curse upon all of you! *(Trapped between brightening sunlight and circle of crosses, he cringes and cowers, hissing and snarling. He is forced to the edge of window; he turns, blinded, and falls through window with a strangled cry. All rush to look out.)*

MINA *(Turning back into room):* Now his tormented soul may find peace at last!

HARKER: Now this horror is ended. (*Holding* MINA) We are free of Dracula forever! *(Curtain)*

THE END

PRODUCTION NOTES

Dracula

Characters: 6 male; 5 female.

Playing Time: 35 minutes.

Costumes: British dress of the 1900–1910 period. Seward, white doctor's coat. Dracula, black suit, long black cape, pale make-up, fangs. Lucy, nightgown. Renfield, institutional pajamas. Karnes, white uniform. Vampires, long, white gowns, pale make-up, blood-red lips.

Properties: Luggage; handkerchief; notebook and pencil; candle; paper; pen and inkwell; coffeepot and cups on tray; box of "garlic flowers" on string; wreath of "garlic flowers"; doctor's bag; newspaper; five crosses on chains; pocket watch.

Setting: Scene 1: a gloomy room in Castle Dracula. At left is a window, low to floor. It must be large enough to allow easy passage by Dracula. Door is at right. Stone fireplace, center. Large table and heavy wooden armchairs are at center, and couch is at right. Table is set with "gold" plates, bowls of food, goblets, and wine bottle. Walls are hung with tapestries and lighted torches. Scene 2: before the curtain. Bare stage with two coffins, center, and board on floor nearby. Scene 3, before the curtain, desk and chair are at right. Scene 4, Lucy's hospital room. The fireplace set in Scene 1 may be used here, with different coverings and decoration on furnishings. Add curtains at windows, paintings on walls. Bed is at left, near window. Small table and chairs are center. Mina's desk remains down right.

Lighting: Flickering light from torches; dim lighting for entrance of Vampires; subdued light in Dracula's burial vault; bright light in Lucy's room; lightning flashes; spotlight with yellow gel for sunlight in Scene 4; blackouts, all as indicated in text.

Sound: Creaking and slamming of door; howling of wolves; thunder; fluttering and banging at window. Appropriate music may also add to the mood of the play.

The Purloined Letter

by Edgar Allan Poe

Characters

AUGUSTE DUPIN, *a detective*
PIERRE, *his friend*
PREFECT, *Paris Police Department*
MINISTER
LADY
GENTLEMAN

SCENE 1

TIME: *Paris, 1840's.*

SETTING: *A room in Auguste Dupin's apartment, furnished with two armchairs, small table, desk and chair center. There is a tray with glasses and decanter of wine on table. Door to outside hall is right. Down left is small, ornate table, representing Lady's chamber.*

AT RISE: AUGUSTE DUPIN *sits in armchair, reading newspaper.* PIERRE *stands behind table, pouring glass of wine.*

PIERRE *(Gesturing at newspaper):* There! You see, my friend, all of Paris is still talking about those hideous murders in the Rue Morgue! The murders so quickly and cleverly solved by the finest detective in Paris, my friend and colleague, Auguste Dupin. *(Hands* DUPIN *glass of wine)* Don't you find it satisfying to have the police come to you for assistance?

DUPIN: They come to me only as a last resort, Pierre.

PIERRE *(Gleefully):* I know! Even then that pompous Prefect of the Police can hardly bring himself to ask your advice. But, oh, how he tries to take all the credit after you have solved the case. If only he were more appreciative of your talents.

DUPIN: Our friend the Prefect appreciates me when it suits him.

PIERRE: When he is at his wits' end and has nowhere else to turn! *(There is a knock at door.)* Do you think that could possibly be. . . ? *(Opens door)* Why, what a surprise! Monsieur, the Prefect! (PREFECT *enters, brushing past* PIERRE.)

PREFECT *(Removing his hat):* Good evening, Dupin. I hope I am not interrupting anything.

DUPIN: Not at all! Come in. I believe you know Pierre?

PREFECT *(Stiffly):* Your servant?

DUPIN: My assistant. Won't you sit down?

PIERRE *(Smiling; pulling up chair for* PREFECT): You will find this chair quite comfortable. May I take your hat?

PREFECT *(Sitting):* No, thank you. *(Holds his hat on his knee; to* DUPIN) I was just attending to some business in this neighborhood, and I saw your lights. I thought I would see how you're getting on.

PIERRE: We are both quite well, thank you. Completely rested and recovered from our exertions in the Rue Morgue murder case. *(Offers* PREFECT *a glass of wine)*

PREFECT: I do not drink wine when on duty. Ah . . . Dupin, I was wondering . . . I thought I might mention a little matter to you. A case . . .

PIERRE: Which has caused you a bit of trouble, Monsieur?

PREFECT *(Frowning at* PIERRE): It is very simple! I have no doubt that I can manage it perfectly well! *(To* DUPIN) I thought you might like to hear the details, Dupin, because it is so very odd.

DUPIN *(Calmly sipping wine):* Simple and odd. I see.

PREFECT: The police have been quite puzzled because the affair *is* so simple. It baffles us completely.

DUPIN: Perhaps it is the very simplicity of the matter that baffles you.

PREFECT *(Laughing heartily):* The very simplicity? What nonsense! Really, Dupin, you surprise me!

PIERRE: A perfectly reasonable suggestion, Monsieur. What, exactly, is this problem that baffles you?

PREFECT *(Huffily turning his back to* PIERRE): The business demands the greatest secrecy, Dupin. I could lose my position if it were known that I confided this matter to anyone. *(Glances doubtfully at* PIERRE)

DUPIN: You know you may rely on me, *and* my friend.

PIERRE *(Perching on edge of table):* We are all attention! Proceed, Monsieur!

PREFECT *(Scowling at* PIERRE, *then speaking directly to* DUPIN): I have received personal information from a high government source that a letter of great importance has been purloined from the royal apartments!

PIERRE: Aha! *(To* DUPIN) See how quickly your reputation will rise now, my friend!

PREFECT *(Ignoring* PIERRE): The man who took the letter is known. He was seen taking it, and he still has it in his possession.

DUPIN: And the letter is extremely sensitive.

PREFECT: Disclosure of the letter's contents to a third person, who shall be nameless, would bring into question the honor of a lady of most exalted station. Possession of this letter gives the thief great power over her.

DUPIN: But this power depends upon the thief's knowing that the lady knows he has the document. (PREFECT *leans closer to* DUPIN; PIERRE *also leans closer.)*

PREFECT: He knows! He is one of the high ministers at court. A plotter! An unprincipled villain! A man who dares anything to further his own interests.

DUPIN: I believe I know him, without your mentioning his name.

PREFECT: His theft was exceedingly bold. The lady was helpless. She received the letter while alone in her chamber, several months ago. (*Lights fade out on* DUPIN's *apartment and come up left on* LADY's *chamber.*)

LADY (*Entering left, with letter*): Yes! This is the letter I have been waiting for! It will mean much to the security of France! (*Looks around anxiously*) But no one must know of it! No one would understand what I do in all innocence for my country.

GENTLEMAN (*Entering left*): Ah, here you are, my dear. (LADY, *startled, whirls to face him, holding letter behind her.*)

LADY: Oh!

GENTLEMAN: Forgive me, my dear. I did not mean to startle you.

LADY: I did not hear you come in. (*Casually places letter on table behind her*) What is it?

GENTLEMAN: The Minister has asked to see us about some urgent business. (MINISTER *enters, with papers; bows slightly.*)

MINISTER: Your pardon, madam, but I have some papers that require your approval.

LADY (*Nervously*): Can they not wait until another time?

MINISTER: No, madam. They are of the utmost importance. May I use this table?

LADY: If . . . you wish. (*Watches anxiously as* MINISTER *spreads papers on table. He notices her letter, looks up at her sharply, then crosses to* GENTLEMAN *with papers.*)

MINISTER: Will you be good enough to look these over? (*Hands papers to* GENTLEMAN, *who moves left, studying them.* MINISTER *crosses to* LADY, *speaks aside to her.*) I recognize the handwriting on that letter, madam. Do you dare carry on such dangerous correspondence?

LADY: Do you dare question me?

MINISTER: You are on treacherous ground, madam!

LADY: Not nearly as treacherous as yours will be if you try to interfere with me!

MINISTER: What if your husband were to learn of this? (*Nods toward* GENTLEMAN)

LADY: He must never know! He would not understand!

MINISTER: No, madam, nor anyone else at court. Secret correspondence with an enemy!

LADY: Your enemy, perhaps, not mine. Do not interfere!

MINISTER *(Slyly):* We shall see, madam.

GENTLEMAN *(Crossing to them):* This is in order, Minister. *(To
LADY)* My dear, you are pale. Are you not feeling well?

LADY: I . . . I am only a little tired. *(Takes paper, glances at it
hastily, then hands it to MINISTER)* Yes, this is correct. Is that
all?

MINISTER: Yes, that is all . . . for now. Thank you. *(Takes papers
from table, leaving letter)* I will see that these are dispatched
at once. Ah! I missed one. *(He picks up letter.)* Good evening.
*(Bows slightly, glances slyly at LADY, who stares at him
angrily, then quickly exits)*

GENTLEMAN: You must lie down and rest, my dear. I will send
your maid to you, and see that you are not disturbed.

LADY: Yes, I will rest for a while. (GENTLEMAN *exits.*) My
letter! The Minister took it, knowing I could say nothing in the
presence of my husband. I must get it back at once, before he
uses it against me! *(Exits; lights fade out left, and come up on
DUPIN's apartment.)*

DUPIN: Then the lady clearly saw the Minister take her letter?

PREFECT: Yes. And he has since used the power attained
through that letter to further his own political purposes.
(Proudly) The lady tried to get it back herself, but when she
failed, she committed the matter to me—secretly, of course.

PIERRE: And now you commit it to us. Very wise, Monsieur!

DUPIN: The lady has my deepest sympathy. I have guessed who
she is, and I know her. I would do her any service within my
power.

PREFECT: As would I. My first act was to make a thorough
search of the Minister's apartments. His habits are regular,
and he is frequently out at night. His servants sleep at a
distance from his rooms, and, as you know, I have keys that
can open any door or cabinet in Paris.

PIERRE: Very clever of you, Monsieur!

PREFECT: For the past three months I have been personally engaged in ransacking the Minister's apartments. Two of my best men and I investigated every nook and corner in which the letter might be concealed. I am absolutely convinced that the letter was not there.

PIERRE: Then the Minister has hidden it somewhere else.

DUPIN *(Rising, slowly pacing):* That is possible, but I believe he would keep the letter near him, where he could produce it at a moment's notice.

PREFECT: That is exactly what *I* thought! But where?

PIERRE: Surely he does not keep it upon his person?

PREFECT: No. I hired pickpockets to waylay him, and they found no letter on him.

DUPIN: Suppose you tell us the details of your search. Did you examine all the furniture?

PREFECT: Every piece in the every room. We missed nothing.

DUPIN: The drawers?

PREFECT: Every possible drawer! To a properly trained police agent, there is no such thing as a secret drawer.

DUPIN *(Calmly):* The chairs?

PREFECT: We probed all chair cushions with long needles. *(He rises and draws long needle from his pocket and jabs it into the seat cushion of* DUPIN's *chair.)* We did the same with the mattresses.

DUPIN: What about the tables?

PREFECT: We removed all table tops. Sometimes a person will try to conceal an article in a hollowed-out table leg. The same theory applies to bedposts, all of which we examined closely— as well as the rungs of all pieces of furniture.

DUPIN: His papers and books?

PREFECT: We not only opened every book, but turned over every page. *(Seizes a book and demonstrates)* Nothing!

DUPIN: The paper on the walls?

PREFECT: We've gone over all the walls!

DUPIN: The cellar?

PREFECT: Every corner!

DUPIN: The grounds around the house?

PREFECT: Every brick, every blade of grass! The letter is not there! *(Urgently)* It *must* be recovered, Dupin. The lady is desperate. Her situation becomes more and more unbearable every day.

PIERRE: And *your* situation, Monsieur, becomes equally uncomfortable, does it not?

PREFECT: The Lady has offered a generous reward, which I would enjoy claiming. However, I am prepared to give my own check for fifty thousand francs to anyone who would assist me in obtaining that letter.

PIERRE: Fifty thousand francs! You are considerably more baffled in this matter than I supposed!

DUPIN: Surely, Monsieur, you have not exerted yourself to the utmost in this affair?

PREFECT: But I have! Would I swallow my pride and come to you, if I had not?

DUPIN: In that case *(Opens desk drawer and takes out checkbook)* . . . I would not take a single franc from the lady, but *you* may write the check for fifty thousand francs to me. When you have signed it, hold it until tomorrow night. Then you will hand the check to me, and I will hand the purloined letter to you.

PREFECT *(Astonished):* You are not serious!

DUPIN: I am perfectly serious. Come at nine o'clock, tomorrow night.

PREFECT: Nine o'clock. *(Sits at desk and writes check)* To Auguste Dupin, the sum of 50,000 francs. *(Shows check to DU-PIN, who examines it and nods his approval)*

DUPIN: Thank you. Good evening, Monsieur. (PREFECT *takes hat, puts check into pocket, crosses to door.)*

PREFECT: Good evening, gentlemen. *(Exits)*

PIERRE: Did you see the look on his face? Tell me, my friend, how are you going to get that letter?

DUPIN: By using my own methods. The Paris police are exceedingly able in their way. They are ingenious, cunning, and well trained. I feel confident that the Prefect and his men made a satisfactory investigation—as far as their labors extended.

PIERRE: But they did not extend far enough.

DUPIN: Had the letter been hidden in any of the places they searched, they would have found it. But the Prefect searched only in places where *he himself* might have hidden the letter.

PIERRE: Then he did not consider that the Minister is a clever courtier of high birth and vast experience, who might have had other ideas.

DUPIN: The Minister's frequent absences from home at night, hailed by the Prefect as an aid to his success, were deliberate opportunities for the Prefect to search undisturbed, and quickly satisfy himself that the letter was not there.

PIERRE: The Minister is extremely clever.

DUPIN: Yes, and the more I reflect upon his cleverness, and the fact that he must keep the letter near him if he intends to make use of it, the more convinced I am that he has not tried to conceal it at all.

PIERRE: I am sure that idea never occurred to Monsieur the Prefect.

DUPIN: In the morning I will call upon the Minister. He is an old enemy of mine. Several years ago our paths crossed in Vienna, but he escaped me. I told him then I would not allow him to escape again. Pierre, will you see if you can find a pair of dark spectacles?

PIERRE: There is a pair in the desk drawer.

DUPIN: I will wear them to the Minister's apartment. I want you to come with me, Pierre. I will require your assistance.

PIERRE *(Pleased):* I am entirely at your service! *(Curtain)*

*   *   *   *   *

SCENE 2

TIME: *The next morning.*

SETTING: *The Minister's apartment. Two armchairs and desk*

*from Scene 1 may be placed in a different arrangement.
Papers, books, and wooden letter holder are on desk. The table
is removed.*

AT RISE: MINISTER, *in dressing gown sits in chair, drinking
cup of coffee.* DUPIN, *wearing dark glasses, sits opposite him.*

MINISTER: Your visit is most unexpected, Dupin.

DUPIN: I heard that you were living here, and I wished to call
and inform you that I, too, have returned to Paris.

MINISTER: It has been four, no, five years since we last met in
. . . Madrid?

DUPIN: Vienna.

MINISTER *(With a laugh):* Ah, yes! Vienna! I got the best of you
there! You really should have known better than to try to
connect me with that little intrigue.

DUPIN: You should know better than to involve yourself in such
intrigues. It is true, you managed to escape me . . . that time.

MINISTER: You were not wearing dark spectacles in Vienna.

DUPIN: My eyes have grown weak. They are sensitive to light.

MINISTER *(Amused):* That must be quite a disadvantage to you
in your little amateur detective adventures.

DUPIN *(Mildly):* Not at all. I am used to it.

MINISTER *(Yawning):* Perhaps you should pursue some other
occupation, Dupin, something more lucrative. You do not appear to be doing well. Isn't that the same coat you were
wearing in Vienna?

DUPIN: I am perfectly content in my present line of work,
Minister. And you seem satisfied in yours.

MINISTER: Yes, I do very well, and I have expectations of doing
better. Much better!

DUPIN: Indeed?

MINISTER: Yes. I have considerable influence at Court these
days. *(Sound of several gunshots is heard offstage, followed
by shouts of crowd.)* What is that?

DUPIN: It sounds like gunshots . . . out in the street. (MINISTER
*rushes down center and looks out over audience, as if through
window.)*

MINISTER: Some lunatic is firing a pistol into the air. The fool! What does he mean? *(As soon as* MINISTER *turns his back,* DUPIN *quickly snatches a torn letter from letter holder on desk, thrusts it into his pocket, then carefully puts another letter from desk into letter holder. He then joins* MINISTER *down center.)*

DUPIN: Who would dare create such a disturbance outside your house? The man must be mad.

MINISTER: There! He has been disarmed.

DUPIN: He looks rather desperate. Perhaps I can be of some assistance down there. You will excuse me, Minister, until we have cause to meet again.

MINISTER: I assure you, Dupin, there will be no reason for us to meet again.

DUPIN: One never knows. Good day, Minister. *(Exits;* MINISTER *looks after him sharply, then shrugs and laughs.)*

MINISTER: Dupin! What a fool! More so now than ever. For a moment I thought he might suspect . . . but, no! That is impossible! *(Exits; curtain)*

* * * * *

SCENE 3

TIME: *The next evening.*

SETTING: *Same as Scene I.*

AT RISE: DUPIN *and* PIERRE *sit at desk.* PREFECT *stands behind them, staring at letter on desk.*

PREFECT: You actually found the letter in the Minister's apartment? Where was it?

Dupin: The Minister very carefully dirtied it, crumpled it, tore it nearly in half, and wrote an address to himself on the reverse side. Then he thrust it carelessly into the letter holder on his desk.

PREFECT: The letter holder! Why, I . . . I never thought to look in so obvious a place!

DUPIN: I looked very carefully from behind my dark spectacles. The Minister had no idea my eyes were scanning every item in the room while he sat there, insulting me. The fact that this torn and dirty letter was so inconsistent with the neatness of every other item in the room convinced me that it had to be the stolen letter. The Minister had tried to hide it by placing it in full view of every visitor.

PREFECT: But how did you get it without his seeing you?

DUPIN: As soon as Pierre fired a pistol outside, the Minister jumped up to look out his window, and a moment later I had the letter in my pocket and a substitute, from his desk, in the letter holder.

PIERRE: But you were almost too late in coming to my rescue. I thought I was going to be arrested!

DUPIN: You were perfect in the role of a pistol-waving lunatic, Pierre.

PIERRE: Thank you. But it is not an occupation I wish to pursue further. (*To* PREFECT) Monsieur, do you have the check?

PREFECT: The check? Oh, yes, the check! (*Fumbles in his pocket and pulls out check, thrusts it at* DUPIN)

DUPIN: Thank you. And you have the purloined letter. (*Hands him letter*)

PREFECT (*Staring at letter; joyfully*): Yes! Yes! I have it! The lady is saved! France is secure! I will be rich! There is no time to be lost! (*Dashes out*)

PIERRE: He did not even thank you!

DUPIN (*Waving check*): This is all the thanks I require.

PIERRE: How long will it be, do you think, before the Minister discovers his loss?

DUPIN: That will depend upon the lady. By tomorrow morning, she may confront him with confidence, knowing that she has destroyed the letter herself, and that *he* is now in *her* power. (*Lights fade out on* DUPIN's *apartment and come up left on* LADY's *chamber.* LADY *enters.* MINISTER *follows, with papers.*)

MINISTER: I require your approval and signature on these papers, madam.

LADY *(Glancing at papers):* I do not approve, and shall not sign.

MINISTER: I believe you will, madam! Or do you forget that I can bring you to your knees by showing a certain letter to your husband?

LADY *(Calmly; firmly):* It is *you*, Minister, who shall be on your knees, begging for mercy, if you do not desist at once from your attempts to undermine the welfare and security of France! *(Tears papers in half)* I no longer accept your advice! I no longer fear you, or anything you may say or do! *(Drops papers on floor, exits)*

MINISTER *(Angrily; picking up papers):* She will regret this! I'll . . . *(Hesitates)* She was so calm . . . she held up her head. *(Anxiously)* Could it be she has somehow recovered that letter? But how? How? *(Suddenly)* Ah! Dupin! It was he! I am undone! *(Rushes out; blackout)*

THE END

PRODUCTION NOTES

The Purloined Letter

Characters: 5 male; 1 female.

Playing Time: 25 minutes.

Costumes: French, 1840's. Dupin, Pierre, and Prefect wear plain black suits; Prefect has top hat. In Scene 2, Dupin wears dark glasses. Lady and Gentleman wear elegant clothing. Minister wears black suit in Scene 1 and 3; silk robe or dressing gown in Scene 2.

Properties: Newspaper; two letters; papers; long needle, such as knitting needle; cup and saucer; check.

Setting: Scenes 1 and 3: Dupin's modest apartment. A small table and two armchairs are center. Tray of glasses and decanter are on table. Desk and chair are at right. Books, papers, and ink bottle are on desk; checkbook and pen are in desk drawer. Door to outside hall is right. Down left, small ornate table represents Lady's chamber. Scene 2: Minister's apartment. Dupin's desk and armchairs may be placed in a different arrangement at center. More letters and books are on desk; also on desk is wooden letter holder with torn and dirty letter.

Sound: Gunshots, shouts of a small crowd.

The Miraculous Eclipse

from A Connecticut Yankee in King Arthur's Court *by Mark Twain*

Characters

OLD HANK MORGAN
BOY
HANK MORGAN, *a young man*
SIR KAY, *knight of the Round Table*
CLARENCE, *page*
KING ARTHUR
MERLIN THE MAGICIAN
FOUR GUARDS
COURTIERS, *lords and ladies*
KNIGHTS
SERVANTS
HERALD

SCENE 1

TIME: *1879.*
SETTING: *A street in Hartford, Connecticut. A barrel stands center.*
BEFORE RISE: OLD HANK MORGAN *enters slowly right, followed by* BOY.
BOY: Excuse me, Mr. Morgan.

91

OLD HANK *(Stopping and turning):* Yes?

BOY: Some of the boys have been telling me that . . . well, that you sure can tell a whale of a story!

OLD HANK: That's what they told you, is it? *(Fumbles in coat pockets, pulls out pipe)* You're new in town, aren't you?

BOY: Yes, sir. The boys dared me to ask you to tell *your* version of the story of King Arthur and his knights of the Round Table.

OLD HANK: They did, eh? Well, son, it just so happens I knew King Arthur well when I was a young man, so I can tell you anything you want to know about him.

BOY *(Amazed):* You knew King Arthur?

OLD HANK *(Nodding):* I knew all the folks at Camelot, including that cagey old humbug, Merlin.

BOY *(In awe):* You knew Merlin the Magician? But they all lived in the sixth century!

OLD HANK *(Tamping his pipe):* That's right. And if it weren't for Merlin, I might still be in the sixth century myself! *(Smiles)* You don't believe me, do you?

BOY: Well, sir, if you've got some time, I'd like to hear your story. Then I'll tell you if I believe you.

OLD HANK: I've got all the time in the world. *(Sits on barrel and hunts through his pockets as he talks, finally coming up with tobacco pouch.* BOY *sits cross-legged on ground.)* You see, I was born and brought up right here in Hartford, Connecticut, so I am a Yankee of the Yankees, and very practical.

BOY: That's what the boys said about you, Mr. Morgan.

OLD HANK: As a young man, I first went to work as a blacksmith. Then later I went over to the Colt Arms Factory and learned how to make guns, cannons, boilers, engines—all sorts of labor-saving machinery. If there wasn't a quick, new-fangled way to make a thing, I'd invent one. I became head supervisor and had a couple of thousand men under me.

BOY *(Impressed):* A couple of thousand? Whew!

OLD HANK: Some of them were pretty rough characters, too. *(Stands)* Say, you just come on home with me and we'll sit on my front porch. It'll be more comfortable. *(Starts left.* BOY *follows, carrying barrel.)* I was a man full of fight when I was supervisor, but one day I met my match. A big fellow named Hercules and I had a misunderstanding, and we went after each other with crowbars.

BOY: That must have been some fight!

OLD HANK: It was! Hercules knocked me down with a crusher to my head that made everything crack! My world just went out in total darkness, and when I came to, I wasn't at the arms factory any more. (OLD HANK *and* BOY *exit left. Lights dim to indicate shift of scene to a country road in England. Lights come up full again on* HANK MORGAN *as a young man. He holds his head in pain.)*

YOUNG HANK: Oh, my aching head! Hercules will pay for this, or my name isn't Hank Morgan! *(Looks around)* Where am I? This doesn't look like any place I've seen around Hartford. (SIR KAY, *wearing full armor, bounds in left with sword drawn and takes threatening position in front of* HANK.)

SIR KAY: Will you joust, fair sir?

HANK *(Staring rudely):* Will I what?

SIR KAY *(Waving sword):* Will you fight with me to win land or lady or—

HANK *(Interrupting):* Now look here, who do you think you are, wearing that outlandish getup and swinging that dangerous weapon around? Get along back to the circus where you belong, or I'll report you!

SIR KAY *(Holding swordpoint to* HANK's *chest):* My name is Sir Kay, and in the name of the King, I take you captive! You are now my property and must come with me at once!

HANK *(Aside):* If this fellow isn't part of a circus, he must be crazy. But I'd better play along with him, or he might get nasty with that sword. *(Raises his hands in surrender and turns back to* SIR KAY) All right, Sir Kay, you've got me. Where to?

SIR KAY: This way! *(Starts off left, pushing* HANK *in front of him with sword)*

HANK: Uh, by the way, Sir Kay, how far are we from Hartford?

SIR KAY *(Puzzled):* I have never heard of that place.

HANK *(Stopping):* Never heard of Hartford? *(Aside)* I reckon he must be from out of state. *(Turns back to* SIR KAY*)* Well, what town are we headed for? Bridgeport?

SIR KAY *(Shaking his head):* Camelot! *(Pushes* HANK *forward)*

HANK: Camelot? There isn't any town by that name in Connecticut!

SIR KAY: You are not in Connecticut.

HANK *(Stopping agian):* Well, where in the world am I?

SIR KAY: England! (HANK's *mouth drops open in astonishment, as* SIR KAY *pushes him off left.)*

*   *   *   *   *

TIME: *England, in the year 528.*

SETTING: *A courtyard in Camelot. At center is a throne on platform.*

AT RISE: COURTIERS, KNIGHTS, GUARDS *and* SERVANTS *move busily back and forth.* SIR KAY *and* HANK *enter left. At the sight of* HANK, *all stop to stare and point at him.*

COURTIERS *(Ad lib):* Look there! Did you ever see anything like it? Look at his strange clothes! Be careful, don't get too close! *(Etc.)*

SIR KAY *(Poking* HANK *with sword):* I warn you, don't try to escape. (HANK *looks around, puzzled, as* CLARENCE *enters, smiling and looking* HANK *over from head to foot.)* My page, Clarence *(Pointing to him)*, will keep you in charge until I come back for you. *(Exits right)*

HANK: Page, did he say? Go on! A boy your size can't be much more than a paragraph!

CLARENCE: You have an unusual way of speaking, sir, but you are welcome! I hope you will find me to be your true friend.

HANK: Well, my boy, if you're really my friend, you can tell me where I am. That escapee from a circus who brought me here said this was England, but he's obviously not in his right mind.

CLARENCE: Nay, sir, my master, Sir Kay, spoke the truth. You are in England.

HANK: England. *(Shakes his head)* Well, either *I'm* crazy or something just as awful has happened. Now tell me, honest and true, what is this place?

CLARENCE: Camelot, the court of King Arthur.

HANK: The King Arthur who had the Round Table?

CLARENCE: Is there any other, sir?

HANK *(Hesitantly):* And according to your notions, what year is it?

CLARENCE: The nineteenth of June, in the year five hundred twenty-eight.

HANK *(Repeating words mechanically):* Five twenty-eight? *(Turns away; in a daze)* Five twenty-eight. *(Looks at* COURTIERS, *then at himself)* I'm sure it was 1879 when I got up this morning. *I* look like 1879, but all these people look like . . . five twenty-eight. *(Pacing)* Five twenty-eight . . . that was the year when a total eclipse of the sun occurred . . . on June 21st at three minutes past noon. Just two days from now. *(Suddenly)* I've got an idea! If I can just keep hold of my senses for forty-eight hours, I'll know for certain if this boy is telling me the truth. *(Turns back to* CLARENCE) Tell me, Clarence, who is this Sir Kay?

CLARENCE: A brave knight, sir, and foster brother to our liege the King. You are his prisoner, and as soon as dinner is finished, he will exhibit you before the King and brag about capturing you. He'll exaggerate the facts a little, but it won't be safe to correct him. Then you'll be flung into a dungeon.

HANK *(Horrified):* Flung into a dungeon? What for?

CLARENCE *(Casually):* It is the custom. But never fear, I'll find a way to come and see you, and I'll help you get word to your friends who will come and ransom you.

HANK: Well, I'm much obliged to you, Clarence, but you see, all my friends won't even be born for more than thirteen hundred years. *(Fanfare of trumpets is heard off right.)*

CLARENCE: King Arthur is coming now. (HERALD *enters right, holding trumpet, and walks center.*)

HERALD: His Royal Majesty, King Arthur! (KING ARTHUR *enters, followed by* MERLIN, *and attended by several* KNIGHTS. *He sits on throne center.* COURTIERS *bow low and stand in groups at either side of throne.* SIR KAY *enters right, seizes* HANK *by arm and pushes him to his knees in front of* KING ARTHUR.)

SIR KAY *(Bowing low):* My lord King, most noble knights and ladies of the realm! Behold this curious captive I have conquered!

KING ARTHUR: And where did you find this strange creature, Sir Kay?

SIR KAY: I came upon this horrible ogre, my liege, in a far land of barbarians called Connecticut. Everyone there wears the same ridiculous clothing that he does, but I warn you, do not touch him! His clothing is enchanted! (COURTIERS *gasp and step back.*) It is intended to secure him from harm, but I overpowered the enchantment through my strong will and great courage! I killed his thirteen attending knights in a three hours' battle and took him prisoner!

HANK *(Starting to rise):* Now, just a minute—

SIR KAY *(Pushing* HANK *down):* Behold this enchanted, man-devouring monster who tried to escape from me by leaping into the top of a tree at a single bound!

HANK *(Starting up again):* Now, look here, you're carrying this thing a little too far—

SIR KAY *(Pushing him down roughly):* Behold this menacing barbarian while you may, good people, for at noon on the twenty-first he shall die!

HANK *(Jumping up):* What? What have I done to deserve death? I haven't even been in this century more than half an hour!

SIR KAY: You have suffered defeat at my hands, and I decide if you live or die. You must die!

KING ARTHUR: Well done, Sir Kay. But if his clothing is enchanted, how do you propose to put him to death? (COURTIERS *murmur excitedly.*)

SIR KAY: Surely Your Majesty's mighty magician, Merlin, can break the enchantment.

COURTIERS *(Ad lib):* Yes, yes! Merlin will know what to do! Try, Merlin! *(Etc.)*

MERLIN: Make way, please. (*He steps forward, makes several sweeping passes with his arms.* COURTIERS *fall back respectfully, and watch him intently.*) How can all of you be so dull? Has it not occurred to anyone here but me that the thing to do is to remove the enchanted clothing from this—(*In disgust)* this creature, and thus make him helpless and harmless? Proceed.

HANK *(Starting to back away):* Now, hold on here. . . . Hey! (FOUR GUARDS *seize* HANK, *push him to floor, pull off his boots, stockings, overalls, sweater, etc., leaving him wearing only his suit of long underwear.*)

MERLIN *(With a wicked laugh):* Now he is powerless!

SIR KAY: To the dungeon with him!

KING ARTHUR: A cheer for Sir Kay, truly a brave knight of the Table Round! (HANK *is dragged out left by* GUARDS, *as* COURTIERS *cheer* SIR KAY. *Curtain)*

*　*　*　*　*

SCENE 2

SETTING: *Dungeon cell. Pile of straw and low stool are center. May be played before curtain.*

AT RISE: CLARENCE *sits on stool, watching* HANK, *who lies sleeping on straw.* HANK *stirs, stretches, his eyes still closed.*

HANK *(Not seeing* CLARENCE*):* What an astonishing dream I've just had! King Arthur's Court! What nonsense! *(Yawns and stretches)* I reckon the noon whistle will blow shortly, and then I'll go down to the factory and have it out with Hercules.

(Turns over, opens his eyes sleepily, sees CLARENCE, *and sits up abruptly)* What! Are you still here? Go away with the rest of the dream! Scat!

CLARENCE *(Laughing):* Dream? What dream? *(Stands up)*

HANK: Why, the dream that I'm in the court of a king who never existed, and that I'm talking to you who are nothing but a work of my imagination!

CLARENCE *(Sarcastically):* Indeed! And is it a dream that you're going to be burned tomorrow?

HANK: Burned! *(Jumps up)* I'm still in the dungeon! This dream is more serious than I thought. *(Pleading)* Clarence, my boy, you're the only friend I've got. Help me think of a way to escape from this place.

CLARENCE: Escape? Why, the corridors are guarded by at least twenty men at arms. You cannot hope to escape. Besides . . . *(Hesitantly)* . . . there are other obstacles more overpowering than men at arms.

HANK: What are they?

CLARENCE *(Nervously):* Oh, I dare not tell you!

HANK: But you must! Come, be brave! Speak out!

CLARENCE *(Looking around fearfully, then speaking close to* HANK's *ear)*: Merlin, that terrible and mighty magician, has woven wicked spells about this dungeon. No man can escape it and live! *(Nervously)* There, I have told you. Now be merciful, and do not betray me, or I am lost!

HANK *(Laughing):* Merlin has cast a few spells, has he? That cheap old humbug? Bosh!

CLARENCE *(Falling to his knees in terror):* Oh, beware of what you say! These walls may crumble on us at any moment. Call back your awful words before it is too late!

HANK *(Turning away; to himself):* If everyone here is as afraid of Merlin's pretended magic as Clarence is, certainly a superior man like me with my nineteenth-century education ought to be shrewd enough to take advantage of this situation. *(Thinks a moment, then turns back to* CLARENCE) Come on, Clarence, get up and pull yourself together. (CLARENCE *stands*.) Do you know why I laughed at Merlin?

CLARENCE *(Timidly):* No, and I pray you won't do it again.

HANK: I laughed because I'm a magician myself.

CLARENCE *(Recoiling):* You?

HANK: I've known Merlin for seven hundred years, and—

CLARENCE: Seven hundred years?

HANK: Don't interrupt! He has died and come alive again thirteen times. I knew him in Egypt three hundred years ago, and in India over five hundred years ago. He's always getting in my way everywhere I go, but his magic doesn't amount to shucks compared to mine. Now, look here, Clarence, I'll be your friend, and you must be mine.

CLARENCE: I *am* your friend, I assure you!

HANK: Good. Now, you get word to the King that I am the world's mightiest and grandest magician, and that if any harm comes to me I will quietly arrange a little calamity that will make the fur fly in these realms.

CLARENCE *(Terrified):* Yes, yes, at once! *(Backs off right, then turns and runs out)*

HANK: That should get me off the hook pretty quick. *(Struts back and forth confidently for a moment, then suddenly stops)* Ah! What a blunder I've made! I sent Clarence off to alarm the King with the theat of a calamity I haven't thought of yet! These sixth-century people are childish and superstitious. They believe in miracles. Suppose they want to see a sample of my powers? Suppose the King asks me to name my calamity? (HANK *sinks down onto stool, chin in hands, as lights fade out. In a moment, lights come up again.* HANK *remains on stool in same position.)* I've got to stall for time. I can't think of anything. *(Looks off right)* Here's Clarence. I have to look confident. (CLARENCE *enters right, dejectedly.)* Well?

CLARENCE: I took your message to my liege the King, and he was very much afraid. He was ready to order your release, but Merlin was there and spoiled everything.

HANK: I might have known.

CLARENCE: He persuaded the King that you are crazy, and that your threat is nothing but foolishness because you have not named your calamity. Oh, my friend, be wise and name it, or you may still be doomed! (HANK, *deep in thought, frowns, then suddenly smiles.*)

HANK: Ah! I have it! Just in time, too. (*Turns to* CLARENCE *and draws himself up haughtily*) How long have I been shut up in this miserable hole?

CLARENCE: Since yesterday evening.

HANK: Then today is the twentieth of June?

CLARENCE: Yes.

HANK: At what time tomorrow am I to be burned?

CLARENCE (*Shuddering*): At high noon.

HANK: Listen carefully. I will tell you what to say to the King. (*In deep, measured tones*) Tell him that at high noon tomorrow I will smother the entire world in the dead blackness of midnight!

CLARENCE (*Falling to his knees*): Oh, have mercy!

HANK (*Dramatically*): I will blot out the sun, and it will never shine again! The fruits of the earth shall rot for lack of light, and the people of the earth shall famish and die to the last man! Go! Tell the King! (CLARENCE *staggers to his feet and backs off right, in terror.*)

HANK: (*Slapping his knee*): Ha! The eclipse will be sure to save me, and make me the greatest man in the kingdom besides! Furthermore, I'll be the boss of the whole country within three months. After all, I have thirteen hundred years' head start on the best educated man in the kingdom! (*Sits down, smiling, then suddenly frowns*) Hm-m, I hope my threat won't be too much for these simple people. Suppose they want to compromise? Then what do I do? (*Lights fade out for a moment to indicate brief passage of time, then come up again.* HANK *remains seated.*) Of course, if they want to compromise, I'll listen, but I'll have to stand my ground and play my hand for all it's worth. (1ST *and* 2ND GUARDS *enter right.*)

1ST GUARD: Come! The stake is ready!

HANK (*Terrified*): The stake! (GUARDS *seize him.*) But . . . but . . . wait a minute! The execution is tomorrow!

2ND GUARD: The order has been changed and set forward a day. Come! (GUARDS *drag* HANK, *speechless, out right. Curtain*)

* * * * *

SCENE 3

SETTING: *Courtyard in Camelot. There is a stake center, with bundles of wood stacked around it.*

AT RISE: COURTIERS, CLARENCE, KING ARTHUR, *and* MERLIN *stand right and left, as* HANK *is dragged in right by* 1ST *and* 2ND GUARDS. CLARENCE *goes over to* HANK, *speaks to him quietly.*

CLARENCE (*To* HANK): My friend, it was through *my* efforts that the change was made for the day of your execution.

HANK: *Your* efforts? (GUARDS *tie* HANK *to stake and pile wood around him.*)

CLARENCE: Yes, and hard work it was, too. When I named your calamity, the King and all his court were stricken with terror. Then I had an idea. I told them that your power would not reach its peak until tomorrow, and that if they would save the sun, they must kill you today while your magic is still working. In the frenzy of their fright, they swallowed my lie, and here you are!

HANK (*Miserably*): Clarence, how could you!

CLARENCE (*Excitedly*): You only need to make a *little* darkness, and the people will go mad with fear and set you free. They will take me for a featherheaded fool, and you will be made great! But I beg of you, spare our blessed sun, for me—your one true friend! (*Backs away into crowd*)

HANK (*Miserably*): My one, true, featherheaded friend! You have ruined me!

MERLIN (*Approaching* HANK, *waving his arms and sneering*): You call yourself a magician? Then stop the devouring flames if you can! I defy you! (*Beckons to* GUARD, *who comes forward with torch.* HANK *throws up his arms in an attitude of de-*

spair, and suddenly lights begin to dim. All gasp and look up.)

COURTIERS *(Ad lib):* Look! The sun is disappearing! It's getting dark, and it's only noon! *(Etc.)*

HANK *(Looking up in surprise):* The eclipse! It's starting! I don't know where it came from, or how it happened, but I'd better make the most of it, or I'm done for! *(Strikes grand attitude, pointing upward)*

MERLIN *(Frantically):* Apply the torch!

KING ARTHUR: I forbid it! (MERLIN *snatches torch from* GUARD *and starts toward stake.)*

HANK: Stay where you are! If any man moves, even the King, I will blast him with thunder and lightning! (COURTIERS *step back.* MERLIN *hesitates, then hands torch to* GUARD, *and backs away.)*

KING ARTHUR *(To* HANK): Be merciful, fair sir. It was reported to us that your powers would not reach their full strength until tomorrow, but—

HANK: That report was a lie. My powers are at full strength *now!* (COURTIERS *crowd around* KING ARTHUR *frantically.)*

COURTIERS *(Ad lib):* Oh, save us! Give him whatever he wants! Do whatever he wants, only save the sun! *(Etc.)*

KING ARTHUR: Name your terms, reverend sir, but banish this calamity!

HANK *(Looking up):* Well . . . I must have some time to consider.

KING ARTHUR: But it grows darker every moment!

COURTIERS *(Ad lib):* It's getting colder and colder! The night winds are blowing at noon! It's the end of the world! *(Etc.)*

HANK: Nevertheless, I must think! *(Looks up as lights continue to dim to almost complete darkness; to himself)* What *is* this? How am I to tell whether this is the sixth century or not with this eclipse coming a day early? *(Pulls sleeve of* 3RD GUARD) What day of the month is this?

3RD GUARD *(Stepping back, terrified):* The twenty-first, reverend sir.

HANK: The twenty-first! *(To himself)* That featherheaded Clarence told me today was the twentieth! *(With sigh of relief)* But his mistake about the date, and his good intentions in changing my day of execution, have saved me after all! I'm in King Arthur's court, all right, and there's only one course for me to take. *(Turns to* KING*)* Sir King, whether or not I blot out the sun forever, or restore it, is up to you. You shall remain King and receive all the glories and honors that belong to you. But you must appoint me your perpetual minister, and give me one percent of all increases in revenue I may create for the state.

KING ARTHUR: It shall be done! Away with his bonds! Do him homage, all of you, for he is now at my right hand and clothed with power and authority! Now, sweep away this darkness and bring the light again. (GUARDS *untie* HANK.)

HANK *(To himself)*: I wish I knew how long this eclipse is supposed to last! *(To* KING*)* Sir King, I may be clothed in power and authority in your eyes, but in my eyes, I am practically naked. I must have my clothes back.

KING ARTHUR: They are not good enough. Bring him costly garments! Clothe him like a prince! (KING *claps his hands several times, and* SERVANTS *rush in with rich robe, plumed hat, jeweled sword, etc., and start to put them on* HANK.)

HANK *(As he is being clothed)*: Let it be known that I shall be called The Boss, and all who do as I say and don't get in my way will be spared any further calamities. *(Turning)* As for you, Merlin, beware! Your magic is weak, and I have knowledge of enchantments that can knock you out of commission forever!

MERLIN *(Menacingly)*: You have not seen the last of me!

KING ARTHUR: Everything shall be as you say, Sir Boss, only bring back the sun!

CLARENCE *(On his knees)*: For your one true friend's sake, bring back the sun!

HANK *(To himself)*: I hope it's time. *(Solemnly lifts his arms and gazes upward)* Let the enchantment dissolve and pass harmlessly away! *(Darkness continues. The people stir un-*

easily. HANK *waves his arms in grand flourish. Still it re-mains dark.* HANK *makes more flourishes, and slowly lights begin to come up, gradually becoming brighter and brighter.* COURTIERS *shout for joy.*)

CLARENCE: Oh, thank you, Sir Boss! You have worked a won-drous miracle, but I beg of you, never do it again!

HANK: Don't worry, Clarence, I won't perform this particular miracle again. Come, my boy, I'll find some suitable quarters in the castle and set up a factory. You can be my assistant, and I'll show you how to make all kinds of other miracles. (*Starts off left with his arm around* CLARENCE's *shoulders, then suddenly stops, scratching his head*) A Connecticut Yankee in King Arthur's Court! You know, a situation like this has all kinds of possibilities! And if I ever get back to Hartford, what a story I'll have to tell! (*Exits left with* CLARENCE *as* COUR-TIERS *bow to him, and curtain falls*)

THE END

PRODUCTION NOTES

THE MIRACULOUS ECLIPSE

Characters: 12 male; as many male and female extras as desired for Courtiers, Servants, and Knights.

Playing Time: 25 minutes.

Costumes: Old Hank, Boy, and Young Hank wear work clothes and boots, vintage 1879. Young Hank also wears long underwear. All other players wear medieval dress: capes, leotards, plumed caps, swords, etc. King Arthur wears a crown, Merlin a tall conical hat, Sir Kay a suit of armor.

Properties: Pipe; tobacco pouch; swords and spears; torch (colored cellophane may be used to represent flame); rich-looking robe, hat and sword.

Setting: Scene 1, Before Rise: Street in Hartford, with barrel at center stage; country road in England. At Rise: Courtyard in Camelot. A throne on a platform is up center. Benches may be placed here and there. Artificial shrubbery and flats painted to represent stone walls and gateways may be added. Scene 2: Dungeon cell, played before curtain. A pile of straw and low stool are center. A flat painted to represent a dirty stone wall with a barred window may be added. Scene 3: Same as Scene 1, with the addition of a stake and bundles of wood. The stake should be anchored or propped up so it is held steady.

Lighting: If possible, lights should dim slowly to effect the eclipse coming and going. If lights cannot be dimmed, they should be turned off gradually one or two at a time to effect growing darkness and light returning.

Sound: A trumpet fanfare.

The Sacrifice

from Les Misérables
by Victor Hugo

Characters

MARIUS, *young lawyer*
COURFEYRAC, *his friend*
EPONINE, *poor girl, 16*
JEAN VALJEAN, *old man*
COSETTE, *his daughter, 16*
MONSIEUR GILLENORMAND, *Marius' grandfather*
GAVROCHE, *street boy, 12*
ENJOLRAS, *revolutionary*

SCENE 1

TIME: *May, 1832.*
SETTING: *A street in Paris. Bench, tree, and lamppost are right. A backdrop painting of shabby shops and tenements may be used. Another bench is down left.*
AT RISE: MARIUS *sits on bench at right, a book in his hands, daydreaming.*
MARIUS *(Suddenly closing book):* It's no use. I can't work. I can only think of Cosette!
COURFEYRAC *(Entering right):* Marius?
MARIUS *(Turning):* Courfeyrac! *(Shaking his hand; warmly)* My friend!

COURFEYRAC: I came to tell you that there will soon be a new revolution.

MARIUS: I heard the rumors, but I paid little attention to them.

COURFEYRAC: What? Why, Paris is like a loaded cannon! The tiniest spark will set her off, and knock King Louis Philippe off his royal throne! *(Fervently)* We will fight, and we need you with us!

MARIUS: I have changed, Courfeyrac.

COURFEYRAC *(Sitting beside* MARIUS*)*: What's the matter with you? Are you sick?

MARIUS: I suppose you could call it that. I am hopelessly in love.

COURFEYRAC *(Surprised)*: In love? With whom?

MARIUS: With the most beautiful angel on earth!

COURFEYRAC *(In disbelief)*: You're joking!

MARIUS: No! *(Rises; excitedly)* She and her father used to come to the Luxembourg Gardens. I passed her as I took my daily walks, and each day I fell more and more in love with her. Once I heard her father call her Cosette. For weeks I adored her from a distance, and then one day our eyes met, and I saw that she loved me, too! *(Lights on bench dim, and spotlight comes up, left.* MARIUS *walks left as* COSETTE *and* JEAN VALJEAN *enter, cross to bench, left, and sit.* MARIUS *passes them, walking slowly.* COSETTE *looks up at* MARIUS *and they hold glance a moment. Then* MARIUS *turns and crosses right, as* COSETTE *and* VALJEAN *rise and exit left. Spotlight goes out, and lights rise on bench, right, where* COURFEYRAC *is sitting.)*

COURFEYRAC: So, Marius, where is your Cosette now?

MARIUS *(Sitting)*: I wish I knew! I dared to follow her home one day, but her father saw me and gave me a look I'll never forget. For the next three days, they didn't come to the Gardens. In desperation I went to their house and learned they had moved without leaving a new address. I have searched for her for six months, and I will continue until I find her!

COURFEYRAC: Marius, this is not the time for such nonsense!

The common people of Paris stand on the brink of rebellion, and you are one of them!

MARIUS: Of course, I am, but now I am in love.

COURFEYRAC *(Scolding):* Have you suffered and starved with us for nothing? Have your forgotten your father's heroism at Waterloo? Surely, you didn't break all ties with your royalist grandfather just to fall foolishly in love!

MARIUS: I am and shall always be a true son of the French Revolution! And I am with you and the people always in spirit, but now I can think of nothing but Cosette!

COURFEYRAC *(Rising, pacing):* Marius, it has been forty-three years since the fall of the Bastille. Seventeen years since Waterloo. But the masses are still hungry, oppressed, without hope. Why waste your energies on a futile search?

MARIUS *(Shaking his head):* I must find her. She is all that matters to me now.

COURFEYRAC *(With a long sigh):* I don't understand you. Still, you are my friend, and I shall always be yours. We've gone through much together. Do what you must. *(Claps him on shoulder)* If you change your mind, you know where I am.

MARIUS: Yes, Courfeyrac, and when I find my Cosette, I'll bring her to meet you! (COURFEYRAC *exits left, shaking his head.* EPONINE *slowly enters right, and crosses to* MARIUS.)

EPONINE *(Awkwardly):* I beg your pardon. Monsieur Marius?

MARIUS *(Looking up):* Yes?

EPONINE *(Timidly):* My name is Eponine. I live down the hall from you. I've had nothing to eat for two days. *(Hesitating)* I thought perhaps . . . you might . . . help me?

MARIUS *(Fumbling in his pockets):* I'll see what I have.

EPONINE *(Smiling wistfully):* Monsieur Marius, I think you are a very handsome young man. *(He looks up, startled.)* I see you often in the streets. *(Timidly)* Do you ever notice me?

MARIUS *(Gently):* No, I've never seen you before. *(Hands her a coin)* I have only five francs.

EPONINE *(Protesting):* I couldn't take your last coin, monsieur.

MARIUS: I've eaten today. You haven't. Take it.

EPONINE *(Taking coin):* Thank you, monsieur. You are very kind. Now I am going to meet an old gentleman and his daughter. Sometimes they are kind to me, too. Good morning, Monsieur Marius. *(She smiles, then moves right, looking back at him, and waits by lamppost.)*

MARIUS: Poor girl. I didn't know she lived near me. I've been so busy with my search. *(He drops his head into his hands.)* My search! When will it end? (JEAN VALJEAN *enters right with* COSETTE, *who carries small basket.* MARIUS *does not notice their entrance, or following dialogue.)*

EPONINE *(Approaching them and curtsying awkwardly):* Good morning, monsieur! Good morning, mademoiselle!

VALJEAN *(With concern):* How are you feeling today, Eponine?

EPONINE: A little weak, monsieur, but that is only because I am hungry.

COSETTE: We've brought you some bread and cheese, and some vegetables. *(Hands basket to* EPONINE*)*

EPONINE *(Eagerly looking into basket):* Thank you, mademoiselle! *(She takes piece of bread and eats hungrily.)*

MARIUS *(Rising):* I accomplish nothing by sitting here. I must walk. Perhaps today . . . *(Turns right, then stops as he sees* COSETTE; *aside)* It is she! *(Steps quickly behind tree and watches* COSETTE; *aside)* I have found her! Cosette!

VALJEAN: We will see you again, Eponine. Come, Cosette. *(He takes* COSETTE's *arm and starts off right.)*

EPONINE *(Gratefully):* Bless you, monsieur! Bless you, mademoiselle!

MARIUS *(Aside):* I must follow them, but cautiously. Her father mustn't see me. *(Moves left, his gaze fixed on* COSETTE*)*

EPONINE *(Turning right and bumping into* MARIUS*)*: Oh! Monsieur Marius! Look! Look at the good things! *(She blocks his way.)* Please don't go away! I will share my food with you.

MARIUS *(Looking anxiously off left):* I can't stop now. *(Frantically)* They are getting into a carriage! *(Rushes off left)*

EPONINE: Monsieur Marius! Where are you going? *(Looks after him)* What is he doing? He acts like a madman, running after that carriage. He will never catch it. There are too many people in the street. *(After a pause)* Ah! He is coming back.

MARIUS *(Slowly re-entering left; miserably):* Too late! I have lost her again!

EPONINE: Monsieur Marius, you look so sad. What is the matter?

MARIUS *(Harshly):* Leave me alone!

EPONINE: Oh, please, be kind to me. *(Eagerly)* Can I do anything for you?

MARIUS *(Furiously):* You can stay out of my way! *(She draws back as he starts off right, then he stops.)* No, wait. *(Turns back to her)* Perhaps you *can* help me.

EPONINE *(Smiling):* Yes, only speak gently to me. I will do anything for you!

MARIUS: Do you know the old gentleman and young lady who just left?

EPONINE: Yes. They are very kind to me.

MARIUS *(Eagerly):* Do you know where they live?

EPONINE *(Puzzled):* Why do you want to know . . . *(Suddenly, her smile fades, and she looks at him suspiciously.)* You mean, you want to know where *she* lives!

MARIUS *(Desperately):* Yes! I must find her!

EPONINE *(Turning away):* Mademoiselle is very pretty, isn't she!

MARIUS: I think she is beautiful!

EPONINE *(To herself):* Once, I was pretty. *(Turns back to him)* Will it make you happy to know where she lives?

MARIUS: Yes, Eponine! Happy beyond words!

EPONINE *(Sullenly):* What will you give me if I tell you?

MARIUS: Anything you wish.

EPONINE: Anything I wish? Do you promise?

MARIUS: Yes!

EPONINE *(Smiling):* Then, come! I will show you her house! *(She takes his hand and leads him off left. Curtain)*

* * * * *

SCENE 2

TIME: *An hour later.*

SETTING: *Jean Valjean's garden. Bench from Scene 1 is moved center and tree placed behind it. An L-shaped brick wall is placed across rear of stage and downstage right. There is gate in right wall.*

AT RISE: COSETTE *sits on bench, writing on lap desk.* MARIUS *enters right, peers over wall, sees her, then enters garden through gate. He stands, hat in hand, watching her with a joyful expression.*

COSETTE *(Looking up suddenly, seeing him, and dropping her pen):* Oh! *(Joyfully)* It is you!

MARIUS *(Breathlessly):* Yes, I have come at last. I've been searching for so long!

COSETTE: I prayed that you would find me!

MARIUS *(Hurrying to her and taking her hand):* I have thought of you every moment since I last saw you. I love you!

COSETTE: Then our thoughts of each other have been the same. *(Smiling happily)* And I don't even know your name.

MARIUS: Marius. And yours?

COSETTE: Cosette.

MARIUS: What about your father?

COSETTE: Monsieur Valjean, the dearest and best man in the world! He is all I have, and I am everything to him.

MARIUS: You must be. He snatched you away from me before I could say a single word to you.

COSETTE: He is a very cautious man, and very protective of me. He doesn't know you yet, and mustn't until the time is right. But I want to know all about you.

MARIUS: I'm a lawyer, but a very poor one. My father was a hero at Waterloo. When I was born, my mother died, and so I was raised by my grandfather, a supporter of the King. I, however, have accepted the people's view, and because of this my grandfather threw me out four years ago. Since then I've been free, but penniless. Now, tell me your story, Cosette. I'm sure it's much more interesting than mine.

COSETTE: I'm afraid not. I was reared in a convent where my father was gardener. My mother, too, is dead. Now my father is retired and we live here very quietly.

MARIUS: I'm sure there is more to you than that! When can I see you again?

COSETTE: Come in the evening after ten o'clock. My father will be asleep then. I'll meet you here.

MARIUS: I'll come every evening! We have so much to say to each other. *(Rising)* I thank heaven I found you! *(Kisses her gently, then exits through gate, looking fondly at her)*

COSETTE *(Looking after him):* Dear Marius! How happy you've made me! *(Runs off left. Lights fade out to indicate passage of time. When they come up again, it is night, one month later. MARIUS enters right and approaches gate. EPONINE, dressed in men's clothing and cap, follows him.)*

EPONINE: Monsieur Marius!

MARIUS *(Startled):* Eponine? I hardly know you in those clothes.

EPONINE: I am part of the new revolution. There will be fighting soon, maybe tonight.

MARIUS: Then you'd better get off the streets.

EPONINE: The streets are my home now. Why did you move away? It's been a month since I last saw you.

MARIUS: I couldn't find work. I had to move to a cheaper room.

EPONINE: When my landlord threw me out, I had no place to go and no friend but you, but I couldn't find you. Then I remembered this place. You've come here to see *her*, haven't you?

MARIUS: Yes, she is expecting me.

EPONINE: You come here often, don't you? Have you forgotten it was I who showed you this place?

MARIUS *(Uncomfortably):* No, I haven't forgotten. I'm very grateful, Eponine. Now, you must excuse me. *(Turns to gate)*

EPONINE *(Stepping in front of him):* Don't you remember your promise? You said you would give me anything I wished!

MARIUS: Very well. What do you want?

EPONINE *(Suddenly timid):* Would you . . . would you come and walk with me?

MARIUS: I can't now.

EPONINE *(Pleading):* Only for a little while. I have something to tell you.

MARIUS: I'm sorry, I can't.

EPONINE *(Upset):* But you promised me something!

MARIUS *(Fumbling in pocket and offering a coin):* This is all I have.

EPONINE *(Knocking coin out of his hand):* I don't want your money!

MARIUS *(Abruptly):* Then I have nothing else to give you. I must go now. Cosette is waiting for me. *(Brushes quickly past her through gate and shuts it firmly behind him, then moves to bench)*

EPONINE *(Bitterly, looking after him):* I am waiting, too! But you don't see me! *(Choking back a sob)* Somehow, I will *make* you see me! *(Sits down angrily on ground by wall. As MAR-IUS waits restlessly by bench, COSETTE enters left, sobbing.)*

MARIUS *(Alarmed):* Cosette! What is the matter? Why are you crying? *(Draws her to bench and sits)*

COSETTE: Marius, this morning my father told me we must go to England.

MARIUS *(Stunned):* No! When? Why?

COSETTE: In three days. He said that Paris is not safe for us now. I don't understand.

MARIUS: There is trouble in the streets. Sometimes innocent people become victims. *(Hopefully)* Did your father say you would come back when the trouble is past?

COSETTE: He didn't say. *(Brightening)* Marius, I will write to you and you can come to me in England!

MARIUS: My love, I have no money to pay for my passport! I have nothing, no one, but you.

COSETTE: Then what will happen to us?

MARIUS *(Holding her close):* I can't live without you. You are my life! If you go away, I must die!

COSETTE: Don't say that! There must be something we can do.

MARIUS *(Thinking a moment):* Yes, there is one chance. Cosette, I must leave you for a while. If all goes well, I'll be back within two hours.

COSETTE: Where are you going?

MARIUS: To see my grandfather.

COSETTE: But he said he never wanted to see you again.

MARIUS: That was four years ago. *(Embraces her)* Wait for me here! *(He releases her, reluctantly, then hurries out gate and off right.)*

COSETTE *(Looking after him):* Marius, hurry back to me! *(Shivers)* It is chilly out here. I'll get my shawl. *(Exits left)*

EPONINE *(Rising and looking after MARIUS):* I don't know where he is going, but when he comes back, I'll be waiting for him. *(Sounds of shots and men shouting are heard off right; she moves to gate.)* What is that? Shooting! *(Excitedly)* The fighting has begun! Ah! Someone is coming. *(Ducks down by wall as VALJEAN enters hurriedly right, looking anxiously over his shoulder. He enters garden and sits on bench.)*

VALJEAN: This hopeless rebellion moves closer and closer. The police are everywhere, questioning everyone. Thieves and bandits are looting houses, destroying property. This house is not safe for Cosette!

EPONINE *(Overhearing VALJEAN):* Not safe? No, it isn't safe. Here is my chance! *(Rises and enters gate)* Monsieur Valjean!

VALJEAN *(Turning sharply):* Who are you? What do you want?

EPONINE *(Taking off cap):* It is I, Eponine. You have been kind to me, and now I bring you a warning. The crowds are getting bigger every moment. They must come through this street on their way to the Square. They might even tear down your garden wall to make a barricade here! For your own good, monsieur, and the welfare of your daughter, leave here at once! Farewell, monsieur! *Vive la Révolution!* *(Runs out gate, shuts it, crouches beside wall)*

VALJEAN: I mustn't lose a moment! *(Starts off left)*

COSETTE *(Entering left with shawl):* Father! What's the matter?

VALJEAN: Cosette, we must leave at once.

COSETTE *(Alarmed):* At once? Why?

VALJEAN: It isn't safe here. We will go to the house I have rented on the other side of the city. Then in three days we will be safely in England.

COSETTE: But Father, it is so late. Can't we wait until tomorrow?

VALJEAN: No, there is greater safety under cover of darkness. Come at once! *(Starts to exit left)*

COSETTE *(Aside):* What can I do? How can I let Marius know?

VALJEAN *(Urgently):* Cosette!

COSETTE *(Noticing lap desk under bench):* Father, I left my writing desk in the garden. I'll get it and come right in.

VALJEAN *(Exiting left):* Hurry!

COSETTE: I must write Marius a letter! *(Unaware that EPONINE is watching her over the wall, COSETTE hastily writes letter, blots it, folds and seals it.)* I will leave it here for him. *(Kisses letter and lays it on bench)* Please understand, Marius. Don't desert me! *(Hurries out left with desk)*

EPONINE *(Cautiously entering garden through gate):* When Marius comes back he will find her gone, but I will be here. *(Picks up letter and puts it into her pocket)* He will never see this letter. He will be mine now. *(Moves to gate as COURFEYRAC, ENJOLRAS and GAVROCHE enter down right.)* Ho, citizens! Where are you going?

COURFEYRAC: To the barricade in the Rue de la Chanvrerie! If you love France, come with us!

EPONINE: I will come later!

ENJOLRAS: *Vive la Révolution!* *(The three salute and march off up right.)*

EPONINE *(Returning to bench and sitting behind it):* Now I must wait for Monsieur Marius. *(Curtain)*

* * * * *

SCENE 3

TIME: *A short while later.*
SETTING: MONSIEUR GILLENORMAND's *house. May be played*

before a curtain. A wall flat, with rich painting on it, and armchair are at right.

BEFORE RISE: MONSIEUR GILLENORMAND, *wearing velvet dressing gown and slippers, sits in chair, his hand on a gold-headed cane.* MARIUS *stands nervously before him, hat in hand.*

GILLENORMAND *(Sharply):* Why have you come here at this late hour?

MARIUS: Grandfather, I know my presence displeases you, but I must ask something of you.

GILLENORMAND *(Eagerly):* Ah! You have come to ask my pardon! You have seen your faults and changed your political views!

MARIUS *(Uncomfortably):* No, Grandfather. I come to ask your permission to marry.

GILLENORMAND *(Astonished):* What! You wish to marry? You, who stand before me dressed as a beggar? Tell me, how much do you earn at your lawyer's trade?

MARIUS *(Helplessly):* Nothing.

GILLENORMAND: Nothing! Then the girl is rich?

MARIUS: No.

GILLENORMAND *(Frowning):* She has expectations?

MARIUS: I think not.

GILLENORMAND: Who is her father?

MARIUS: Monsieur Valjean, a retired gardener.

GILLENORMAND: Monsieur who? A retired what? Have you lost your senses?

MARIUS *(Dropping to his knees):* Grandfather! I love her! I will die if I cannot have her! I beg of you, allow me to marry her!

GILLENORMAND *(Furious):* You wish to throw your career to the dogs, along with your future! You wish to plunge into misery with a wife at your neck, and I am to consent? Never!

MARIUS *(Pleading):* Grandfather, please!

GILLENORMAND: Never!

MARIUS *(Struggling to control himself, then rising):* Very well. I have nothing more to say.

GILLENORMAND: Fool! Ask my pardon, then see what my answer will be!

MARIUS: I have done nothing for which I should ask your pardon, Grandfather. If you cannot accept me because of my political views, then nothing has changed between us. *(Turns to leave)*

GILLENORMAND: Stop! Where are you going?

MARIUS *(Turning to face* GILLENORMAND): What does it matter? You will not see me again.

GILLENORMAND: Shall you go the way of your father and join this wretched rebellion in the streets?

MARIUS: Perhaps. I have friends among the people.

GILLENORMAND: Friends? They are all miserable thieves, beggars, assassins! Traitors to their king! You would dare be a part of such rabble?

MARIUS *(With conviction):* Yes, Grandfather! I am very much a part of them! *(Bows respectfully)* Good night. *(Exits right)*

GILLENORMAND *(Enraged):* Marius! *(Rises with difficulty, waving cane)* Marius! You disgrace this family! You could be so much, but you are nothing! Marius! *(Sinks back into chair)* I wish never to hear your name or see your face again! *(Chokes back sob as he stares after* MARIUS. *Blackout)*

*   *   *   *   *

SETTING: *Same as Scene 2.*

AT RISE: EPONINE *is asleep behind bench.* MARIUS, *downcast, enters right.*

MARIUS: Cosette? *(Looks around anxiously)* Cosette? *(Moves left)* Where are you?

EPONINE *(Rising):* Monsieur Marius!

MARIUS *(Startled):* Eponine! What are you doing here?

EPONINE: Waiting for you. The fighting has begun *(Taking his arm)* Come, I will lead you to the barricade!

MARIUS *(Pulling away):* No! I must find Cosette! *(Desperately calling)* Cosette! Where are you?

EPONINE *(Impatiently):* She is gone. The garden is empty, the house is dark.

MARIUS *(Dazed):* Gone? *(Distraught)* Yes, she is gone, lost to me forever! I'll never see her again. *(Slumps onto bench)* Without Cosette, I have nothing. I *am* nothing.

EPONINE *(Urgently):* Monsieur Marius, come with me to the barricade!

MARIUS *(Dully):* Barricade? Yes, the barricade . . . the revolution. I will fight in this civil war, just as my father fought at Waterloo. I will join my friends again. *(Turns to* EPONINE*)* Show me the way, Eponine, I will follow you.

EPONINE *(Joyfully):* This way, Monsieur Marius! *(Pulls him off right, as he looks back desperately. Curtain)*

*   *   *   *   *

SCENE 4

SETTING: *The barricade. Tree and bench from preceding scene have been removed, and brick wall is reversed to reveal stone and wooden barricade across rear of stage.*

AT RISE: *Sounds of gunfire and shouting are heard off left and right.* COURFEYRAC, ENJOLRAS, GAVROCHE, MARIUS, *and* EPONINE, *holding guns, crouch in front of barricade.*

COURFEYRAC: The Municipal Guards are forming for a direct attack on us. The streets behind us are blocked.

GAVROCHE: I have no weapon. Enjolras, give me a musket!

ENJOLRAS *(Grinning):* A musket for you, little Gavroche?

GAVROCHE *(Fiercely):* I'm not too little to fight!

ENJOLRAS: I would send you home, if you had a home to go to. Here, work your way forward and report the first enemy movements to us.

GAVROCHE *(Eagerly):* All right! I can do that better than anyone else because I am small! *(Scampers off right)*

MARIUS: Do children fight with us now, Courfeyrac?

COURFEYRAC: Some of the most desperate are children, my

friend. Enjolras, take your men and move to the right. We will
stay here. (ENJOLRAS *nods, exits right.*)

MARIUS: How long do you think we can hold this barricade?

COURFEYRAC: An hour, maybe two. We are badly outnumbered.
I'm glad you are here, Marius.

MARIUS *(Grimly):* I had no choice.

GAVROCHE *(Running in):* They are coming!

COUREFYRAC: We are ready! Take positions and wait for a good
shot! (*Loud shots are heard off right.* MARIUS, COURFEYRAC
and EPONINE *spread out and take firing positions, aiming up
right over barricade.*)

ENJOLRAS *(Entering; beckoning to* COURFEYRAC): Courfeyrac!
Over here, quickly!

COURFEYRAC: I'm coming! *(Fires a shot, then follows* EN-
JOLRAS *quickly off right)*

MARIUS: Keep down, Courfeyrac! (*Rises, fires, then whirls
around, dropping his gun and holding his head)*

EPONINE *(Alarmed):* Monsieur Marius! You are hit!

MARIUS *(Binding handkerchief around his head):* It's not bad.
Stay down!

EPONINE: Let me help you! (*Rises and starts toward him just as
another volley of shots is heard. She is hit, cries out, and falls
to ground beside* MARIUS.)

MARIUS: Eponine! *(Bends over her)* Eponine! You've been hit!
Why didn't you stay down? You know nothing of fighting. You
shouldn't have come here at all. *(Gently helps her to rise and
lean against wall)*

EPONINE *(Weakly):* I am happy here . . . because you are with
me. Soon . . . you will be with me forever. *(Pulls out letter)* I
didn't want you to have this . . . but now, it doesn't matter.
(MARIUS *takes letter; she coughs, then smiles faintly.*) Poor
Monsieur Marius . . . didn't you know . . . I was . . . in love
with you? *(Falls back, dead)*

MARIUS: Eponine! Poor girl! I'm sorry! (*Lays her down gently
and covers her with his coat, then moves right with letter and
tears it open)* It is from Cosette! *(Reading)* My beloved,

forgive me. My father wishes to go at once. We shall be tonight in the rue de l'Homme Arme, Number 7. In three days we will be in England. Yours forever, Cosette. *(Kneels a moment, overcome with grief)* I must write her a farewell letter. *(Takes small notebook and pencil from pocket and writes, then folds letter and writes address)* Gavroche! Gavroche!

GAVROCHE *(Running in, right):* Yes, monsieur?

MARIUS: I want you to carry this letter for me. You can easily slip out of the barricade and along the back streets.

GAVROCHE: But I will miss the fighting!

MARIUS: You shouldn't be gone long. It's urgent!

GAVROCHE: All right, monsieur. *(Takes letter and exits left)*

MARIUS: If he is gone long enough the fighting may end here and he might be spared. *(Picks up gun)* Cosette! Do not forget me! *(Curtain)*

* * * * *

SCENE 5

SETTING: *Valjean's house. Two chairs and table are left, in front of a wall flat on which mirror hangs directly above table.*

BEFORE RISE: VALJEAN *and* COSETTE, *in hats and cloaks, enter left. He carries a valise, she carries lap desk.*

VALJEAN: You see, my daughter, we have made a safe journey. The fighting no longer threatens us. *(Looks closely at her)* You are so pale! Are you ill?

COSETTE: No, Father, I'm just tired. *(Sets lap desk on table and sits, untying her bonnet)*

VALJEAN: You will be your usual cheerful self in the morning. Take off your cloak. I will carry your little desk into the other room and . . . *(Stops, staring at mirror above lap desk)* what is this?

COSETTE *(Not looking up):* What, Father?

VALJEAN *(His voice shaking):* There is some writing on your blotter . . . reflected in the mirror.

COSETTE *(Not realizing):* Some writing?

VALJEAN *(Reading, slowly):* My beloved, forgive me . . . (CO-SETTE *looks up sharply with a cry.)* . . . my father wishes to go at once. We shall be tonight in the . . . *(Turns to her in disbelief)* Cosette? *(She turns away, sobbing.)* So this is why you are so pale? So unhappy at leaving. There is someone you call your beloved. *(Suddenly)* That young man from the Luxembourg Gardens!

COSETTE *(Sobbing):* Yes, Father. His name is Marius. We love each other!

VALJEAN *(Groping his way to chair and sitting, staring sadly at her):* Why didn't you tell me?

COSETTE *(Dropping to her knees beside him):* Father, forgive me! I was afraid if you knew, you wouldn't let me see him again, and I couldn't bear that!

VALJEAN: Do you love him that much?

COSETTE: Oh, yes!

VALJEAN *(Sadly):* I knew this day would come, the day I would lose you, but I didn't expect it so soon.

COSETTE: You haven't lost me! I love you as I always have and always will!

VALJEAN *(Fervently):* Cosette, you are all I have! All these years, you have been my reason for living! How can I give you up? *(Knock at door;* VALJEAN *calls out.)* What? What is it?

GAVROCHE *(Offstage):* A letter for Cosette Valjean.

COSETTE: A letter! It must be from Marius! *(Rises quickly)*

VALJEAN: Wait! I will answer. *(Goes to door and opens it.* GAVROCHE *enters.)* I am Monsieur Valjean. My daughter is expecting the letter.

GAVROCHE *(Handing letter):* Then you know Monsieur Marius sent me?

VALJEAN: Of course. Were is the answer to be sent?

GAVROCHE: To the barricade in the rue de la Chanvrerie. Am I to wait, monsieur?

VALJEAN: No, you may go now. (*Hands* GAVROCHE *a coin*)

GAVROCHE (*Tossing coin, pleased*): You are a fine fellow, monsieur! (*Exits*)

COSETTE: Did the boy say he had come from a barricade?

VALJEAN (*Closing door*): Yes. (*Hands her letter*) Your letter.

COSETTE (*Tearing open letter and reading*): "My beloved, our marriage is impossible, my grandfather refuses permission. I love you above all else, but I cannot have you. Therefore, I die. Marius." (*Anguished*) Oh, no! Father, he is in the fighting! He will die! (*Drops letter on table and sobs*)

VALJEAN: He is either very brave or very foolish. (*Slowly picks up letter and looks at it, reading*) I love you above all else . . . I cannot have you . . . I die. (*Looking at her*) He loves you this much?

COSETTE: I didn't know how much until now! Oh, Father, is there no way to save him?

VALJEAN (*With difficulty*): I am an old man. When I am gone, there must be someone to love and protect you. I will try to find him.

COSETTE: Oh, Father, can you?

VALJEAN: There is no doubt in your mind? You do love him?

COSETTE: Yes, Father! Please bring him back to me!

VALJEAN (*Turning quickly away*): I know that part of the city well. I make no promises, for many do not survive these street fights. But I will try, for you. (*She goes to him; he embraces her, kisses her on forehead, then quickly takes hat and exits.*)

COSETTE (*Clutching letter*): Oh, Marius, will I ever see you again? (*Blackout*)

* * * * *

TIME: *An hour later.*

SETTING: *Same as Scene 4.*

AT RISE: COURFEYRAC *and* ENJOLRAS *lie on ground, dead.* MARIUS *lies face down, badly wounded and unconscious.*

Shooting is heard in distance off right. VALJEAN *enters cautiously left, and goes quickly from one body to the next.*

VALJEAN: Is there no one left alive? (*He comes to* MARIUS *and gently turns him over.*) This is he! But am I too late? How he bleeds! (*Feels* MARIUS' *temples*) Still a pulse, very faint.

MARIUS (*Moaning faintly*): Cosette . . .

VALJEAN: Very well, young man, even in your delirium you speak her name. (*He struggles to pull* MARIUS *upright and over his shoulders*) Listen to me, if you can hear me. Do not die! She is waiting for you! (*Slowly, he half drags, half carries* MARIUS *off left. Curtain*)

THE END

PRODUCTION NOTES

THE SACRIFICE

Characters: 6 male; 2 female.

Playing Time: 35 minutes.

Costumes: Appropriate 19th century French clothing. Cosette wears
dress, light shawl, cloak, bonnet. Marius, Courfeyrac, and Enjolras
wear shabby coats and pants, frayed shirts, worn boots and hats;
Gavroche is in rags, Eponine is barefoot, her face is dirty, and she
wears a ragged dress in Scene 1, then changes to ragged men's pants
and shirt with cap in Scene 2. Valjean wears a black suit and hat.
Gillenormand wears a rich velvet dressing gown and slippers.

Properties: Book, coins, small basket with bread, lap desk with pens,
paper and blotter, four carbines or pistols of the period, handkerchief, gold-headed cane, small notebook and pencil, small valise.

Setting: Scene 1: A Paris street, with a bench at right beside tree,
lamppost at left and another bench down left. Backdrop painting of
poor shops and tenements may be used. Scene 2 and 3, At Rise:
Valjean's garden. The bench and tree are moved to center, other
bench and lamppost removed. An L-shaped wall painted with bricks
is placed across rear of stage and downstage right. There is a
working gate in the wall. Scene 3, Before Rise: Monsieur Gillenormand's house. A small wall flat hung with a rich painting and a chair
are stage right. Scenes 4 and 5, At Rise: The barricade. Tree and
bench are removed from garden, and brick wall is reversed to show
stone and wooden barricade painted on other side, forming barricade
across stage. Scene 5, Before Rise: Valjean's house. Small wall flat
used in Scene 3 is used, with mirror replacing painting. Two chairs
and small table are placed stage left.

Lighting: Dim lighting may be used to indicate night; blackouts, spot-
lights as indicated.

Sound: Gunshots and men shouting.

Nicholas Nickleby

by Charles Dickens

Characters

NICHOLAS NICKLEBY, *19*
MRS. NICKLEBY, *his mother*
KATE NICKLEBY, *his sister, 17*
RALPH NICKLEBY, *his uncle*
NEWMAN NOGGS, *Ralph's clerk*
MR. SQUEERS, *schoolmaster*
MRS. SQUEERS, *his wife*
SMIKE, *a drudge at the school*
SCHOOLBOYS, *6 to 8 extras of various ages*
BOLDER
COBBEY
MOBBS
MR. CHEERYBLE, *London merchant*

SCENE 1

TIME: *1830's; winter.*
SETTING: *Ralph Nickleby's moneylending office in London. Scene may be played before curtain, with desk and three chairs at center.*
BEFORE RISE: RALPH NICKLEBY, *sour-faced old man, sits at desk, frowning at a letter.* NEWMAN NOGGS, *shabbily dressed, waits beside him.*

RALPH *(Unpleasantly):* So, my long-lost relatives are waiting outside, Noggs?

NOGGS: Yes, sir. They are eager to see you.

RALPH *(Impatiently):* People who don't have money are always eager to see people who do. Show them in. Let me get this disagreeable matter settled as quickly as possible.

NOGGS: Yes, sir. *(Crosses left, and calls offstage)* Mr. Ralph Nickleby will see you now. (MRS. NICKLEBY, KATE, *and* NICHOLAS, *all dressed in black, enter left)* Please sit down, ladies.

MRS. NICKLEBY: Thank you. *(She and* KATE *sit.* NICHOLAS *stands behind them.* NOGGS *stands left of desk.)*

RALPH *(Briskly):* Well, ma'am, I received your letter last week, informing me that my brother, whom I haven't seen in forty years, died penniless. Now you, a widow with children, come to London to apply to me for assistance.

MRS. NICKLEBY *(Tearfully):* It was my husband's dying wish that we come to you, sir. He thought you would be able to help the children find employment. This is my daughter, Kate, and my son, Nicholas. (KATE *nods;* NICHOLAS *bows politely.)*

RALPH *(Frowning):* Humph! Young, innocent, and ill-prepared to face the world, I'll wager!

MRS. NICKLEBY: The loss of our dear husband and father has been very hard on us, sir.

RALPH *(Coldly):* Nonsense, ma'am. Husbands and fathers die every day.

NICHOLAS *(Indignantly):* And brothers, too, sir!

RALPH: Mind your tongue, young man! My brother never did anything for me, nor I for him. How old are you?

NICHOLAS *(Trying to keep his temper):* Nineteen, sir.

RALPH: And what do you intend to do now to earn your living?

NICHOLAS *(Proudly):* I don't know just yet, but whatever I do, I won't live on my mother's savings.

RALPH: You'd have little enough to live on if you did! Have you ever worked at anything?

NICHOLAS *(Hesitantly):* No, sir, but—

RALPH: I thought not! You were raised to be a gentleman, I suppose?

MRS. NICKLEBY *(Emphatically):* Oh, yes, he was, sir. And Nicholas has completed all the education his poor father could give him.

RALPH *(Eyeing* NICHOLAS; *drily):* Which was scant indeed, it seems. *(To* NICHOLAS) Are you willing to work?

NICHOLAS *(Proudly):* Of course. I will undertake any honest labor and apply myself diligently.

RALPH: Then listen to me. I noticed this in the morning paper. *(Holds up paper and reads aloud)* "Wanted: Able assistant for Mr. Wackford Squeers' School at Dotheboys Hall in Yorkshire, where young boys are boarded, clothed and instructed. Annual salary, five pounds." *(Looks up; to* NICHOLAS) There! With that in hand, your fortune is made!

MRS. NICKLEBY *(Bravely):* That sounds quite suitable for you, Nicholas.

KATE: But, mother, the salary is so small, and Yorkshire is so far away from London.

NICHOLAS *(To* RALPH): Surely, Uncle, I can earn more than five pounds a year.

RALPH *(Sneering):* Can you? Where? If you don't like this position, find your own! Without friends, money, recommendation or knowledge of business, you'll have a good time of it.

NICHOLAS: But if I leave London, what will become of Mother and Kate?

RALPH: I will see that they have board and lodging until the girl can secure employment. I can probably find a place for her with a dressmaker.

MRS. NICKLEBY: I'm sure we'll be all right, Nicholas. Do consider carefully what your uncle is offering you.

NICHOLAS: Very well, Mother. If Mr. Squeers will have me, I'll try my fortune with him in Yorkshire.

RALPH *(Slyly):* Oh, he'll have you. I happen to know him. He is in London now looking for new pupils, as well as a new assistant. I'll arrange for you to get the position. But see here, you must keep the situation, or I shall have nothing more to do with you or your mother and sister. I never deal with beggars.

NICHOLAS *(Angrily):* We are not, nor shall we ever be beggars, sir.

RALPH: Very well! I'll send Noggs for you at eight in the morning. Be prompt! Good day. *(Nods roughly to them and exits left)*

KATE *(Rising; fretfully):* Oh, dear! Our uncle has such a sharp temper.

MRS. NICKLEBY: I'm sure he's more kindly disposed than he appears, Kate.

NICHOLAS: No, Mother, I'm afraid he is a miserly, heartless man, but I must follow his advice until I can make my own way.

MRS. NICKLEBY: Do be patient, Nicholas, and you will succeed.

KATE *(Encouragingly):* You'll make a fine schoolmaster's assistant.

NICHOLAS: I hope so, for all our sakes. Come, let's go back to our lodgings. (NICKLEBYS *exit left, and* NOGGS *watches them, shaking his head regretfully. Blackout)*

*   *   *   *   *

SCENE 2

TIME: *The next morning.*

SETTING: *Outside coach office. Played before curtain, after desk and chairs have been removed. Boxes and bundles are stacked at right.*

BEFORE RISE: MR. SQUEERS, *a rough–looking man wearing an eyepatch and carrying cane, enters right, pushing two frightened* SCHOOLBOYS, *each carrying a bundle.* RALPH *follows them on.*

MR. SQUEERS *(Roughly):* Climb up on top of that coach, you little scoundrels, and stop sniveling!

SCHOOLBOYS: Yes, sir. *(They hurry off left.)*

RALPH *(Slyly):* I suppose those boys will be model pupils at your school, Mr. Squeers?

MR. SQUEERS *(Grinning wickedly):* If they aren't models now, sir, they soon will be. *(Brandishing cane)* Boys learn quickly at Dotheboys Hall!

RALPH: Up to what age do you keep them?

MR. SQUEERS: For as long as their tuition is paid, or until they run away, sir. *(Chuckles)*

RALPH *(Thoughtfully):* Run away, do they? But you must find replacements quite easily.

MR. SQUEERS: Always, sir, with no trouble at all.

RALPH: I would like to have the same arrangement with your new assistant, my nephew.

MR. SQUEERS: Eh? How do you mean?

RALPH *(Confidentially):* I mean that I don't want to see him after today. Set him to work. Don't spare him. If he should happen to leave your service without permission, then I am rid of a pauper relative, and you are rid of an incompetent assistant. In either case, we both come out for the better, so do with him as you please.

MR. SQUEERS: Oh, I do as I please with everyone at Dotheboys Hall, Mr. Nickleby.

RALPH: I knew I could depend on you. *(Looks off right)* Well! Here comes my nephew. (NICHOLAS *enters with luggage, followed by* NOGGS, KATE *and* MRS. NICKLEBY.) Come here and meet your employer, Mr. Wackford Squeers.

MR. SQUEERS *(Grinning slyly, extending his hand):* How do you do, Nickleby?

NICHOLAS *(Nobly):* I am quite well, thank you, sir.

MR. SQUEERS: Your uncle has assured me that you are just what I want in an assistant. *(Nodding to* KATE *and* MRS. NICKLEBY) Good morning, ladies.

RALPH: Well, go along now, nephew, and remember the conditions I hold you to.

NICHOLAS: I will. And you remember, Uncle, that my mother and sister depend on you.

RALPH: Don't worry. I'll take care of them. *(Scowling, he exits right.)*

MR. SQUEERS *(Roughly):* Come along, Nickleby! *(Nodding)* Good day, ladies! *(Exits left)*

MRS. NICKLEBY: Dear me! What a rough-looking man!

KATE: Nicholas, if that vulgar fellow is the schoolmaster, what kind of a school can Dotheboys be?

NICHOLAS: I don't know, Kate. I suppose the Yorkshire folk are rather uncultivated.

MRS. NICKLEBY: Then I'm sure you will be a good influence on them, my dear.

NICHOLAS: I'll try to be, Mother. Write to me and tell me how you are provided for, and I will write to you.

MRS. NICKLEBY *(Hugging him):* We will, Nicholas. Goodbye, dear son. We shall miss you.

KATE *(Hugging him):* I know you'll succeed, Nicholas! Goodbye!

NICHOLAS: Goodbye! *(As he turns to exit left, NOGGS suddenly runs on right.)*

NOGGS: Wait, sir! *(Thrusts a letter at NICHOLAS)* Take this. Read it in private. Mr. Ralph Nickleby isn't to know about it! *(Turns to ladies and bows awkwardly)* If you'll come with me, ladies, I've been instructed to show you the way to your new lodgings. *(He escorts KATE and MRS. NICKLEBY off right. NICHOLAS waves after them and starts off left, just as MR. CHEERYBLE, a pleasant-faced old gentleman, enters left, holding some letters. He bumps into NICHOLAS and drops his letters.)*

NICHOLAS: I beg your pardon, sir! Let me get your letters for you. *(Stoops to pick up letters)*

CHEERYBLE *(Pleasantly):* No offense, young man. *(Taking letters)* Thank you. You must be in a hurry. Going on the Yorkshire coach, are you?

NICHOLAS: Yes, sir. I'm going to teach at a school for boys in Yorkshire.

CHEERYBLE: Indeed! A teacher, are you? Splendid! Education is

a very fine thing. You couldn't have chosen a better calling in
life. May I ask your name, sir?

NICHOLAS: Nicholas Nickleby, sir.

CHEERYBLE: I'm pleased to know you, Mr. Nickleby. *(Shakes
his hand warmly)* My name is Cheeryble—Charles Cheeryble. I have a counting house off Threadneedle Street. You
must come and call on me when you are in London again. I
take keen interest in young men who show promise!

NICHOLAS: Why, thank you, sir. That's very kind of you.

CHEERYBLE: Have a pleasant journey, sir, and good luck to you!

NICHOLAS: Thank you. Good day, sir. (CHEERYBLE *nods pleasantly and exits right.* NICHOLAS *looks after him.)*

SQUEERS *(From off left):* Nickleby!

NICHOLAS: I'm coming! *(Hurries off left. Blackout)*

* * * * *

SCENE 3

TIME: *Later that day.*

SETTING: *Mr. Squeers' School at Dotheboys Hall in Yorkshire, a
dimly lit, dirty room with several benches and two teachers'
desks at left and center. There are doors at right and left, and
a table with two chairs at right.*

AT RISE: SQUEERS *and* NICHOLAS, *with* SCHOOLBOYS, *shivering and stamping, enter right.*

SQUEERS: Hurry in, Nickleby! The wind blows hard enough to
knock a man off his legs! *(Calling harshly)* Smike! Bring
something hot to drink, do you hear? *(Removing hat and coat)*
Boys! Go upstairs and find a place to sleep. Any corner will do.
Go along! *(Shoves* BOYS *across room and they stumble sleepily off left)* This is Dotheboys Hall, Nickleby, although no one
in these parts calls it that. I only use that name when I'm in
London. It sounds better. *(Laughs)*

NICHOLAS *(Looking around dejectedly):* Indeed, sir, it's not quite what I expected. (SMIKE, *a dirty, ragged boy in his teens, limps in right with two cups, which he sets on table.*)

SQUEERS *(Roughly):* Well, Smike, why didn't you come at once, eh? *(Cuffs him)*

SMIKE *(Cowering):* Please, sir, I fell asleep by the fire.

SQUEERS *(Fiercely):* What? Who told you to waste wood and build a fire? You keep awake better in the cold. *(Cuffs him again and* SMIKE *creeps into upper right corner.* MRS. SQUEERS, *in nightgown, shawl, and nightcap, enters right and hugs* SQUEERS.)

MRS. SQUEERS *(In a hoarse voice):* Here is my Squeery, safely back from London! How are you, Squeery?

SQUEERS: I'm quite well, my love. I've brought back a new assistant, Mr. Nicholas Nickleby.

MRS. SQUEERS: Oh? *(Looks scornfully at* NICHOLAS*)* Is this the best you could do?

SQUEERS: Oh, he'll do very well, my love.

NICHOLAS *(Proudly):* I shall do the best I can, ma'am.

MRS. SQUEERS: Oh, will you? We'll see about that! *(Tosses her head and takes letters from her pocket)* Here are your letters, Squeery.

SQUEERS: Ah, yes, thank you, my dear.

MRS. SQUEERS: When you are finished, I have a nice juicy steak in the kitchen for you. *(Scowls at* NICHOLAS *and exits right)*

SQUEERS: Thank you, my love. Nickleby, drink some of that hot stuff, and stop shivering! *(As he opens letters,* NICHOLAS *sits opposite him and drinks, obviously displeased with the contents of the mug.* SMIKE *creeps up behind* SQUEERS *and looks anxiously over his shoulder.)* What are you staring at, Smike?

SMIKE *(Timidly):* Please sir. Is there . . .

SQUEERS *(Sharply):* Is there *what?*

SMIKE: Did anybody . . . I mean, has nothing been heard about me, sir?

SQUEERS *(With a sneer):* About *you,* Smike? *(Laughs)* Not a word now and never will be! Fine thing, too, that you've been left here all these years with no money paid after the first six, and no clue found as to whom you belong. It's a fine thing that I have to feed you and never hope to get one penny for it, isn't it?

SMIKE (*Turning away; sadly*): I'm sorry, sir. (*Exits right, wiping his eyes on his sleeve*)

SQUEERS: I think that boy gets more thick-headed every day! At least he's cheaper than a servant. Nickleby, you'd better get to bed. Be up at seven sharp! Good night. (*Exits right*)

NICHOLAS (*Rising*): Good night. (*He looks about in dismay; to himself*) Can this dreary, dirty place really be a school? That poor lad, Smike, lame and filthy—can he be one of the pupils? I think my uncle sent me here just to get me out of his way. But I must try to make the best of this, for the sake of Mother and Kate. (*He takes off his coat and pulls out letter from pocket.*) The letter from Mr. Noggs. I had forgotten it. (*Opens letter and reads*) "My dear young man, your father did me a kindness years ago, and now I'll try to do you one. If you ever need a friend or shelter in London, come to me at the sign of the Crown in Silver Street. In the meantime, I will help your mother and sister as much as I can, for you cannot depend on your uncle. Newman Noggs." (*Folding letter*) How kind of him! I won't forget this. (*Curtain*)

* * * * *

SCENE 4

TIME: *Next morning.*

SETTING: *The same.*

AT RISE: NICHOLAS *sits shivering at table, buttoning his coat.*

SQUEERS (*Entering right*): Well, Nickleby, I'm afraid the well is frozen, so you won't be able to wash.

MRS. SQUEERS (*Entering; impatiently*): Drat it! I can't find the school spoon, and this is brimstone morning.

SQUEERS: So it is! We purify the boys' blood now and then, Nickleby.

MRS. SQUEERS: Purify, fiddlesticks! *(To NICHOLAS)* They have brimstone and treacle partly because if they didn't have something in the way of medicine, they'd always be ailing and giving us a world of trouble, and partly because it spoils their appetites and comes cheaper than breakfast and dinner. *(Calls off right, sharply)* Smike!

SMIKE *(Entering right, with heavy kettle):* Yes, missus?

MRS. SQUEERS: Where's the school spoon? *(Cuffs him)* Speak out! What have you done with it?

SMIKE: Please, missus, I believe it's in your pocket.

MRS. SQUEERS: What? *(Finds spoon in her pocket)* Wretch! *(Cuffs him)* Bring the brimstone, and no dawdling! (SMIKE *follows* MRS. SQUEERS *left and sets kettle on bench.* SCHOOL-BOYS, *including two new boys, as well as* BOLDER, COBBEY *and* MOBBS—*all ragged, dirty and shivering—enter left and form a line in front of* MRS. SQUEERS. *She spoons each of them a dose from kettle, pulling their hair and shoving them about.* BOYS *make horrible faces and huddle together on benches.)*

SQUEERS *(Watching, with glee):* Mrs. Squeers is a most invaluable woman, Nickleby!

NICHOLAS *(Watching with ill-disguised alarm):* Indeed, sir!

SQUEERS: Why, she does things for them that half the mothers anywhere don't do for their own sons.

NICHOLAS *(Quietly):* I should think they would not, sir.

SQUEERS: Come along, Nickleby, and meet your pupils. *(Crosses to desk and raps sharply on it with his cane, making* BOYS *jump in fright. To* MRS. SQUEERS) My love, is the doctoring finished?

MRS. SQUEERS: Just finished. Smike, take this away. *(She holds out kettle, frowning fiercely at* BOYS. SMIKE *exits left with kettle, then returns and waits by door at left.)*

SQUEERS: First class present themselves! (1ST, 2ND, *and* 3RD BOYS *stand and form a line in front of him.)* This is the first class in English spelling and philosophy, Nickleby. Boys, this is your new teacher. (*To* 1ST BOY) Now then, what job did you perform this morning?

1ST BOY: Please sir, I cleaned the back parlor window.

SQUEERS: So you did! We go upon the practical mode of teaching, Nickleby. Clean! *(Spells out)* C-l-e-a-n. To make bright, to scour. (*To* 2ND BOY) You! How did you earn your keep today?

2ND BOY: Please, sir, I weeded the garden.

SQUEERS: To be sure! Botany! A knowledge of plants. That's our system, Nickleby. *(Eyeing him sharply)* What do you think of it?

NICHOLAS: It's . . . it's a very useful system, Mr. Squeers.

SQUEERS: Of course it is! (*To* 3RD BOY) You! What's a horse!

3RD BOY: A beast, sir.

SQUEERS: So it is! As you're perfect in that, go and look after my horse and rub him down well! (3RD BOY *exits left, others return to their seats.* SQUEERS *addresses his wife.*) Now, my love, let me have the letters I brought back with me from the boys' relatives. (BOYS *murmur among themselves and watch anxiously as* MRS. SQUEERS *hands over letters.*) Silence! Let any boy speak a word without permission, and I'll break my cane on his back! *(Silence)* Now, then! *(Scanning a letter)* What's this? Bolder's father is two pound ten short in his tuition! Where's Bolder?

BOLDER *(Rising, timidly):* Here, sir.

SQUEERS: Come here, Bolder! (BOLDER *comes to desk apprehensively.*) Bolder, you are an insolent scoundrel, just like your father! As the last thrashing did you no good, we must see what another will do toward beating the insolence out of you. Smike, lock him in the cellar until I'm ready for him! (SMIKE *reluctantly hustles* BOLDER *off left, then returns.* SQUEERS *picks up another letter and scans it.*) Here's a letter for Cobbey. Stand up, Cobbey!

COBBEY *(Frightened):* Yes, sir. *(Stands)*

SQUEERS: Your sister sends eighteen pence, which will just pay for that pane of glass you broke. Mrs. Squeers, my love, will you take charge of the money? (*Hands coin to* Mrs. Squeers) Sit down, Cobbey! (Cobbey *sits.* Squeers *looks at another letter.*) Ah! Here is one from Mobbs' stepmother. Stand up, Mobbs! (Mobbs *stands.*) Your stepmother is sorry to hear that you are discontented, which is sinful and horrid, and hopes Mr. Squeers will thrash you into a happier state of mind. *(Smiles)* Well! Cheerfulness and contentment must be upheld. Smike, lock Mobbs up with Bolder! I'll be there directly. (Smike *leads the whimpering* Mobbs *off left.*) Now, Nickleby, you will hear the second class in their reading. The rest of you boys will go outside and break the ice in the well and draw water for the washtubs. Classes will resume at one o'clock. (4th, 5th *and* 6th Boys *come to* Nicholas, *with books.* Other Boys *shuffle dejectedly off left.*)

Mrs. Squeers *(Chuckling):* Now, Squeery, let us see to Bolder and Mobbs!

Squeers *(Swinging his cane):* Yes, my love. (Squeers *exits left, followed by* Mrs. Squeers.)

Nicholas (*To* Boys): Boys, sit down and read over your lesson, and then I'll hear you recite. (Boys *sit and look at books.* Nicholas *paces down center. To himself*) What a mockery of learning! This is no school—it is a workhouse! What can I possibly do to help these poor boys? (Smike *enters left and approaches* Nicholas *timidly. As* Nicholas *notices him, he shrinks back as if expecting a blow.*) You need not fear me, Smike. I won't harm you, poor fellow.

Smike *(Desperately):* Oh, sir, you will be kind to me, won't you? *(Covers his face, sobbing)*

Nicholas *(Gently placing his hand on* Smike's *shoulder):* Hush! Be a man. You are nearly one by years.

Smike *(Miserably):* Oh, how many years have passed since I was a little child here, younger than any that are here now.

Nicholas: Have you no parents or relatives to help you?

Smike: None that I know of.

NICHOLAS: You mustn't give up hope, Smike. Someday, someone will come for you.

SMIKE *(Wringing his hands):* No, no one will ever come. I have no hope.

MRS. SQUEERS *(Harshly, off right):* Smike!

SMIKE: I must go now.

MRS. SQUEERS *(Entering right, angrily):* Smike! Come here at once! *(As SMIKE creeps toward her, she cuffs him sharply, knocking him down.)* Where's the wood for the kitchen fire? Why haven't you cleaned the stable yet? Disturb the new assistant, will you?

NICHOLAS: If you please, Mrs. Squeers, Smike was not disturbing me.

SQUEERS *(Entering right; angrily):* Smike! Why aren't my boots polished?

MRS. SQUEERS: Because he's been chattering away with the new assistant, keeping them both from their work.

SQUEERS: What's this, Nickleby? Come, come! The boys are waiting for their lesson!

NICHOLAS *(After a moment's hesitation):* Yes, sir. *(Turns back to BOYS and begins a lesson, in pantomime, during following dialogue)*

MRS. SQUEERS: Go on! Get to work! *(Hauls SMIKE to his feet and shoves him off right)*

SQUEERS: Well, my love, what do you think of Nickleby?

MRS. SQUEERS: I think he's a proud, haughty peacock!

SQUEERS *(Grinning):* What do you expect from a gentleman's son who is forced to work for his living?

MRS. SQUEERS: The nasty, stuck-up monkey! I watched him when you sent Bolder and Mobbs off to be caned. He looked as black as thunder, and once I thought he meant to interfere. He must learn who is master here!

SQUEERS: Oh, he will, my love, he will. He comes very cheap, you know, and he's ours for as long as we wish. He won't make any trouble, my love, none whatsoever! *(Confidentially)* He's got a mother and sister back in London who would come to very dire straits should he fail in his new position.

MRS. SQUEERS: Hah! Well, just let me catch him meddling with Smike again. They'll both pay for it.

SQUEERS: My dear, I believe there's not a spirit anywhere that we can't break! *(Chuckles, and leads* MRS. SQUEERS *off right; curtain)*

* * * * *

SCENE 5

TIME: *One month later.*

SETTING: *The same.*

AT RISE: NICHOLAS *sits at desk, reading a letter.* SMIKE *sits near him, bent over a book.*

SMIKE *(In dismay):* I can't read it. I can't make sense of it.

NICHOLAS *(Looking up; gently):* Stop for now. You can try again tomorrow.

SMIKE: I have always wanted to learn to read, but Master Squeers never took the time to teach me. He works me harder than ever, and Mrs. Squeers won't be satisfied no matter what I do.

NICHOLAS *(Grimly):* I know. It's because I have been your friend. They do it to hurt me as much as you. But you will do better when I am gone.

SMIKE *(Anxiously):* Are you going away?

NICHOLAS: I'm afraid I will be forced to leave soon. The Squeers hate me, and I am powerless to help the boys.

SMIKE: But you have helped me! You have been my friend!

NICHOLAS: My friendship has only brought you more suffering, I'm afraid. And my being here seems to have brought hardship to my mother and sister. Today I received a letter from Kate. She works long hours in a dreary place, for very little pay, and my mother is left alone all day. My uncle has neglected them. They are helpless and unprotected, and I can't bear to think of them that way. I must return to London.

SMIKE: But what will you do there?

NICHOLAS: I don't know, Smike. Perhaps I can find a school where the children are taught and cared for properly, a place where I could be proud to teach and could earn a decent living.

SMIKE: Is there such a place?

NICHOLAS: Oh, yes, somewhere. All schools are not like this.

SMIKE: But if you go away, I'll never see you again.

SQUEERS *(Angrily, from off right):* Smike!

SMIKE *(Urgently):* I would fear for my life if you weren't here.

NICHOLAS: They wouldn't dare threaten your life.

SQUEERS *(Furiously, off right):* Smike! Do you want a thrashing?

SMIKE: Please don't go! Please! *(Frightened, he runs off left.)*

SQUEERS *(Entering right):* Confound that brat Smike! Nickleby!

NICHOLAS: Yes, sir?

SQUEERS: Where is that obstinate scoundrel?

NICHOLAS: I don't know where he is.

SQUEERS *(Scowling):* Oh, don't you?

NICHOLAS *(Angrily, but calmly):* No, I don't, and I'm glad I don't, for then it would be my duty to tell you.

SQUEERS: Which, no doubt, you would be very sorry to do?

NICHOLAS: I would, indeed.

SQUEERS: You go too far, Nickleby. You think you're too good for me and my school, don't you? Well, I'll take you down, sir. You'll take your meals in the kitchen and sleep with the boys. I'll give you more classes to teach and keep you at them for longer hours. And when I find Smike, he'll have a lesson he won't soon forget!

MRS. SQUEERS *(Triumphantly, from off left):* I've got him! *(Enters left, dragging a frightened SMIKE)* Here he is, the young devil! I found him trying to hide, and all his morning chores not finished! But then, when you have a proud teacher to set him rebelling, what can you expect? (*Scowling at* NICH-OLAS) You wouldn't be in the house another hour if I had my way.

NICHOLAS (*Calmly*): Nor would you, ma'am, if I had mine.

SQUEERS (*Seizing his cane and collaring* SMIKE): Well, Smike, we can't have this, you know! (NICHOLAS *rises, angrily*) Keep your place, Nickelby! I am master here! (*Raising cane*)

SMIKE (*Desperately*): Spare me, sir!

SQUEERS: Spare you? Oh, yes, I'll flog you within an inch of your life and spare you that! (*He strikes* SMIKE *twice with cane.* SMIKE *cries out.*)

NICHOLAS: Stop! Stop this at once! Touch him again at your peril! I will not spare you, sir, if you persist in this senseless cruelty!

SQUEERS: Beggar! Stay back!

NICHOLAS: I will not!

SQUEERS: Oh, won't you? (*Enraged, he stikes* NICHOLAS *with cane.* NICHOLAS *seizes cane, knocks* SQUEERS *down, and begins to beat him.* SMIKE *creeps to right, terrified.* SQUEERS *roars,* MRS. SQUEERS *shrieks and tries to pull* SQUEERS *away, but* NICHOLAS *continues until the bellowing* SQUEERS *finally rolls away, jumps up, and runs off right, followed by his hysterical wife. Gasping for breath,* NICHOLAS *flings down the cane.*)

NICHOLAS: Well, I've sealed my fate here, but he got what he deserved!

SMIKE: Are you going away now?

NICHOLAS: Yes, Smike. Are you hurt?

SMIKE (*Kneeling at his feet*): No. Oh, take me with you. Please! I'll be your faithful servant. I'll do anything you ask, but please don't leave me here!

NICHOLAS: Come, stand up. (SMIKE *stands.*) We'll go to London together. I have a friend there who may be able to help us. His name is Newman Noggs. (*Curtain*)

*   *   *   *   *

SCENE 6

TIME: *Two weeks later.*

SETTING: *The Crown Inn; may be played before curtain. A table and two chairs are center.*

BEFORE RISE: NICHOLAS *and* SMIKE, *looking tired and worn, sit at table, while* NOGGS *bustles about, setting out bread and drink.*

NOGGS: I can hardly believe my eyes, Mr. Nickleby. You and your friend walked all the way from Yorkshire—and in such miserable weather! *(Concerned)* I wish I had more to offer you.

NICHOLAS: Please, sit down, Mr. Noggs, and trouble yourself no further. You've been very kind.

SMIKE: Indeed, sir, we are very grateful to you.

NICHOLAS: Tell me, what has my uncle heard from Yorkshire?

NOGGS *(Hesitantly):* Nothing good, I'm sorry to say. Mrs. Squeers wrote to him, saying that you attacked Mr. Squeers, hurt him severely, and ran away—taking with you, as she puts it, a boy of desperate character. She and Squeers demand justice.

NICHOLAS *(Angrily):* Do they, indeed? I shall never regret what I have done. I will never be a coward and stand tamely by while a black-hearted scoundrel cruelly abuses an innocent and unfortunate boy.

NOGGS: I am proud to hear you say that, sir. I would have acted just as you did. But sir, you should know that your uncle means to inform your mother and sister about this incident tomorrow—and cast them off entirely!

NICHOLAS: The villain! Would he really be so heartless?

NOGGS: He would.

SMIKE *(Timidly):* My friend, I'm afraid you are in this great trouble because you brought me away with you. I should have stayed behind and spared you this hardship.

NICHOLAS: Smike, I would not have deserted you for the world.

My uncle must be dealt with and my mother and sister cared for.

NOGGS: And the sooner we find a way to do it, the better. (CHEERYBLE *enters right, and stops in surprise as he sees the group at table.*)

CHEERYBLE: Why, it's the young gentleman who went off to Yorkshire to teach boys! Mr. Nickleby, isn't it? *(Offers his hand)*

NICHOLAS *(Rising and taking his hand):* Yes, Mr. Cheeryble. How do you do, sir?

CHEERYBLE: I'm very well, sir, thank you. But, dear me, if you'll pardon my saying so, you don't look well at all.

NICHOLAS: No, sir. I'm afraid I've met with considerable misfortune.

CHEERYBLE: I'm very sorry to hear it! You must tell me all about it. *(To* NOGGS*)* Sir, will you kindly order a round of good hot punch for everyone?

NOGGS: With pleasure, sir. *(Exits left)*

CHEERYBLE *(Taking off his coat and putting it around* SMIKE's *shoulders):* Here, young man, you're shivering. *(Sits)* Now, Mr. Nickleby, begin at the beginning and tell me all. *(Curtain)*

* * * * *

SCENE 7

TIME: *The next day.*

SETTING: *The Nicklebys' flat in London. A few chairs and table are placed around stage.*

AT RISE: MRS. NICKLEBY *and* KATE *are seated, in tears.* RALPH *stands to one side.*

RALPH: This is a very pretty turn of events, isn't it? I recommended Nicholas, against my better judgment, for a position he could have retained in comfort for years. And what has happened? He has beaten his employer and may very well be arrested.

MRS. NICKLEBY: Surely you are mistaken, sir!

KATE: I cannot believe it! It is some conspiracy against Nicholas by that horrid Mr. Squeers.

RALPH: Young woman, you wrong a worthy man. Your brother assaulted Mr. Squeers, then ran away, taking a boy with him. He has broken our agreement, and I want nothing more to do with any of you. You must vacate these lodgings at once.

KATE: Oh, if only Nicholas were here!

RALPH: If he were, it would be my duty to deliver him to justice! *(Door suddenly bursts open at left, and* NICHOLAS *enters, followed by* CHEERYBLE, NOGGS *and* SMIKE.*)*

MRS. NICKLEBY: Nicholas!

KATE *(Running to him):* Dear Nicholas!

RALPH *(Calmly):* Well, nephew, this is both foolish and bold of you. Just what do you mean by coming here?

NICHOLAS: Sir, you knowingly sent me to a den of sordid cruelty, where children are ill used. And while you promised to aid my mother and sister, you have purposely neglected them!

RALPH *(Sneering):* Have I? *You* are the one accused of attacking your master and kidnapping a boy!

NICHOLAS: I rescued the boy from a cruel and degrading beating, and brought him away with me for safety. Here he is!

RALPH *(Scowling at* SMIKE*):* He must be sent back at once.

NICHOLAS: Never! He will stay with me. And as for you, sir, trouble yourself with me and my family no more. We renounce you!

RALPH: Take care what you say, sir. I can ruin you!

NICHOLAS: Take care what *you* say, Uncle! I am not without friends.

RALPH: What good are friends when you have no way to earn your living?

CHEERYBLE *(Stepping forward):* Oh, but he does, sir. I have offered him a position as secretary in my firm, beginning at a salary of 120 pounds per year.

RALPH: What? You must be mistaken, sir!

CHEERYBLE: Not in the least, sir. It is *you* who have been

mistaken in your dealings with this fine young man. May I show you to the door? *(Takes RALPH's arm and propels him toward door at left)*

RALPH *(Turning; fiercely):* Noggs! Are you coming?

NOGGS: I am not.

RALPH: What do you mean, you are not?

NOGGS: I mean that Mr. Cheeryble has offered me a place as clerk at three times the salary you have paid me, and I have accepted.

RALPH: Bah! Good riddance! (CHEERYBLE *pushes him out the door.*)

MRS. NICKLEBY: Dear Nicholas, everything is happening so quickly. What does all this mean?

NICHOLAS: Why, it means we shall all live very comfortably now, Mother, thanks to Mr. Cheeryble's generosity. Not only has he taken me into his firm, but he has provided a cottage for all of us, at very reasonable rent.

KATE *(To CHEERYBLE):* Sir, we shall be forever grateful! But what of this trouble with Mr. Squeers?

CHEERYBLE: Oh, you mustn't worry about him, my dear young lady. I shall see that he and his school are thoroughly investigated. He won't remain a schoolmaster for long.

NOGGS: Indeed he won't, sir! Nor will Mr. Ralph Nickleby make any further trouble. He has been beaten, and I'm very glad of it.

NICHOLAS *(Leading SMIKE forward):* Mother, Kate, here is my friend, Smike. We must make room for him in our new house.

KATE: Smike, you shall have a home with us for as long as you wish.

SMIKE: Thank you. You are all so kind.

CHEERYBLE *(Heartily):* Come, now, everyone! We are going out for the finest dinner London can offer, to celebrate this most happy occasion! *(All rise happily, as lights dim. Curtain)*

THE END

PRODUCTION NOTES

Nicholas Nickleby

Characters: 15 to 17 male; 3 female.

Playing Time: 35 minutes.

Costumes: English dress of the 1830's, winter: Black dresses, bonnets and capes for Mrs. Nickleby and Kate; black suits and overcoats for Nicholas, Ralph and Cheeryble; shabby suit for Noggs; rustic suit, eyepatch for Squeers; nightgown, shawl, nightcap, then plain dress and apron for Mrs. Squeers; ragged shirts, breeches and shoes for Smike and Schoolboys.

Properties: Letter; quill pen; cups; bunches of letters; large kettle; spoon; cane; several books; two letters for Nicholas; plate of bread; traveling bags; coin.

Setting: Scene 1: Ralph Nickleby's office; a desk and three straight chairs. Scene 2: Outside a London coach office. Boxes and bundles are stacked at stage right. Scenes 3, 4, and 5: Dotheboys Hall in Yorkshire. Several benches and two desks at left and center stage; a table with two chairs at right; doors at right and left. Scene 6: The Crown Inn in London; a table and two benches at center. Scene 7: Nicklebys' flat in London. Few chairs and a table.

Lighting: No special effects.

The Imaginary Invalid

by *Molière*

Characters

ARGAN, *hypochondriac*
TOINETTE, *his maidservant*
ANGELIQUE, *his daughter*
BELINE, *his wife*
MONSIEUR BONNEFOY, *lawyer*
CLEANTE, *in love with Angelique*
DR. PURGON, *Argan's physician*
THOMAS DIAFOIRUS, *clumsy suitor*
BERALDE, *Argan's brother*

SCENE 1

TIME: *Mid-seventeenth century.*
SETTING: *Richly furnished sitting room of Argan's house in Paris. Sofa, table, and chair are center, two or three side chairs, music stand and two chairs are far right. On table are medicine bottles, piles of bills, and small hand bell. Entrance to hall is left, door to rest of house, right.*
AT RISE: ARGAN, *dressed in nightcap, dressing gown, and slippers, sits at table, his legs covered with shawl. A cane is propped against chair.*
ARGAN (*Looking through bills*): Hm-m. These medical bills total sixty-three francs for twelve bottles of medicine and

twenty injections this month. But I'm not as well this month as I was last month! *(Impatiently)* Where is Toinette? She's never here when I want her! *(Rings bell furiously; shouting)* Toinette! *(Shakes bell harder and shouts)* Toinette!

TOINETTE *(Entering left, carrying feather duster; calmly):* Here I am, master.

ARGAN: You good-for-nothing! You've left me alone for a whole hour! I might have died! *(Coughs)* Here! Take these pesky bills away.

TOINETTE *(Picking up bills):* Humph! *(Looks them over)* Dr. Purgon plays fine games with your carcass. I'd like to ask him just exactly what's wrong with you that you need all these medicines.

ARGAN: Hold your tongue! Who are you to question my doctor's orders? You know I am deathly ill.

TOINETTE *(Mildly):* Ah, yes! Everyone knows that Monsieur Argan is the sickest man in Paris! You've seen to that. *(Puts bills into table drawer, then dusts room with feather duster)*

ANGELIQUE *(Entering left):* Good morning, Father. *(Gives ARGAN a hug)*

ARGAN: Angelique, my dear daughter! I want to talk to you about something very important.

ANGELIQUE: And I must have a word with you, Father. But Dr. Purgon is waiting in the hall to give you your injection.

ARGAN: Ah! Good! I'll be back in a moment. *(Hobbles out)*

ANGELIQUE *(In confiding tone):* Toinette! Can you guess what I want to talk to my father about?

TOINETTE: I expect it's about that young man, Cleante. You are never happy unless you are talking about him.

ANGELIQUE *(Dreamily):* You *do* think he's very handsome, don't you?

TOINETTE: Very!

ANGELIQUE: Toinette, do you think he really loves me as much as he says he does?

TOINETTE: You'll soon find out. Didn't he say that he was going to ask your father for your hand? (ANGELIQUE *nods.*) That's a very good way of testing his true intentions. (ARGAN *re-enters.* TOINETTE *resumes dusting.*)

ARGAN: Well now, Angelique, I've some good news. *(Sits slowly)* I have received and accepted an offer of marriage for you. (ANGELIQUE *gasps, beams with joy.*) Ah, you are smiling! I see there's no need to ask you if you want to be married.

ANGELIQUE *(Smiling):* It's my duty to obey you in everything, Father. I'm so grateful for your goodness! *(Kissing him on forehead)*

TOINETTE *(Turning):* I really must give you credit for agreeing to this marriage, master. It's very sensible of you.

ARGAN *(Frowning):* Toinette, I did not ask for your opinion! *(She shrugs, goes back to dusting.)* I haven't yet seen the young man, Angelique, but I'm told that I shall be pleased with him, and that you will, too.

ANGELIQUE: Oh, you may be sure I shall!

ARGAN *(Surprised):* Why? Have you seen him?

ANGELIQUE: Why, yes, Father. We met a week ago at the theater and fell in love at first sight.

ARGAN: Oh? I didn't know that, but I'm glad to hear it. I've heard that he's a very trustworthy young man.

ANGELIQUE *(Nodding happily):* Yes, Father.

ARGAN: And he comes from a good family.

ANGELIQUE *(Proudly):* Yes, Father.

ARGAN: And he speaks excellent Latin and Greek.

ANGELIQUE *(Startled):* He does? (TOINETTE *watches them, surprised.*)

ARGAN: Why, he's taking his degree as a doctor in three days!

ANGELIQUE: He is?

ARGAN: Of course. Didn't he tell you?

ANGELIQUE: Why, no, Father. Who told you?

ARGAN: My physician, Dr. Purgon.

ANGELIQUE: Does Dr. Purgon know him?

ARGAN: Of course, he knows him. He's his own nephew!

ANGELIQUE *(Incredulous):* Cleante is Dr. Purgon's nephew?

ARGAN: Cleante? Who is Cleante? I thought we were talking about the young man who wants to marry you.

ANGELIQUE *(Confused):* Yes, of course . . . that is . . . I mean . . .

ARGAN: Very well, then. His name is Thomas, not Cleante. Thomas Diafoirus. Dr. Purgon and I arranged the marriage yesterday, and Thomas is coming here to see you this afternoon. *(He looks at* ANGELIQUE, *who is speechless.)* Why, Angelique, what's the matter? You look completely astonished!

ANGELIQUE *(Faintly):* Father, you have been talking about one person, and—and I thought you meant someone else. *(Weeps)*

TOINETTE *(Interrupting):* Master, this is ridiculous! How can you think of marrying your daughter to a doctor? You already have plenty of money.

ARGAN *(Impatiently):* If you must know, I want my daughter to marry a doctor so that I can have a ready supply of medicine and consultations. *(Loudly)* You know how feeble and ill I am!

TOINETTE *(Skeptically): Are* you feeble and ill, master?

ARGAN *(Shouting):* You impudent creature! Of course I am!

TOINETTE: Very well, if you insist. *(Sharply)* But your daughter isn't ill, so there's no need for her to marry a doctor.

ARGAN *(Pompously):* A daughter should be pleased to marry someone who will attend to her father's poor health.

TOINETTE: Master, you are much too kindhearted to force your daughter to marry a man she doesn't love.

ARGAN: I am not! *(Stands and shakes his fist at* TOINETTE*)* I can be very hardhearted when I want to!

TOINETTE: Easy, master. Don't forget you are feeble and ill. (ARGAN *quickly sits down, then glares at* TOINETTE.)

ARGAN *(Banging his fist on table):* Stop trying to confuse me, Toinette. I command Angelique to marry the man I have chosen for her! (ANGELIQUE *weeps loudly.)*

TOINETTE *(Belligerently):* And I absolutely forbid it!

ARGAN: What! How dare you, a common servant, speak to me like that!

TOINETTE *(Calmly):* When a master does not think sensibly, it is up to his sensible servant to correct him.

ARGAN: You impudent creature! *(Jumps up, seizing cane)* I'll beat you for your impudence! (*Starts after her.* ANGELIQUE *watches.*)

TOINETTE (*Dodging him*): But it's my duty to keep you from disgracing yourself, master.

ARGAN (*Chasing her around table*): Stand still! I'll teach you your duty!

TOINETTE (*Shouting defiantly*): I'll never agree to this marriage! Never! *(He swings cane at her wildly.)*

ANGELIQUE (*Taking him by the arm*): Oh, Father, do sit down! You'll make yourself ill.

TOINETTE (*Laughing*): You're really quite light on your feet, master. (ARGAN *flops into chair, breathless.*)

ARGAN: Oh, I'm done for! You will be the end of me!

BELINE (*From offstage*): Argan? (TOINETTE *grabs* ANGELIQUE *and they hurry off right, as* BELINE *enters left.*)

ARGAN: Beline, my dear wife! Come and rescue me! (*She crosses to* ARGAN.)

BELINE (*Soothingly*): What is the trouble, my dearest?

ARGAN: That horrible Toinette!

BELINE (*Smoothing his brow*): Now, now, don't get excited.

ARGAN: She infuriates me! She dared to tell me I'm not ill!

BELINE: Oh, the impudence!

ARGAN: You know how weak I am, my love.

BELINE: Yes, my dearest. I'll speak to her. (*Sternly*) Toinette!

TOINETTE (*Entering right, and curtsying*): Madame?

BELINE: Toinette, why have you been upsetting my husband?

TOINETTE (*Sweetly*): Why, madame, I don't know what you mean. I always try to please him in everything.

ARGAN (*Angrily*): You deceitful creature! You *never* please me in anything!

TOINETTE: It's just that he told me he meant Angelique to marry Thomas Diafoirus, and I said I thought it was a terrible idea.

BELINE: I think you are quite right, Toinette, but if you annoy my husband again, I'll have to dismiss you. Now, hand me those pillows and help me make him comfortable. (TOINETTE *gives her pillows from sofa.* BELINE *arranges them around*

ARGAN.) I'll just put this pillow beside you, and one to support you here, and another at your back.

TOINETTE *(Putting pillow on his head):* And this one to keep the morning dew off you! *(Laughs and runs out right)*

ARGAN *(Jumping up and throwing pillows after her):* You wretch! You devil! Oh! I can't bear any more of this! That wicked girl has completely upset me. I'll have to take eight doses of medicine and a dozen injections to put myself to rights again!

BELINE: There, there! Sit down. She doesn't mean any harm. You know she's really quite fond of you. *(He sits.)*

ARGAN: But she never cares for me the way you do, my dear. You are my only consolation and comfort.

BELINE *(Sweetly):* My love!

ARGAN: I want to show you how much you mean to me, my dear. As you know, I am going to make my will soon.

BELINE: Please don't talk about it! *(Greedily)* The word "will" makes me tremble.

ARGAN: But I asked you to talk to your lawyer about it.

BELINE: I did! In fact, he's here now, waiting to see you.

ARGAN: Then ask him to come in.

BELINE *(With mock concern):* I really can't bear the thought of all this. *(Calls off left; eagerly)* Monsieur Bonnefoy, won't you please come in right away? (MONSIEUR BONNEFOY *enters.*)

BONNEFOY *(Bowing):* Madame! Monsieur Argan!

ARGAN: Please sit down, sir. My wife has told me that you are a most trustworthy man and in her confidence. I wish to make my will, sir, and leave my entire estate to her.

BONNEFOY *(Sitting):* Yes, your wife has told me of your intentions, sir, but I understand that you also have a daughter?

ARGAN: Yes, I do, but she is about to marry a doctor who will be quite wealthy. I intend to give her a handsome dowry, but my wife is to have everything else.

BELINE: Oh, my dear, if anything happens to you, I won't want to go on living. *(Pretending to sob)* I should follow you to the grave to prove my love for you.

ARGAN: My dear wife, don't cry. To ease your grief, I will give you twenty thousand gold francs, which I keep behind the wall in my closet, for your birthday next week.

BELINE: Oh, no, no, no, my dear! I don't want them! I couldn't accept them! *(Suddenly)* Uh . . . how much did you say you had in your closet?

ARGAN: Twenty thousand gold francs, my love.

BELINE: Twenty thousand gold francs! Oh, but money is nothing to me, my dear. All I want is you! Uh . . . did you say I couldn't have the money until next week?

BONNEFOY *(Breaking in):* Ahem! Do you wish to draw up the will now, sir?

ARGAN: Yes, indeed! Please step into my study, sir. *(Reaches for cane and starts to rise.* BELINE *helps him.)*

BELINE: My poor boy, lean on me. Such a dreadful, tiresome business, making a will. (ARGAN *stands and starts left.* BELINE *and* BONNEFOY *exchange satisfied glances, as they exit left with* ARGAN. TOINETTE *and* ANGELIQUE *enter right.)*

TOINETTE: I'm sure your stepmother is forcing your father into something that will be against your interests, Angelique.

ANGELIQUE: I don't care what he does with his money as long as he doesn't force me to marry a man I don't love. Oh, Toinette, please don't desert me in my trouble!

TOINETTE: Desert you? Never! I'll do everything I can to help you, but from now on, I must change my tactics and pretend to agree with your father, or he will suspect me.

ANGELIQUE: Very well, and please, Toinette, try to see Cleante and tell him about this marriage Father has arranged.

TOINETTE: Don't worry about a thing! You can rely on me! *(They exit left. Curtain)*

*   *   *   *   *

SCENE 2

TIME: *Late that afternoon.*
SETTING: *Same as Scene 1.*

AT RISE: TOINETTE *enters left, looks around.*

TOINETTE *(Calling off):* There's no one here. Come in! (CLEANTE *and* ANGELIQUE *enter.* TOINETTE *remains near door, listening attentively and looking off watchfully.)*

ANGELIQUE: Cleante, I was so surprised to find you here.

CLEANTE: When Toinette told me about this dreadful marriage your father has arranged, I knew I had to see you at once.

ANGELIQUE *(Anxiously):* Oh, but if my father should see you . . .

CLEANTE: Don't worry. Toinette will introduce me to him as a substitute for your singing teacher. *(Leads her to sofa)* Now, please tell me what you intend to do. I must know. *(They sit on sofa.)*

ANGELIQUE: I . . . I really don't know. It's my duty to obey my father, but . . .

CLEANTE: Surely he won't force you to marry a man you don't love—a man you've never even met!

ANGELIQUE: Oh, but I'm to meet him this very afternoon.

CLEANTE: But he cannot love you half as much as I do!

ANGELIQUE *(Turning away shyly):* And how do I know that?

CLEANTE *(Kneeling and taking her hand):* Dearest Angelique, you must marry no one but me! This very morning I asked your Uncle Beralde to speak to your father and offer my plea for your hand.

ANGELIQUE *(Turning to him, smiling):* Oh, Cleante, you really do love me! (CLEANTE *kisses her hand.)*

TOINETTE *(Urgently):* The master is coming! (CLEANTE *and* ANGELIQUE *quickly move to music stand, pick up sheets of music, sit down and pretend to study them.* ARGAN *enters left, leaning on cane.)*

TOINETTE: There's a young gentleman here, sir.

CLEANTE *(Rising and bowing):* Good afternoon, sir. I'm happy to see you are feeling much better.

TOINETTE *(Pretending to be angry):* What do you mean, feeling better? He's still very ill!

CLEANTE: Oh, but I heard that he was better, and I think he looks quite well.

TOINETTE: Why, he's never looked so bad as he does today.

ARGAN: She's quite right, sir. I'm not very well today.

TOINETTE: Just because he can move around, eat, drink, and sleep as well as anyone, doesn't mean he isn't extremely ill. (*Knock is heard.* TOINETTE *starts off left.*) Excuse me, someone's at the door. (*Exits left*)

ARGAN: Well! For once that girl is speaking sensibly! (*Sits*)

CLEANTE: Sir, I have come in the place of your daughter's singing teacher, who had to go out of the city today.

ARGAN: I see. Well, continue with your lesson, Angelique, but sing very softly. My ears are so sensitive, you know.

TOINETTE (*Re-entering*): Upon my word, master, I take back everything I said against the marriage you have arranged. Here are Dr. Purgon and his nephew. (*Smothers a laugh*) What a good-looking and intelligent son-in-law you are going to have!

CLEANTE (*Starting out*): Excuse me.

ARGAN: Oh, you need not go, sir. My daughter is about to see her future husband for the first time. You must meet him and come to the wedding.

CLEANTE: You are too kind, sir. (*Returns to music stand and sits as* DR. PURGON *and* THOMAS DIAFOIRUS, *a clumsy young man with a stupid expression and poor posture, enter left.*)

ARGAN: Dr. Purgon, I receive you and your nephew with the greatest of pleasure! You'll pardon me if I don't rise.

DR. PURGON: By all means, remain seated, sir. Thomas, make your compliments.

THOMAS: Do I begin with the father?

PURGON: Of course. (THOMAS *walks over to* ARGAN *and bows.*)

THOMAS (*Standing stiffly and speaking mechanically*): Sir, I come to salute, cherish and honor you as a second father, and to thank you humbly and respectfully for making possible my future alliance with your daughter and her generous dowry. (*Bows clumsily and steps back beside* DR. PURGON)

TOINETTE (*Aside to audience*): Hail to our colleges that send such clever graduates into the world!

THOMAS: Was that all right, uncle?

PURGON: Quite.

ARGAN: Angelique, come and greet the gentleman. (ANGELI-QUE *steps forward reluctantly.*)

THOMAS *(Bowing awkwardly):* Madame! Heaven has rightly given you the title of mother, and—

ARGAN: Sir, this is my daughter! (CLEANTE *chuckles behind his hand.*)

THOMAS: Oh! *(Confused)* Well, where is your wife?

ARGAN: She will be here in a moment.

PURGON: Thomas, make your compliments to the young lady!

THOMAS *(Staring over* ANGELIQUE's *head):* Madam, I find myself entranced by your beauty, and offer to you this day my devoted heart, which seeks no greater glory than to be your humble and devoted servant and husband.

TOINETTE *(Aside, mockingly):* How hard he must have studied to learn that original speech!

ARGAN: Please be seated, gentlemen. (THOMAS *sits on sofa.*) Angelique, sit there on the sofa with your intended. (ANGEL-IQUE *looks helplessly at* CLEANTE, *then sits on sofa.*) Dr. Purgon, you are most fortunate to have such a fine nephew.

PURGON: I have good reason to be proud of him, sir. As a doctor, he follows my example and rejects the alleged medical discoveries of these modern times, such as the circulation of the blood.

THOMAS: I have written a thesis against those who uphold the circulation of the blood. With your permission sir, I offer it to the young lady as the first fruits of my genius. *(Hands a rolled paper to* ANGELIQUE) And very soon I would like to invite her to see a dissection and hear my dissertation upon it. (ANGEL-IQUE *moves away from* THOMAS. CLEANTE *edges his chair closer to* ANGELIQUE.)

TOINETTE *(Aside):* How amusing! Some young gentlemen take young ladies to the theater, but I'm sure a dissection would be much more entertaining!

ARGAN *(To* PURGON): Tell me, sir, have you ever thought of promoting your nephew's career before the Royal Family?

PURGON: My experience, sir, has been that it is better to prac-

tice among the general public. They are less exacting. People
of royal blood always insist on being cured when they are ill.

TOINETTE *(Aside):* Ha! As if fellows such as he could cure
anyone! His job is to collect fat fees and prescribe useless
remedies. (BELINE *enters left.*)

ARGAN: Ah, here is my wife. Beline, my love, here (*Indicates*
THOMAS) is the future bridegroom.

THOMAS *(With a stiff bow):* Madame! Heaven has rightly given
you the title of mother, since in your visage I behold—

BELINE *(Abruptly):* I am happy to meet you, sir.

ARGAN: Come, Angelique, my dear. Give this gentleman your
hand and pledge him your troth as your husband to be. (AN-
GELIQUE, *dismayed, jumps up and moves closer to*
CLEANTE.)

ANGELIQUE: Please, Father, don't rush things. Give us time to
get acquainted.

THOMAS: As far as I am concerned, mademoiselle, we can get
acquainted after we are married.

CLEANTE: Pardon me, sir, but I have heard that such an arrangement is rarely, if ever, satisfactory.

THOMAS *(Rudely):* No one asked for your opinion, sir!

ANGELIQUE (*Handing rolled paper back to* THOMAS): I must
confess, sir, that you have not yet favorably impressed me. If
you are an honorable gentleman, you will not want a wife who
is forced to marry you.

THOMAS *(Giving rolled paper back to her):* On the contrary,
mademoiselle, I can accept you and your handsome dowry
from the hands of your father, and remain a man of honor.

ANGELIQUE *(Pushing paper back at him):* Forcing yourself upon
me, sir, is a poor way to make me love you. (*Moves closer to*
CLEANTE)

CLEANTE: I quite agree with the young lady, sir.

THOMAS (*Ignoring* CLEANTE): May I point out, mademoiselle,
that in ancient times young men carried off by force the
women they intended to marry. Love had nothing to do with
it.

ANGELIQUE: But we are living in modern times, sir, and as far as I am concerned love has *everything* to do with it!

ARGAN: Angelique! That is no way to speak to your future husband!

BELINE (*To* ARGAN): If I were you, I wouldn't insist that she marry anyone. I would send her directly to a convent.

TOINETTE (*Aside*): Where she wouldn't need her generous dowry!

ANGELIQUE: Father, if you will not allow me to marry a man I love, then I beg you not to force me to marry a man I could never love. (CLEANTE *nods encouragement to her.*)

THOMAS: Well! (*Goes to stand by* DR. PURGON, *pouting*)

ARGAN: Oh, Thomas, Dr. Purgon, I am so sorry about this! Angelique, apologize at once!

ANGELIQUE: I'm sorry, Father, but I regard marriage as a lifelong bond to be approached with caution. (*Turns to* BELINE) Some women, however, marry only in hopes of becoming rich upon the death of their husbands.

BELINE (*Sharply*): What do you mean by that?

ANGELIQUE (*Mildly*): Only what I have said, madame.

ARGAN: Angelique, listen to me! You will marry Thomas Diafoirus within three days, or you will enter a convent! Make your choice! (ANGELIQUE *looks tearfully at* ARGAN, *then helplessly at* CLEANTE, *then runs out left, sobbing.* CLEANTE *rises from his chair, then sits again, agitated.*) Don't worry, Dr. Purgon, I'll bring her to her senses.

TOINETTE (*Aside*): Poor Angelique! But her Uncle Beralde is expected to call on her father this afternoon. He is very fond of her and will do all he can to help her, especially when I tell him my plans! (*Beckons to* CLEANTE *to follow her, and they slip out left, unnoticed*)

BELINE: I doubt that your daughter will ever be sensible, my dear. But I must be off. I have legal business with Monsieur Bonnefoy.

ARGAN: Yes, yes. Goodbye, my love. (*She exits.*)

PURGON (*Stiffly*): We must be going, too, sir.

ARGAN: Oh, but you aren't forgetting my injection, are you, sir?

PURGON: I will return in a moment. *(Turning)* Say good day, Thomas.

THOMAS *(Sulkily):* Good day, sir.

ARGAN: Good day, Thomas. And don't worry. I am sure my daughter will soon become your wife. (PURGON *and* THOMAS *exit. Shortly,* BELINE *re-enters, wearing hat and gloves.)*

BELINE: My dear Argan, as I passed your study door on my way out, I saw that young man with Angelique. He left when he saw me.

ARGAN: What young man? *(Hopefully)* Thomas?

BELINE: No, the one who was sitting by the music stand.

ARGAN: The singing teacher?

BELINE: I don't know, but *(Sarcastically)* when I saw him, he certainly wasn't giving Angelique a singing lesson. I must be going. *(Exits left)*

ARGAN *(Enraged):* Oh, that crafty daughter of mine! No wonder she was so obstinate! She's in love with that singing teacher! *(Sinks down in chair)* Oh, what trouble that child brings me! I haven't had time to think of my illness for the past hour. Oh-h-! (BERALDE *strides in left.)*

BERALDE *(Briskly):* Good afternoon, brother! How are you feeling today?

ARGAN: Beralde, how good of you to come see me. I'm very bad.

BERALDE: Oh? That's a pity, but I think I can cheer you up. I have come with an offer of marriage for my niece.

ARGAN *(Standing, angrily):* Don't mention my daughter to me! She has deceived me and I'm sending her to a convent!

BERALDE: What? Why do you want to put that dear child into a convent?

ARGAN *(Angrily):* Because I'm the master of this house, and I will do as I think fit with my daughter! (BERALDE *sits.)*

BERALDE: You never mentioned anything about a convent until your wife advised you on the matter, brother.

ARGAN: Now my poor wife is brought into it! You have always been against her!

BERALDE: All right, I won't speak of her. But tell me, why do

you wish to have Angelique marry a doctor? Are you determined to be an invalid for the rest of your life?

ARGAN: What do you mean?

BERALDE: I mean that you have a perfectly healthy constitution.
Look how you have survived all the medicines and injections
your doctors have forced upon you!

ARGAN: But, brother, the medicines are what keep me alive. Dr.
Purgon tells me that without his strict attendance, I wouldn't
survive three days.

BERALDE: Nonsense! He will attend you into your grave, if you
keep him as your doctor. But, come, brother, I urge you to
make some concession to your daughter's wishes about marriage. (PURGON *enters left with his bag, followed by*
TOINETTE, *carrying tray of wine glasses and decanter.*)

ARGAN: Excuse me, brother. Here is Dr. Purgon with my injection.

BERALDE: Another one? *(Stands)* You must be mad! *(Goes to*
TOINETTE) Can't you pass an hour without an injection or a
dose of something? *(Takes glass of wine from tray and winks
at* TOINETTE) Send him away and enjoy yourself for a while!

PURGON *(Insulted):* How dare you try to prevent my patient
from having his injection!

BERALDE *(Pushing* PURGON *toward door):* Oh, go away, sir! Let
your patient enjoy a glass of good wine instead!

ARGAN *(Anxiously):* Beralde, please!

TOINETTE *(Pretending to be indignant):* Really, sir!

BERALDE: Brother, is there no way to cure you of this disease of
being doctored?

ARGAN: If you were in my state of health, you wouldn't talk like
that!

BERALDE: And what exactly *is* the matter with you?

ARGAN: Well, Dr. Purgon hasn't said exactly what it is, but—

PURGON *(Furiously):* Monsieur Argan, are you rebelling against
me?

ARGAN *(Apologetically):* Oh, no, sir! I . . .

PURGON: Are you rejecting this injection which I formulated
just for you?

ARGAN: Heavens, no, I . . .

BERALDE (*To* PURGON): It appears that he is, sir!

PURGON: It's unnatural! (*To* ARGAN) I declare I'll have nothing
more to do with you!

ARGAN (*Desperately*): But, Dr. Purgon, I—

PURGON: Furthermore, the marriage between my nephew and
your daughter is off! (*Starts out left*)

ARGAN: Please, please, Dr. Purgon! (*Starts after him*) Come
back!

PURGON: I predict that within three days you will be in an
incurable contition!

ARGAN (*Falling to his knees*): Have mercy! Don't leave me!

PURGON: It is your own doing! Goodbye, sir! (*Exits left*)

ARGAN: Brother, look what you've done! Now I will die!

BERALDE (*Helping him up*): Don't be ridiculous! Come, pull
yourself together. Here is your chance to be rid of doctors for
good. (*Winks at* TOINETTE, *who winks back*)

ARGAN (*Miserably*): But Dr. Purgon understood my symptoms,
and knew exactly how I should be treated.

TOINETTE: Poor master! Here, sit down. (*Helps him to chair*)

BERALDE: Now, calm yourself, and let me tell you about the
suitor I have in mind for Angelique.

ARGAN (*Banging cane on floor*): No! She has refused to marry
the man I chose for her. I have made up my mind, Beralde!
She will enter a convent!

BERALDE (*With determination*): Brother, I can no longer stand
by and watch you fall into every trap your wife sets for you!

ARGAN (*Angrily*): Trap? What are you talking about?

TOINETTE (*To* BERALDE): Ah, sir, you mustn't talk about the
mistress that way. She loves the master dearly.

ARGAN: That's right! Just ask Beline how fond she is of me.

TOINETTE: Quite so. Would you like me to prove to you just how
much she loves the master?

BERALDE: How will you do that?

TOINETTE: She has just come back from seeing her lawyer and
will be coming in here in a moment for a glass of wine. Master,
you lie down on the sofa and pretend to be dead. Then your

brother will see her great grief when I tell her the sad news.

ARGAN: This seems quite unnecessary, but, very well. Beralde, you will see for yourself that you are wrong.

TOINETTE (*To* BERALDE): Will you hide over there behind the chair, sir? (*Points to large chair, where* BERALDE *goes to hide.* TOINETTE *turns to* ARGAN.) Now, master, lie on the sofa, and don't move. (ARGAN *lies on sofa and closes his eyes.*) Sh-h! I hear the mistress now. (TOINETTE *kneels beside* ARGAN, *pretending to sob loudly, as* BELINE *enters left.*)

BELINE (*Rushing over to* TOINETTE): Whatever is the matter?

TOINETTE (*Sobbing*): Oh, mistress, your husband is dead!

BELINE (*Coolly*): Dead? Are you sure?

TOINETTE: Yes. It happened just a moment ago. See for yourself. (BELINE *looks closely at* ARGAN, *then laughs.*)

BELINE: He's dead, all right! What a relief! Thank goodness he's made his will, leaving everything to me! (*Suddenly*) Toinette, why are you crying?

TOINETTE: I thought it was the proper thing to do, madame.

BELINE: Don't be silly. He was a nuisance to us all, always wanting an injection or a dose of medicine, always coughing and complaining!

BERALDE (*Aside*): I must say, this is a fine funeral oration!

BELINE: Toinette, if you help me carry out my plans, I'll see that you're rewarded. I'll demand that Angelique enter a convent, then I will seize her dowry. I'll give you a third of it. Now, we'll carry him to his bed and keep his death a secret until I get the money out of his closet. But first, I'll get his keys. (*Bends over* ARGAN *and starts to reach into his pocket*)

ARGAN (*Suddenly sitting up*): So, the game is up! This is how you love me!

BELINE (*Shrieking and jumping back*): You aren't dead after all! (*Shrieks*) Oh, oh, oh!

ARGAN (*Shaking his fist after her*): Deceitful woman! How could you do this to me! Leave my house at once! (BELINE *runs off.*)

BERALDE (*Coming out from behind chair*): Well, brother, at last you see how things are.

TOINETTE (*Pretending surprise*): I would never have believed it!

Oh! I hear Angelique in the hall. Why not lie down again, master, and see how she takes the news?

ARGAN *(Reluctantly):* Oh, very well. *(Sprawls on sofa again.* TOINETTE *kneels beside* ARGAN *and pretends to cry loudly.* BERALDE *hides.)*

ANGELIQUE *(Running in left):* Toinette, what's the matter?

TOINETTE: I have sad news, my dear Angelique. Your father is . . . is dead.

ANGELIQUE: My father . . . dead? *(Bursts into tears and throws herself at* ARGAN's *feet)* My dear father, you were all the world to me, and here you have died when you were angry with me! *(*CLEANTE *enters.)*

CLEANTE: Angelique, what is it?

ANGELIQUE *(Sobbing):* I have lost my dear father!

CLEANTE: What a terrible misfortune!

ANGELIQUE: Oh, Cleante, now that I've lost my dear father, we must give up all thought of marriage.

ARGAN *(Sitting up):* My dear daughter!

ANGELIQUE *(Jumping back):* Oh, Father!

ARGAN: Don't be frightened. I'm not dead after all. *(They embrace.)* I'm overjoyed to find you such a loving daughter! *(*BERALDE *comes forward.)*

ANGELIQUE: Father, since you are truly alive, let me beg one favor of you. If you will not allow me to marry my true love, Cleante, please do not force me to marry Thomas Diafoirus.

BERALDE: Come, brother, how can you refuse them? For you see now who truly loves you.

TOINETTE: And surely you see that Angelique and Cleante love each other.

ARGAN *(After a pause):* Young man, if you will become a doctor, you may have my daughter for your wife. *(*ANGELIQUE *embraces* ARGAN.)*

CLEANTE: Oh, willingly, sir! But it will take a few years.

TOINETTE: I will look after you in the meantime, master. Now come, have a glass of wine. *(Pours wine)*

ARGAN: Oh, I can't! I mustn't. Dr. Purgon wouldn't allow it.

TOINETTE *(Handing him glass):* Here! It will do you good.

ANGELIQUE: I'm sure it will taste much better than a dose of medicine.

CLEANTE *(Lifting glass):* To my lovely Angelique!

BERALDE: To the approaching marriage!

ARGAN: To my rescued estate!

TOINETTE: And to my master's good health! *(All raise glasses. Curtain)*

THE END

PRODUCTION NOTES

THE IMAGINARY INVALID

Characters: 6 male, 3 female.

Playing Time: 30 minutes.

Costumes: Period dress of the seventeenth century in France. Argan wears dressing gown, nightcap, and slippers. Toinette wears plain dark dress with white apron and small lace cap. Beline wears hat and gloves in Scene 2.

Properties: Shawl, walking cane, feather duster, rolled paper tied with a ribbon, tray with decanter and five wine glasses, doctor's bag.

Setting: The richly furnished sitting room of Argan's house in Paris. Sofa with pillows, table and chair are center; two or three side chairs, music stand, and two chairs are far right. On table are medicine bottles, piles of bills, and small hand bell. There is an entrance to hall at left, door to rest of house on right.

Sound: Knock at door.

Lighting: No special effects.

The One Million Pound Bank Note

by Mark Twain

Characters

HENRY ADAMS, *young American mining clerk*
ABEL ⎫
EDWARD ⎭ *wealthy English gentlemen*
GEORGE, *their butler*
HARRIS, *café owner*
TOD, *tailor's clerk*
TAILOR
PORTIA LANGHAM, *young English lady*
LLOYD HASTINGS, *Henry's American friend*

SCENE 1

TIME: *1850's.*
SETTING: *A street in a park in London; played before curtain. A park bench is at right.*
BEFORE RISE: ABEL *and* EDWARD *enter left, followed by* GEORGE, *who carries two newspapers.*
ABEL: Brother Edward, are you certain that you wish to settle our argument with a wager?
EDWARD: Quite certain, Abel. We must find a poor, but honest

and intelligent man who is a stranger to London, and put him to the test.

ABEL: Ha! If we should happen to locate such a person, he will most certainly fail our test. He will either be arrested and jailed, or he will starve to death.

EDWARD: Nonsense! I am willing to wager twenty thousand pounds that the man will get along very well for thirty days.

ABEL: Twenty thousand pounds! Very well! But where shall we find such a man?

EDWARD: Look there! (*Points toward* HENRY ADAMS, *in rags, who enters left, looking lost and tired*)

ABEL: Are you referring to that tramp?

EDWARD: He is ragged, yes, but his face looks honest. And we've never seen him here in the park before. Come, let's sit on our bench and quietly observe him. (ABEL *and* EDWARD *sit.* GEORGE *hands each a newspaper, then stands behind them. Brothers pretend to read, but watch* HENRY *closely over tops of their papers.* HENRY *crosses slowly center, unaware that he is being watched.*)

HENRY: If I don't find something to eat soon, I'll have to beg in the streets! *(Turns out pockets)* Not a penny. I've never been so hungry in my life. *(Notices something on ground)* What's that in the gutter? A pear! A luscious, fat, golden pear with only one bite out of it. (*Looks around to see if anyone is watching.* ABEL *and* EDWARD *duck behind their papers.* GEORGE *peers off in another direction.*) I never thought I'd stoop this low, but I'm starving! (*Edges closer to pear; two brothers peer sharply at him over tops of papers.* HENRY *stoops, about to pick up pear.*)

EDWARD *(Putting down paper):* Young man!

HENRY *(Startled; turning):* Are you speaking to me?

ABEL: Yes. Will you step over here, please?

HENRY *(Nervously):* Did I do something wrong?

EDWARD: No, not at all. *(Gestures to bench)* Won't you have a seat?

HENRY *(Warily):* Uh, no, thanks.

EDWARD: You appear to have come upon hard times, young man.

HENRY: I'm afraid so. If I weren't so hungry, I'd think it was all a bad dream.

ABEL: Are you an American?

HENRY *(Proudly):* I sure am. Henry Adams, from San Francisco.

EDWARD *(To* ABEL): A stranger to London! Splendid! *(To* HENRY) What did you do in America, Mr. Adams?

HENRY: I was a mining-broker's clerk. We have a lot of mines in California, you know.

ABEL: Did you come to London to pursue the mining business, Mr. Adams?

HENRY: Oh, no, sir. I didn't want to come here at all. I was sort of kidnapped.

EDWARD: Indeed! Won't you tell us what happened?

HENRY: I was out sailing one Saturday afternoon on San Francisco Bay, when a storm came up suddenly and carried me far out to sea. I drifted for hours and just when I thought I'd never see land again, a ship appeared and took me aboard. I asked the captain to take me back to San Francisco, but he refused. He made me work my passage as a sailor and brought me here to London.

ABEL: Very interesting! Do you have lodgings here?

HENRY: No, sir.

EDWARD: Friends or acquaintances?

HENRY: Not a soul. I'm totally adrift, totally broke, and I don't know what I'm going to do next.

EDWARD *(Breaking into a grin):* Splendid! Young man, you will suit us perfectly. How fortunate that you happened along when you did!

HENRY *(Confused; shaking head):* I don't understand.

EDWARD: George, hand me the envelope, please. (GEORGE *takes envelope from vest pocket, hands it to* EDWARD.) Now, Mr. Adams, you will find a complete explanation of our purpose in this envelope, and all you will need to carry it out. (*Hands envelope to* HENRY)

ABEL: Take care, young man. Don't be hasty or foolish. Use your head!

HENRY: But what is this?

EDWARD: You'll see. (*Rising*) Come along, brother. Good day, Mr. Adams. (*Exits right, quickly, with* ABEL *and* GEORGE)

HENRY (*Calling off*): But . . . but I don't understand. Wait! Please! (*Starts after them, then stops*) Well, how do you like that? I'm starving, and they give me an envelope! I'd do anything for a ham sandwich! (*Tears open envelope and looks inside; pleasantly surprised*) Money! Well, those old gentlemen are all right after all. Now to find the nearest restaurant and order a good hot meal! (*Hurries off left. Blackout, during which bench is removed.*)

* * * * *

TIME: *An hour later.*

SETTING: *Harris's Café. Table and chair are center.*

AT RISE: HENRY *sits at table with several empty dishes before him.* HARRIS *stands nearby, bill in hand, watching him suspiciously.*

HENRY (*Rubbing stomach*): Ah-h! I can't eat another bite. (*To* HARRIS) A very good meal, my man. Nice place you have here.

HARRIS (*Drily*): Thank you. (*Hands bill to* HENRY) Your bill, sir.

HENRY: Oh, yes. I have money right here. (*Takes bank note from envelope and hands it to* HARRIS)

HARRIS (*Surprised*): Very well, sir. (*Takes bill and starts away, then stops, staring at bank note*)

HENRY: Is something wrong? (HARRIS *stares wide-eyed at note, then turns to* HENRY *and stares at him.*) It's enough to pay for the meal, isn't it?

HARRIS *(Gasping):* Enough? Enough? Oh, yes, sir, it's enough! *(His hand shakes as he hands note back to* HENRY.*)*

HENRY: Then what's the matter? Why are you—*(Glances at note and freezes; in a squeaky whisper)* One million pounds!

HARRIS *(Grinning broadly):* One million pounds! (HENRY *looks at* HARRIS, *then at note; coughs, adjusts his clothes, and recovers his composure.)*

HENRY *(In a lofty tone):* Ahem! Yes, of course! Here, my good man. *(Hands note back)* Bring me the change, please.

HARRIS: The change! *(Very accommodating; bowing):* Oh sir, forgive me, I am terribly sorry, but I can't possibly change this note for you.

HENRY: I'm sorry to inconvenience you, but I have nothing else with me.

HARRIS: That's perfectly all right, sir. You can pay me another time.

HENRY: But I may not be in this neighborhood again very soon.

HARRIS: Don't worry about that, sir. I can wait. When you do come back, bring your friends. Order anything you wish and charge it. You may run your account for as long as you please.

HENRY: Well, that's very good of you.

HARRIS *(Laughing):* How clever of you, sir, a wealthy gentleman like you, playing jokes on everyone and dressing like a beggar! *(Escorts him out, brushing his clothes)* Do come again soon, sir. I'll keep a table reserved for you. I'll order the finest wines and meats. Anything you like! Good day, sir! (HENRY *exits.)* To think of it! A millionaire in my humble little café! Oh, just wait until word of this gets around! *(Curtain)*

* * * * *

SCENE 2

TIME: *A few minutes later.*

SETTING: *Same as Scene 1.*

BEFORE RISE: GEORGE *sits on bench.* HENRY *enters.*

HENRY: There's been a terrible mistake! I have to return this note to those two gentlemen before they send the police after me. (*Sees* GEORGE) Oh, what luck! (*Rushes up to* GEORGE) It's you! George!

GEORGE (*Calmly*): Yes, sir?

HENRY: I must see your masters at once!

GEORGE: Impossible, sir. They are in France.

HENRY (*Surprised*): France! When will they be back?

GEORGE: In a month.

HENRY (*Frantically*): A month! But there's been a terrible mistake! I must get word to them.

GEORGE: I'm sorry, sir. I don't know exactly where in France they've gone, and I cannot communicate with them.

HENRY: But I'm sure they'll be back sooner than they expected when they realize what they gave me in this envelope.

GEORGE: They told me that you would probably try to find them within an hour or two, and that I was to tell you it's all right. They'll be back in thirty days' time and will expect to see you again right here.

HENRY: But I can't stay in London that long. I've got to find a way back to San Francisco. (*Holds out envelope*) Here, take this envelope and keep it for them, and be sure to tell them I brought it back right away.

GEORGE: Oh, no, sir, I can't possibly do that. You must keep the envelope and its contents. Those were my strict orders.

HENRY: But I don't understand this at all!

GEORGE: Perhaps you should read the letter, sir. Good day. (*Exits*)

HENRY: Letter? What letter? (*Looks in envelope; pulls out letter*) Oh! (*Sits on bench to read*) "The enclosed sum of money is lent to you for thirty days without interest. Report back to us in thirty days, where you first met us. We have a wager on you. Whichever of us wins shall give you any situation that is within our power to bestow." No signature. No address. (*Looks up*) What a predicament! If I go to the Bank of England with this million-pound note, they'll ask me how I got it, and if I tell them the truth, they'll think I'm crazy. If I lie, I'll be thrown into jail. The note is useless to me, yet I must take care of it for thirty days, and beg my living! Well, I'll have to make the best of things. *(Musing)* I could use a decent suit of clothes. *(Exits)*

* * * * *

SETTING: *Tailor's shop, with rack of men's suits, tall mirror, folding screen, and table piled with old clothes at center.*

AT RISE: HENRY *is trying on a shabby suit that is much too small for him.* TOD *watches him with a scornful, condescending expression.*

TOD: I'm afraid that's the only thing we have that would suit you.

HENRY: It doesn't suit me at all, but I'll take it. *(Casually)* I would appreciate it if you could wait a few days for the money. I haven't any small change with me.

TOD *(Sarcastically):* Well, of course not! I'd only expect a "gentleman" like you to carry large change.

HENRY *(Irritated):* Sir, you shouldn't judge a man by the clothes he wears. I am quite able to pay for this suit. I simply don't wish to put you to the trouble of changing a large note.

TOD: Well, it isn't your business, sir, to jump to the conclusion that we can't change a large note. I'm sure we can.

HENRY: Very well, then! *(Hands bank note to* TOD*)*

TOD *(Surprised):* Yes, sir. *(Takes note, glances at it, then gasps. His hand slowly begins to shake.)* I'll . . . I'll have to call the manager . . . I . . . *(Beckons wildly off;* TAILOR *enters.)*

TAILOR *(Briskly):* What's the trouble here?

HENRY *(Calmly):* There's no trouble. I'm just waiting for my change.

TAILOR: Come, come, Tod, get him his change. What are you waiting for?

TOD: Get him his change! Sir, look at the note! *(Hands note to* TAILOR*)*

TAILOR *(Staring at note):* Good heavens! *(Pulls* TOD *aside)* Tod,

you're a fool! Selling a millionaire such a miserable suit as
that! (*Hands note back to* HENRY)

TOD: But . . . but I didn't know! How could I have guessed?

TAILOR (*Rummaging through suits on rack*): You drive every
millionaire away from this shop because you can't tell a millionaire from a tramp! You never could! Ah! Here's just the
thing! (*Hands a suit to* HENRY) Sir, please take off that
unspeakable rag! Just step behind the screen and try on this
suit. It's a very nice cut, sir. Very good cloth. (HENRY *takes
suit and steps behind screen to change clothes.*) Tod, as soon
as he's out of that other suit, throw it in the fire! (*Hands a
shirt over top of screen; to* HENRY) Sir, try on this shirt. It
goes well with that suit. Just the thing! Plain, rich, modest!
(HENRY *steps out in shirt and trousers.*) Ah! The trousers fit
you well, sir. Tod, the waistcoat! (TOD *hands waistcoat to*
TAILOR; HENRY *puts it on.*) Aha! Right again. Tod, the coat!
(TOD *hands him coat;* TAILOR *helps* HENRY *put it on.*) Perfect!
Just right! I never saw such a triumph in all my experience!
Tod, get the gentleman an ascot! (TOD *finds ascot and* TAILOR
helps HENRY *adjust it.*)

HENRY (*Pleased*): Yes, I believe this will do.

TAILOR: Quite right, sir. It will do for now. But wait until you see
what we make to your own measurements! Tod! Book and
pencil! (TOD *grabs book and pencil and writes as* TAILOR *pulls
measuring tape from around his neck and measures* HENRY
from head to foot.) Length of leg, 32, waist, 34. We'll make you
dress suits, morning suits, shirts, waistcoats—everything,
sir!

HENRY: But I can't order any more clothes unless you can wait
indefinitely or change my note.

TAILOR: Wait indefinitely, sir? I can wait *eternally!* Tod, rush
these things through and send them to the gentleman's address.

HENRY: I'm changing my quarters. I'll have to drop in later and
leave my new address.

TAILOR: Quite right, sir. Very good. (*Ushering* HENRY *out*) Let me show you out, sir. This way. Good day, sir. Thank you, sir! *(As* HENRY *exits, he turns frantically to* TOD.*)* Tod! What are you waiting for? Get to work! Hurry! That man is going to make my fortune! *(Shoves* TOD *off impatiently; curtain)*

* * * * *

SCENE 3

SETTING: *Same as Scene 1.*

BEFORE RISE: HENRY *enters, admiring his new suit.*

HENRY: So this is how it all works! I merely present the one-million pound note and everything comes to me like magic. I shouldn't have any trouble renting the best lodgings in London, furnishing them . . . eating wherever I choose. Who knows? I may even become famous! *(Exits; blackout to indicate passage of time, then lights up on same set.* TAILOR *rushes in left with boxes, followed by* TOD.*)*

TAILOR: Tod! Take these suits to Mr. Adams in Hanover Square—the expensive, private hotel, of course. And hurry! Orders have been pouring into my shop ever since word got around that Adams orders his suits from me! Don't keep him waiting, Tod! Hurry! Hurry! *(Exits right)*

TOD: Yes, sir. One must never keep a millionaire waiting! *(Staggers out with boxes right.* HARRIS *enters left with* HENRY, *who carries newspaper.)*

HARRIS: Mr. Adams, you have made me a rich man. Ever since word got around that you always eat breakfast in my café, I've been swamped with customers. Everyone wants to eat where you eat, sir! I shall never be able to thank you enough! *(Exits right)*

HENRY *(Indicating newspaper):* The American vest-pocket million-pounder! That's what they call me in all the papers. My place is firmly established in London society. My presence is requested at parties, dinners, balls, teas, receptions, luncheons, midnight suppers . . . I hardly have a moment to myself. I'm on speaking terms with knights, dukes, counts, barons, and their ladies, of course. And one particular young lady . . . dear Miss Portia Langham. *(Sighs)* I've spent a fortune, as if I really had a fortune to spend. I'm swimming in glory, and the million-pound note is still safely in my pocket. *(Soberly)* Of course, the day of reckoning will come in just two more weeks. But until then I intend to enjoy every minute of this adventure. (PORTIA LANGHAM, *a beautifully dressed young lady, enters.*)

PORTIA: Oh, there you are, my dear Mr. Adams!

HENRY: My dear Miss Langham! You will allow me to call you Portia, won't you?

PORTIA *(Coyly):* If you insist, Mr. Adams.

HENRY: I do. And you must call me Henry.

PORTIA: If you insist . . . Henry.

HENRY: Splendid! *(Leads her to bench)* Won't you sit down, Portia? It's very pleasant here, and I'm rather fond of this bench.

PORTIA: Fond of a bench? Really! I was hoping you might be fond of me.

HENRY: My dearest girl, I'm not merely fond of you, I have fallen hopelessly in love with you!

PORTIA *(Delighted):* Oh, have you? Then I must be very bold and tell you that I have fallen in love with you, too. Hopelessly!

HENRY *(Ecstatically):* Dear Portia! I am the happiest man in London! And I must be completely honest with you. I must tell you . . .

PORTIA: Tell me what?

HENRY: That I haven't a cent in the world but that million-pound note everyone's heard so much about, and it doesn't belong to me.

PORTIA *(Shocked):* Henry! Whatever do you mean?

HENRY: It all started when I had been in London only a day, reduced to rags, broke, starving, and I met two old gentlemen here on this bench. They spoke to me, and the next thing I knew I was telling them my story, and then they gave me an envelope with the million-pound note, on loan to me for thirty days. *(Shrugs)* I'm the subject of some experiment, some wager. I've gone from rags to riches, but I'm really in a very awkward situation. I'll have to pay back all I've spent at the end of the thirty days, and I don't know how I can.

PORTIA *(Concerned):* You poor dear! Did the two gentlemen tell you their names?

HENRY: No. But they had a butler named George.

PORTIA: A butler named George! Oh, dear! *(Laughs merrily)*

HENRY: My dear girl! What is so funny? I've told you my desperate story, and you laugh?

PORTIA: I can't help it, Henry dear. It's just like a fairy tale.

HENRY: Then I can only love you all the more for being so cheerful when there's nothing to be cheerful about. *(Tenderly)* Portia, I want to marry you, but of course, I can't until I've paid the two old gentlemen all I owe them, and that may take years!

PORTIA: I shan't mind waiting, if only I can see you every day.

HENRY: Will you come with me when I meet the old gentlemen again? I should like to introduce you to them.

PORTIA *(Suppressing a laugh):* Well, if my being here will encourage you, I'll come. But surely you don't intend to meet them with only me to show them?

HENRY: What do you mean?

PORTIA: Surely you intend to win the bet!

HENRY: But my dear girl, I don't know what the bet is! I can only take care of the million-pound note and return it to them.

PORTIA: That's all?

HENRY: What else can I do?

PORTIA: You were in business in America, weren't you, Henry?

HENRY: Yes.

PORTIA: Yet here you've done nothing but wave a bank note in people's faces and the world has fallen at your feet.

HENRY: Yes, that's right.

PORTIA: Henry, dear, I hope you haven't allowed this new-found wealth to turn your mind from honest endeavor.

HENRY: Honest endeavor?

PORTIA: There is more to you than merely living off the face value of a million-pound note, isn't there?

HENRY: I suppose so.

PORTIA: Then show me! *(Kisses him)* And show the two old gentlemen, win the bet and the situation that goes with it! *(Hurries off)*

HENRY: Portia! Wait! Oh, but she's right. I still have two weeks to go, and I really should do something. But what? (LLOYD HASTINGS *enters, looking downcast. He bumps into* HENRY.)

LLOYD: I beg your pardon, sir. I didn't see you.

HENRY: Lloyd? Lloyd Hastings! What on earth are you doing here?

LLOYD: Henry Adams! *You're* the vest-pocket million-pounder I've read about in the papers! I thought the pictures looked familiar, but I couldn't believe it was really you!

HENRY *(Laughing):* I can hardly believe it myself.

LLOYD: To think that only six months ago you and I were working in San Francisco on the Gould and Curry Mine statistics.

HENRY: Have you had success with the mine, Lloyd?

LLOYD: No. The sale fell through, which is why I'm here in London. I can't tell you how poor I am, and how miserable!

HENRY: My dear fellow, don't talk that way! *(Aside)* He makes me all the more aware that I'm standing on the brink of disaster myself.

LLOYD: I came to London to sell the Gould and Curry, hoping I could keep all I might get for it over a million dollars. I worked hard, left no honest effort untried, and spent all the money I had in the world, but no one would believe me. No one would buy it. Now my option on the mine has run out. I'm ruined, unless . . . unless . . .

HENRY: Unless what?

LLOYD: Unless you save me, Henry! You're the only man in the world who can!

HENRY: Why, how can I save you, Lloyd?

LLOYD: You can buy the mine for a million dollars, and lend me enough to get back home to my old job. *(Pleading)* Don't refuse me, Henry! Please!

HENRY *(Apologetically)*: But Lloyd, I can't do that. My hands are tied. The million-pound note . . .

LLOYD: Don't say no, Henry. I know you're a much sharper businessman than I'll ever be! Please!

HENRY: But, Lloyd . . . *(Pauses, thinking)* Wait a minute! Lloyd, I'll save you, but not with a mere million dollars.

LLOYD: What do you mean?

HENRY: I know all about the Gould and Curry mine. I know how valuable it is. You can sell it for at least three million, its real worth, just by using my name as a reference. Then we'll divide and invest the profit!

LLOYD *(Joyfully)*: I may use your name? Henry, buyers will flock to me in droves! These rich Londoners will fight for that stock! *(Grasping HENRY's hand)* Thank you, Henry! Thank you! I'm saved! *(Rushes out)*

HENRY: Thanks to you, Lloyd, I believe I'm saved, too! Now to wait for those buyers to come to me! *(Exits; blackout. When lights come up, EDWARD and ABEL are on bench; GEORGE stands behind them. HENRY enters with PORTIA; they stand at side of stage.)*

HENRY: My dear, you look intolerably beautiful. Come and meet the two gentlemen.

PORTIA: Oh no, Henry, not yet. Finish your business first. I don't want to be a distraction.

HENRY: My dear, you are the sweetest distraction in the world. But if you wish, wait here. (PORTIA *stands at side of stage as* HENRY *approaches* ABEL *and* EDWARD.) Gentlemen, I am ready to report.

EDWARD: We're glad to hear it, Mr. Adams. You look splendid! Have you the bank note we gave you?

HENRY: Yes, sir. Here it is. *(Hands note to EDWARD)*

EDWARD: Ah! And you have managed very well with it over the past thirty days.

HENRY: Yes, sir, better than I could ever have expected.

ABEL: Have you not been arrested, sir?

HENRY: No, sir.

ABEL: And you're not starving? Even a little?

HENRY: No, sir. Not a bit.

EDWARD *(Happily):* Then I've won! *(To* ABEL) He lived for thirty days on a one million-pound note without starving or being arrested! What do you say now, brother?

ABEL: I say that I have fairly lost twenty thousand pounds.

HENRY: I also have this to show you, gentlemen. *(Hands paper to* EDWARD)

EDWARD *(Surprised):* A certificate of deposit for two hundred thousand pounds!

HENRY: I earned it by using your loan as collateral in a business deal.

PORTIA *(Joining others):* Henry, is that really your money? Did you really use your head and do some business on your own?

HENRY: Yes, I did, Portia. I'm not a millionaire, but I'm certainly not a pauper.

EDWARD: Then you may have your choice of the situation you have earned, Mr. Adams.

HENRY: Thank you, sir, but I really don't need it now.

PORTIA: Shame on you, Henry. You haven't thanked the gentlemen properly. *(Kisses* EDWARD *affectionately on cheek)* Dear Papa, I knew he would win for you!

HENRY *(Surprised):* Papa! Portia! Is this gentleman really your father?

PORTIA: Indeed he is. And this is my Uncle Abel, and my dear old butler George. Now do you see why I laughed when you told me your story?

HENRY *(Shocked):* You knew about the wager?

PORTIA: I knew, and oh, how I was rooting for you!

HENRY *(To* EDWARD): Sir, you *do* have a situation I want very much.

EDWARD: Just name it, Mr. Adams.

HENRY *(Beaming at* PORTIA): Son-in-law!

EDWARD (*Shaking* HENRY's *hand*): It's yours! With my warmest blessing! Brother Abel, what do you say we try this little experiment again some day, with this very same million-pound note?

ABEL: Very well. Only next time I shall win! No other man could possibly be as lucky as Henry Adams!

EDWARD: Don't be too sure, brother. It wasn't all luck. Henry Adams used his wits and his head.

HENRY (*Looking fondly at* PORTIA): And I'm richer now than when I had the one-million pound note! (*Blackout*)

THE END

PRODUCTION NOTES

THE ONE MILLION POUND BANK NOTE

Characters: 8 male; 1 female.

Playing Time: 30 minutes.

Costumes: Period dress. Henry wears rags at beginning, then a well-tailored suit. Abel and Edward wear morning suits and top hats; George wears a black suit. Harris wears shirt with sleeves rolled up, trousers, apron; Tod, Tailor, and Lloyd, business suits. Portia wears a pretty dress, hat, and gloves.

Properties: Three newspapers, envelope containing one million pound note and a letter; measuring tape, pencil and paper.

Setting: Scenes 1, 2, 3, Before Rise, a street near a park in London, played before the curtain, with bench at right. Scene 1, At Rise, Harris's Café: a table and chair at center. Scene 2, At Rise, the Tailor Shop: rack of suits, mirror, folding screen and table with old clothes at center.

The Fall of Uriah Heep

from David Copperfield
by Charles Dickens

Characters

DAVID COPPERFIELD
WILKINS MICAWBER, *his old friend*
MR. WICKFIELD, *lawyer*
AGNES WICKFIELD, *his daughter*
URIAH HEEP, *villain*
MRS. HEEP, *his mother*
AUNT BETSEY TROTWOOD, *David's great-aunt*
THOMAS TRADDLES, *David's lawyer friend*

SCENE 1

TIME: *Mid-nineteenth century.*
SETTING: *Law office of Wickfield and Heep in Canterbury, England. Stage is divided: at right and center is the office, with large desk and chair at center, small desk and stool at right, a safe at the back, small table with decanter and glasses on a tray, plus several straight chairs, cabinets, bookcases, etc. Door to an inner office is up right, exit to street down right. At left is sitting room, with sofa, chairs, and small table. Exit left leads to rest of house.*
AT RISE: WILKINS MICAWBER *sits writing at small desk, right.* DAVID COPPERFIELD *enters right.*

179

DAVID: Good morning, sir, I— (MICAWBER *looks up. Both men register surprise.*) Why, Mr. Micawber! My old friend!

MICAWBER *(Jumping up; excitedly):* David Copperfield! (*Shakes hands warmly with* DAVID) How very pleased I am to see you again!

DAVID: It's been months since I last saw you in London. How do you come to be here in Canterbury at the office of Wickfield and Heep?

MICAWBER *(Proudly):* Copperfield, you may recall I always told you that something would turn up for me. I advertised myself in all the papers, and Mr. Uriah Heep answered. As a result I am now employed here as clerk. What brings you here, my friend?

DAVID: I've come to pay a visit to Miss Agnes Wickfield.

MICAWBER: Ah, yes. Now I remember! You boarded here when you were in school. I believe you and Miss Wickfield grew up together.

DAVID: We did, and I think of her as my dear adopted sister. *(They sit.)* Tell me, how do you like working in the law?

MICAWBER *(Expansively):* It is a great pursuit! And I have comfortably settled my family in the house formerly occupied by Uriah Heep and his mother. They have moved in here with the Wickfields.

DAVID *(Surprised):* Here? Uriah has come a long way since *he* was Mr. Wickfield's clerk. How does he treat you?

MICAWBER *(Looking around cautiously, then speaking quietly):* You know, my dear Copperfield, that I am a man who is continually in financial difficulties. However, my friend Heep has been most generous in making loans to me.

DAVID *(Skeptically):* He has? I should not have thought him so free with his money!

MICAWBER *(Surprised):* Oh?

DAVID: I would advise you to be cautious, Mr. Micawber. Uriah claims to be humble, but I know he can be very tricky.

MICAWBER *(Defensively):* Pardon me, but I speak of my friend Heep from my own experience.

DAVID: I am glad *your* experience has been favorable. Mine has not, and it does not appear that Mr. Wickfield's experience has been to his advantage, either.

MICAWBER *(In a superior tone):* I dare say, Mr. Wickfield is a man of excellent intentions, but he is . . . in short, obsolete!

DAVID: I am afraid Uriah Heep seeks to make him so.

MICAWBER *(Uneasily):* Copperfield, I am employed here in a situation of confidence and trust. Therefore, I suggest that we make no further reference to the affairs of Wickfield and Heep. *(Anxiously)* I hope I give you no offense in this.

DAVID: Of course not. You and I have been good friends since my boyhood, and I assure you our happy relationship will continue!

MICAWBER *(Relieved):* Thank you, Copperfield!

DAVID: Tell me, what do you think of Miss Agnes?

MICAWBER *(Enthusiastically):* She is a *very* superior young lady of remarkable attractions, graces and virtues! Charming! (AGNES WICKFIELD *enters left.*)

DAVID *(Standing):* Agnes!

AGNES: David! What a pleasant surprise! *(Moves toward him, smiling and holding out her hand)*

MICAWBER *(Bowing):* Good morning, Miss Wickfield.

AGNES *(Turning to him briefly):* Good morning, Micawber.

MICAWBER: Will you both kindly excuse me? I have some papers to take to the court. *(They nod, as* MICAWBER *takes his hat and papers from desk, then exits right.)*

DAVID *(Leading* AGNES *to sofa in sitting room and sitting beside her):* Agnes, I have missed you so much.

AGNES: Papa and I have missed you, too. You've been away from Canterbury much too long.

DAVID: Back in the happy old days when we were growing up, I came to you so often for advice and support. And now it seems I hardly ever see you.

AGNES: I'm sure you've been busy in London. *(Hesitantly)* Is something troubling you, David? I heard of your Aunt Betsey's recent loss of property. Has this changed her expectations for you?

DAVID: Yes, it has. Not only has she been financially ruined by the loss of her investments, but she has also lost the thousand pounds she paid for my apprenticeship at Doctor's Commons.

AGNES *(With concern):* Does this mean you can no longer study law?

DAVID: Yes, I'm sorry to say I had to give that up. *(Attempting to be cheerful)* However, my aunt and I are quite comfortable in a little flat in London, and she is bearing up quite well.

AGNES: Dear Miss Trotwood. She has always had a will of iron.

DAVID *(Standing; agitated):* You know, of course, Agnes, that my aunt has always entrusted her business affairs to your father. However, her loss of property occurred after Uriah Heep became a partner in your father's firm.

AGNES *(Sadly):* David, there have been many unpleasant changes here since Papa took Uriah into partnership.

DAVID *(Indignant):* I don't see how that mean, fawning fellow ever wormed his way into such a position. Didn't your father consider how unfortunate such a partnership would be?

AGNES: Papa tried to tell me that it was a matter of choice on his part, but I know Uriah forced it upon him. *(Sighing)* Uriah has taken advantage of Papa's illness until . . . until now Papa is quite afraid of him.

DAVID *(Angrily):* Uriah is a villain!

AGNES: He professes humility and gratitude for all that Papa did for him during his years as clerk, but now his position is one of power, and his mother is his accomplice.

DAVID: Where is he now? I'd like to have a few words with him.

AGNES: Oh, David, please, let me earnestly entreat you to be friendly to him. You must, for my sake and Papa's! (URIAH HEEP *enters from inner office door, up right, followed by* MRS. HEEP.)

HEEP: Well! Look who's here, Mother. It's Master Copperfield. . . . I mean *Mister* Copperfield, for he has grown up, hasn't he? *(Rubs his hands together slyly, then offers a limp hand, which* DAVID *shakes reluctantly)*

DAVID *(Coldly):* Uriah. Good morning, Mrs. Heep. You are looking well.

MRS. HEEP *(Whining):* I'm humbly thankful to you, sir, but I'm not entirely well. If only I could see my Uriah well settled in life, then I would be content. *(Glances sharply at* AGNES, *then turns back to* DAVID) How do you think Uriah looks now, sir?

DAVID *(Coldly):* I see no change in him over the years, Mrs. Heep.

MRS. HEEP: Ah, but you don't see him with a mother's eye, sir! *(Sighing)* If only he were settled! *(Turning to* AGNES) Miss Wickfield, won't you join me upstairs?

AGNES *(Politely, but reluctantly):* Very well. *(To* DAVID) If you will excuse me, David. . . . But do come again soon. *(Touches* DAVID's *hand briefly, then exits left with* MRS. HEEP)

DAVID: I hear you are now a partner in the firm, Uriah.

HEEP: Who would have thought it likely? I was much too humble. But the humblest persons may be the instruments of good, and I am glad to think that I have been the instrument of good to Mr. Wickfield. What a worthy man he is, Master Copperfield *(Pause)*, but how imprudent he has been!

DAVID: I am sorry to hear it.

HEEP: If anyone else had been in my place during the last years, he would have had Mr. Wickfield under his thumb. *(Grinds his thumb emphatically on desk)* Under his thumb!

DAVID: Indeed!

HEEP: Oh, there would have been loss and disgrace in the business, but I have humbly served Mr. Wickfield, and he has promoted me to a position beyond my humblest dreams. Did you see *my* clerk, Mr. Micawber?

DAVID: Yes. You know that he and I are old friends.

HEEP *(Slyly):* So you are. Well, he is a man of promise, Master Copperfield, but a poor manager of his money. *(Pauses, scratching his jaw)* I hope you will not think the worse of my humbleness if I make a little confession to you.

DAVID *(With an effort):* Of course not.

HEEP: Oh, thank you, Master Copperfield. *(Pauses, rubbing his hands together)* Master Copperfield, humble as I am, the beautiful image of Miss Agnes has always been before me. Oh, how I love the very ground my Agnes walks on!

DAVID: *Your* Agnes? *(Speechless, then with an effort, composing himself)* Have you made your feelings known to her?

HEEP: Oh, no, I haven't mentioned my feelings to anyone but you. Miss Agnes is so much attached to her father, that I think she may come to be kind to me on his account.

DAVID: I see!

HEEP: But you are quite a dangerous rival. You always have been. I shall take a particular favor if you'll have the goodness to keep my secret and not work against me. *(Menacingly, as* DAVID *is silent)* It would be best for all concerned!

DAVID *(With forced politeness):* Uriah, I will tell you quite frankly that I love, admire and respect Agnes Wickfield as my very dear sister. As it happens, I am presently engaged to another young lady.

HEEP *(Snatching* DAVID's *hand and shaking it vigorously):* Oh, Master Copperfield, I am humbly thankful to hear it!

DAVID *(Pulling hand away):* I think you ought to understand, however, that I believe Agnes Wickfield to be as far above you as the moon.

HEEP: Ah, now, Master Copperfield, confess, you haven't always liked me as I have liked you. All along you've thought me too humble, I'm sure. Well, I am still very humble, but now I have some power! (MR. WICKFIELD *enters from inner office with some papers. He walks and talks unsteadily.)*

MR. WICKFIELD: I have finished these accounts, Uriah, if you wish to look them over. *(Seeing* DAVID; *overjoyed)* David, my boy! Why, you're quite a grown young man now! *(Shakes* DAVID's *hand warmly)*

DAVID: It's good to see you, Mr. Wickfield. I'm sorry I have been away so long.

WICKFIELD *(With an appealing look at* HEEP): Don't you think we might all sit down for a moment?

HEEP: By all means, sir. I was just about to suggest it. And as we seldom see Master Copperfield these days, I propose that we welcome him with a little toast. *(Brings wine glasses from table in corner and sets them on desk)*

WICKFIELD: Yes, of course. Come, sit down, David. (WICKFIELD *and* DAVID *sit in sitting room.* HEEP *fills glasses and passes them to* DAVID *and* MR. WICKFIELD.)

HEEP *(Raising his glass):* Master Copperfield, your health and happiness! *(All drink.)* And I'll give you another toast, gentlemen, to the lovely young lady I admire and adore!

DAVID *(Warningly):* Uriah . . .

HEEP: To Miss Agnes Wickfield! *(With a smirk at* WICKFELD) To be her father is a proud distinction, I'm sure. But *(Gloating)* to be her husband—

WICKFIELD *(Jumping up, dropping his glass; furiously):* You— you villain! How dare you suggest such a thing? *(Lunges wildly at* HEEP, *who moves away from him, as* DAVID *holds* WICKFIELD *back)*

DAVID: Mr. Wickfield, sir! Please calm yourself.

WICKFIELD *(Shaking with emotion and pointing at* HEEP): Look at him, David. There is my torturer! Because of him I have lost my good name, my reputation, and the peace and quiet of my home!

HEEP *(Suddenly humble):* Please, Mr. Wickfield, don't be alarmed. If I have overstepped myself just now, I can go back. I'm just as humble as I always was.

WICKFIELD *(As* DAVID *helps him to his seat):* Oh, David, you can see what I have been reduced to since you lived in this house. My carelessness in the business has ruined me. My grief for my dead wife and concern for my daughter have so distracted me that I honestly do not even know what errors I may have made or what actions were taken in my business without my knowledge—but *(Pointing to* HEEP) he knows!

HEEP: You had better stop him, Copperfield! He's likely to say something he'll be sorry for!

WICKFIELD: Heep has always been a millstone around my neck! And now *(Furious)* he dares to . . . to suggest that he . . . marry Agnes! *(Dropping head into hands)* Oh, my dear daughter! (AGNES *suddenly enters left. She hesitates, then goes to* WICKFIELD.)

AGNES *(Gently):* Papa, you are not well. Let me take you upstairs. *(Helps him up, and he leans against her. Glancing at* DAVID, *she leads* WICKFIELD *left.)*

DAVID *(Following them):* Agnes, is there nothing I can do?

AGNES: I'm afraid it is out of our hands, David.

DAVID *(His hand on her arm; gently):* Agnes, please, promise me you'll never sacrifice yourself to a mistaken sense of duty!

AGNES *(Forcing a smile):* You mustn't worry about me. *(Exits with* WICKFIELD)

HEEP *(Walking center):* I didn't expect Mr. Wickfield to carry on so, Master Copperfield, but *(Slyly)* we'll be friends again in the morning. *(Rubbing hands together)* Perhaps I spoke out too soon, but I can wait! (MICAWBER *enters right.)*

DAVID *(Angrily, clenching his fists):* Uriah, if I had known you've been mistreating the Wickfields since I've been gone—!

HEEP: Now, Master Copperfield *(Sharply),* I'm sure you don't mean to interfere with me! *(Turns to* MICAWBER) Micawber, step into my office at once. I need your assistance. *(Exits into inner office through center door)*

MICAWBER: My dear Copperfield, is something the matter?

DAVID: Yes, Mr. Micawber. Something is very much the matter. And I'm surprised that you haven't noticed it by now.

HEEP *(Calling sharply from inner office):* Micawber! (MICAWBER *glances uncomfortably at* DAVID, *then hurries into inner office.* DAVID *looks after him, then hurries out right. Curtain)*

* * * * *

SCENE 2

TIME: *Several months later.*

SETTING: *A park in London. This scene may be played before the curtain, with bench at center.*

AT RISE: DAVID, AUNT BETSEY TROTWOOD *and* THOMAS TRAD-
DLES *enter right.*

DAVID *(Stopping at bench):* This is where Mr. Micawber wrote
us to meet him, Traddles. I don't know what he is up to, but
the tone of his letter was quite urgent.

TRADDLES: If my services as a lawyer can be useful to him, I will
be happy to serve him. He and his family were very kind to me
when I boarded with them as a student. *(To* AUNT BETSEY)
Won't you be seated while we wait, Miss Trotwood?

AUNT BETSEY *(Sitting on bench):* Thank you, Mr. Traddles. I
hope this gentleman will be prompt. (MICAWBER *enters left,
upset.)*

DAVID *(Going to meet him):* Mr. Micawber!

MICAWBER: Copperfield! *(Shakes hands)* And Mr. Traddles!
Thank you for meeting me here in this sad hour.

TRADDLES: I am sorry to see you in low spirits, Mr. Micawber.

DAVID *(In a worried tone):* Micawber, how is our friend, Heep?

MICAWBER *(Excitedly):* Copperfield, if you refer to my employer as *our friend,* I am sorry for it! And I hope you'll
pardon me if I decline to pursue a subject which has driven me
to the verge of desperation in my professional capacity!

DAVID: I see that your opinion of Uriah has changed since I last
saw you. How are my dear friends, the Wickfields?

MICAWBER: Mr. Wickfield, unfortunately, is very ill. But Miss
Wickfield is the only starry spot in my miserable existence.
(Turns and walks left, wiping his brow nervously)

DAVID *(Taking him by the arm):* Mr. Micawber, please calm
yourself. *(Leading him toward bench)* Allow me the pleasure
of introducing you to my aunt.

TRADDLES *(Taking* MICAWBER's *other arm):* And if confiding
anything to your friends will relieve you, sir, we are all at your
service.

DAVID *(Gesturing):* My aunt, Miss Betsey Trotwood.

MICAWBER *(With exaggerated bow):* Miss Trotwood, your servant!

AUNT BETSEY: I am very pleased to meet you, sir! I know you

are an old friend of my nephew's, and I wish I had had the pleasure of seeing you before.

MICAWBER: Madam, I was not always the wreck you now see before you.

DAVID: I hope your family is well, Micawber.

MICAWBER: Yes, thank you. They are as well as aliens and outcasts can ever hope to be.

AUNT BETSEY *(Impatiently):* Good heavens, sir! What are you talking about?

MICAWBER: The welfare of my family, madam, trembles in the balance. My employer . . . *(Shakily)* my employer, Mr. Heep . . . *(Breaks off, wiping brow excitedly)*

AUNT BETSEY: My dear sir, you are with friends. What is the matter?

MICAWBER *(With a burst):* Matter? Villainy is the matter! Deception, fraud and conspiracy are the matter! And the name of the whole atrocious mass is . . . *Heep!*

AUNT BETSEY: Well, that doesn't surprise me one bit!

MICAWBER: I have come to beg your assistance in rescuing Mr. Wickfield and his daughter from that intolerable scoundrel!

DAVID: We are all entirely at your service, Mr. Micawber.

MICAWBER *(Dramatically):* Then I beg of you all to meet me at the office of Wickfield and Heep one week from today at half past nine in the morning. *(Starts off left, then turns back abruptly)* Miss Trotwood, I also hope at that time to provide you with information regarding your lost property!

AUNT BETSEY: Indeed, sir! Perhaps you share my suspicions that Uriah Heep has something to do with it?

MICAWBER: I do! And *(Turning)* Mr. Traddles, I shall require your legal services, if you please! *(Rushes left again, then stops, turns back abruptly and bows hastily to* AUNT BETSEY*)* My apologies, madam, for this unseemly behavior, but this smoldering volcano *(Thumping his chest),* long suppressed, has finally erupted! *(Rushes out left)*

AUNT BETSEY: Bless him! I never saw a man in such a state!

DAVID: You'd better go after him, Traddles, and see what assistance he needs.

TRADDLES: Yes, of course. *(Stands)* I'll come by to see you later this evening. Good day, Miss Trotwood! *(Hurries out left)*

DAVID: Well, Aunt, it looks as though Uriah Heep may soon be in for a rude surprise.

AUNT BETSEY: I shall be only too happy to be a witness to it!

DAVID: Come, let's go home and wait to hear from Traddles. (DAVID *and* AUNT BETSEY *exit right. Curtain)*

* * * * *

SCENE 3

TIME: *Morning, one week later.*

SETTING: *Same as Scene 1.*

AT RISE: MICAWBER *sits at his desk, writing vigorously.* HEEP *sits at large desk center, busy with papers.* DAVID, AUNT BETSEY *and* TRADDLES *enter right.*

DAVID: Good morning, Mr. Micawber.

MICAWBER *(Looking up):* Ah, good morning! I am glad to see you all, I'm sure. Will you please come with me? *(He leads* DAVID, AUNT BETSEY, *and* TRADDLES *center, and they stop in front of* HEEP's *desk.* HEEP *continues writing, as* MICAWBER *calls out names.)* Miss Betsey Trotwood, Mr. David Copperfield, and Mr. Thomas Traddles. (HEEP *looks up, startled, then stands.)*

HEEP *(Rubbing his hands):* Well, now, this is indeed an unexpected pleasure! Miss Trotwood, things have changed in this office since I was a humble clerk and held your pony at the door for you. But *I* have not changed.

AUNT BETSEY *(Archly):* Well, sir! I think you are pretty constant to the promise of your youth, if that's any satisfaction to you! (AGNES *enters left, joins group at* HEEP's *desk.)*

AGNES *(To* AUNT BETSEY; *warmly):* Dear Miss Trotwood, how good to see you!

AUNT BETSEY *(Embracing her):* And you, my child.

AGNES *(Holding her hand out to* DAVID, *who takes it warmly):* And David, how are you?

DAVID: Well, Agnes, well enough.

TRADDLES: I'm glad you've come, Agnes. Perhaps we can proceed. *(Turning to* HEEP) You are not too busy just now, are you, Mr. Heep?

HEEP: No, Mr. Traddles, although Micawber and I have our hands pretty full, what with Mr. Wickfield being unfit for any occupation now. *(Humbly)* But it's a pleasure to work for him. *(To* MICAWBER) You may go now, Micawber. (TRADDLES *exits left, unnoticed by* HEEP. *All sit, except* MICAWBER, *who remains standing.*) What are you waiting for, Micawber? Didn't you hear me tell you to go?

MICAWBER *(Taking up large ruler from desk):* I did!

HEEP: Then why do you wait?

MICAWBER: Because I . . . *(With a burst)* because I *choose* to wait!

HEEP *(Sharply):* Micawber, I am afraid you'll force me to get rid of you! Go along! I'll talk to you presently. *(Sits behind large desk)*

MICAWBER *(Vehemently):* If there is a scoundrel on this earth with whom I have already talked too much, that scoundrel's name is . . . *Heep!*

HEEP *(Startled, then looking around, suddenly suspicious):* Oho! This is a conspiracy, is it! *(Stands; harshly)* Playing games with my clerk, are you, Copperfield? Well, none of your plots will work against me!

DAVID *(Smoothly):* Mr. Micawber, there is a sudden change in this fellow, which assures me he is ready to be brought to bay. Deal with him as he deserves!

HEEP *(Fiercely):* Buy over my clerk, will you? Well, he's the very scum of society, as you yourself were, Copperfield, before your aunt took you in! Miss Trotwood, I can make you pay for any part you play in this! *(With rising fury)* And, as for you, Miss Wickfield, if you have any love for your father, you had better not join this alliance. *(Raising clenched fist)* I'll ruin him, if you do! Micawber, you know I can crush you! *(Bangs his fist on desk. As all watch him sternly, he looks around uneasily.)* Where's my mother? And where did that fellow Traddles go? (TRADDLES *enters left with* MRS. HEEP.)

TRADDLES: Mrs. Heep is here, sir.

HEEP: And what business do *you* have here?

TRADDLES *(Calmly):* I am acting as the agent and friend of Mr. Wickfield, sir. I have his power of attorney to act for him in all matters.

HEEP: If you have a power of attorney, it has been taken from him by fraud!

TRADDLES: *Something* has been taken from him by fraud, Mr. Heep. You know that better than I.

MRS. HEEP *(Anxiously):* Uriah!

HEEP: Sit down, Mother, and leave this to me! *(Watches uncomfortably as* MICAWBER *picks up ruler, puts it in his vest pocket, clears his throat, and takes paper from his pocket, which he unfolds with a flourish)*

MICAWBER: Miss Trotwood, Miss Wickfield, and gentlemen! I appear before you today to denounce this villain, *Heep!*

HEEP *(In warning tone):* Micawber, you'd better think twice before you continue!

MICAWBER *(Ignoring* HEEP): From my cradle, I, Wilkins Micawber, have been a victim of financial difficulties. One year ago, in order to relieve my financial difficulties, I took employment as confidential clerk here in the office of Wickfield and Heep. But I soon discovered that it was managed entirely by Heep. Heep and only Heep is the forger and the cheat! (HEEP *jumps up and grabs at paper, furious, but* MICAWBER *takes ruler from his vest and strikes* HEEP *sharply on knuckles with it.)*

HEEP: Ow-w! *(Reels back, wringing his hand)* Micawber, I'll get even with you!

MICAWBER: Approach me again, you . . . you *Heep* of infamy, and if your head is human, I'll break it! (HEEP *retreats behind desk, wrapping hand in handkerchief.*) Ahem! *(Grandly)* To continue. . . . My salary at this establishment was a mere pittance. Need I say that it soon became necessary for me to ask for advances from *Heep* in order to support my family? Need I say that those advances were secured by IOU's, and that I soon became entangled in a web of debt that *Heep* had *purposely* spun for me?

HEEP *(Menacingly):* Micawber . . .

MICAWBER: It was *then* that *Heep* began to call upon my services for the falsification of business records and the total deception of Mr. Wickfield.

HEEP *(Jumping up):* Micawber, you will regret this! (MICAWBER *brandishes ruler and* HEEP *falls back.*)

MICAWBER: I now bring the following charges against *Heep:* First! When Mr. Wickfield's faculties for business became weakened and confused, *Heep* deliberately confused all official business transactions.

HEEP *(Fiercely):* You shall prove this!

MICAWBER: I shall, indeed! Mr. Traddles, ask *Heep* who moved into his house when he moved here.

HEEP: You live there, but you won't much longer! I'll throw you out!

MICAWBER: Ask *Heep* if he ever kept a notebook of business accounts in that house, or attempted to burn that notebook in the fireplace in that house! (HEEP *looks up, startled.*) If he says yes and asks you where the ashes are, refer him to Wilkins Micawber, who found those ashes! (*Pulls charred notebook from his pocket and waves it at* HEEP)

MRS. HEEP *(Alarmed):* Uriah, be humble and make terms!

HEEP: Mother, will you keep quiet?

MICAWBER: Second! *Heep* has, on several occasions, forged Mr. Wickfield's signature on various important documents. *(Takes more papers from pocket)* I have here several of *Heep*'s imitations of Mr. Wickfield's signature.

MRS. HEEP: Oh, Uriah, you must be humble and make terms!

(*Turns to others*) I know my son will be humble, gentlemen, if you'll only give him time to think. (*To* HEEP, *anxiously*) I can't bear to hear you provoking these gentlemen and endangering yourself. It's better to be as humble as you always were, my dear.

MICAWBER: Silence, madam. (*Clearing his throat*) And third and last! I am prepared to show by *Heep's* false books that he has deluded and plundered Mr. Wickfield, and in one particular instance, Miss Trotwood, for years. *Heep's* last act was to force Mr. Wickfield to execute a deed, relinquishing his share in the partnership, his house and his furniture! And if it were possible, I believe he would have forced Mr. Wickfield to execute a deed relinquishing his daughter! But fortunately, Mr. Wickfield has friends who will save him and his daughter from this—this monster in the garb of a man! (*Hands burned notebook and papers to* TRADDLES) I have now concluded, and in so doing, I may now return to respectable terms with myself and my fellow man.

HEEP (*Running to safe and throwing it open*): Where are the books? Some thief has stolen the books!

MICAWBER: I did!

TRADDLES: Don't be alarmed, Mr. Heep. The books are now in my possession and I will take care of them.

HEEP: You receive stolen goods, do you?

TRADDLES: Under these circumstances, yes!

AUNT BETSEY (*Suddenly jumping up and seizing* HEEP *by collar*): Do you know what *I* want, Uriah Heep? My property! Agnes, my dear, as long as I thought my investments had been lost by your father, I didn't say a word about them. But now that I know this fellow is answerable for them, I want them back! (*Shakes* HEEP *fiercely*)

DAVID (*Gently pulling her away from* HEEP): Dear Aunt, I assure you that Uriah will restore everything he has wrongly acquired, including your property. Traddles and I will see to it! (*Leads her back to chair*)

TRADDLES: The first thing you must do, Mr. Heep, is turn over to me now Mr. Wickfield's deed of relinquishment. Then you must give up all you have falsely gained and make restoration to the last farthing. Until everything is done to our satisfaction, we shall compel you to keep to your room and have no communication with anyone.

HEEP: I won't do it. (*Starts out right, but* MICAWBER *and* DAVID *block his way*)

TRADDLES: Maidstone Jail is a safer place of detention, Mr. Heep. (*To* DAVID) Copperfield, will you go around to Guildhall and bring a couple of officers?

MRS. HEEP (*Alarmed*): Oh, no! Please, gentlemen, wait! Uriah, if you won't be humble and make terms, I will!

HEEP (*Sullenly, after a pause*): Very well! Let them have that deed. (MRS. HEEP *unlocks desk drawer, takes out deed and hands it to* TRADDLES.)

TRADDLES (*Glancing at deed*): Very good. Now, Mr. Heep, you may go to your room. Mr. Micawber, will you accompany him and see that he remains there?

MICAWBER: With pleasure! (*Grasps* HEEP *by arm*)

HEEP: Copperfield, you've always been against me. You turned your friends against me!

DAVID: It is you who have always been against the world, Uriah. There was never anyone who lived by greed and cunning who did not over-reach himself.

AGNES (*Kissing* MICAWBER *on forehead*): Dear Mr. Micawber! How can we ever thank you!

MICAWBER: Miss Wickfield, it was my pleasure and my duty! (*Bows to all, then pushes* HEEP *out left, followed by* MRS. HEEP, *wringing her hands and almost in tears*)

DAVID: Agnes, when your father hears of this, I'm sure he'll have the will to recover. You are safe from that villain, my aunt is no longer poor, and Traddles and I have the satisfaction of knowing that Uriah Heep won't harm any of us again! (DAVID *and* AGNES *take hands happily, and* AUNT BETSEY *and* TRADDLES *shake hands triumphantly as curtain falls.*)

THE END

PRODUCTION NOTES

The Fall of Uriah Heep

Characters: 5 male; 3 female.

Playing Time: 30 minutes.

Costumes: Appropriate mid-nineteenth century English dress. Uriah and Mrs. Heep wear black.

Properties: Several papers, pens, inkbottles; hat; handkerchiefs; long ruler; partially burned notebook.

Setting: Scenes 1 and 3: The law office of Wickfield and Heep. Area at right and center is furnished as an office with a large desk and chair at center, a small desk and stool at right, a safe at the back, a small table with decanter and glasses on a tray, plus several straight chairs, cabinets, bookcases, etc. A door to an inner office is up right, an entrance to the street down right. The area at left is comfortably furnished as a small sitting room with a sofa and one or two chairs, and a small table. An entrance at left leads upstairs in the house. Scene 2: A park in London. This scene may be played before the curtain. A bench is placed at center.

Lighting: No special effects.

Round-the-Table
Reading Plays

The Hound of the Baskervilles

by Sir Arthur Conan Doyle

Characters

SHERLOCK HOLMES
DR. JOHN WATSON
DR. JAMES MORTIMER
SIR HENRY BASKERVILLE
BARRYMORE, *butler*
MRS. BARRYMORE
JACK STAPLETON
BERYL STAPLETON

WATSON: Of all the mysteries solved by my renowned detective
friend, Sherlock Holmes, I consider the case of the Hound of
the Baskervilles to be one of the most unforgettable. It began
one morning when I entered Holmes's rooms at 221B Baker
Street, and found him at the breakfast table with his back to
the door.

HOLMES: Good morning, Watson! Who is that with you?

WATSON: Holmes! You must have eyes in the back of your head.

HOLMES: Not quite, Watson. I merely have in front of me a well-
polished silver coffeepot that reflects the images of you and
your friend perfectly.

WATSON: Come, turn around and let me introduce Dr. James
Mortimer of Devonshire.

HOLMES: How do you do, Mr. Mortimer?

MORTIMER: It's a great honor to meet the most skilled detective in England. I hope you'll help me with a most extraordinary problem, Mr. Holmes.

HOLMES: Won't you sit down, and tell me more?

MORTIMER: Thank you. A patient and friend of mine, Sir Charles Baskerville, recently died a sudden and tragic death. Before his death he had told me about a strange legend.

HOLMES: What sort of legend?

MORTIMER: In the mid-1600's there lived in Baskerville Hall a wild and cruel man, Hugo Baskerville, who carried off the daughter of a neighboring farmer, intending to marry her against her will. He locked her in an upstairs room at Baskerville Hall, and the frantic girl feared for her life. In desperation she climbed down the ivy outside her window and fled across the moor. When Hugo discovered her gone, he flew into a rage and swore to his servants that he would sell his soul to the Devil if he could recover the girl. He loosed his vicious hounds, gave them the girl's scent from a kerchief she had dropped, then followed after them on horseback across the moor.

WATSON: Why, the man was mad! What happened?

MORTIMER: Hugo's servants rode after him and found his hounds whimpering in a cluster at the edge of a steep hollow. Below them they saw the girl, dead, and beside her, tearing out Hugo Baskerville's throat, a monstrous black hound! It turned its blazing eyes and dripping jaws upon the riders, who fled in terror. According to the legend, this hound has plagued the family ever since. All who have lived in Baskerville Hall have met sudden and mysterious deaths.

HOLMES (Bored): That might be an interesting story to a collector of fairy tales, Dr. Mortimer.

MORTIMER: Perhaps. But I have some very real facts concerning Sir Charles Baskerville's death. On the night of his death, he went out for his usual walk, smoking his usual cigar. He never returned. The butler, Barrymore, found him at the far end of Yew Alley—dead. I was called, and when I arrived I easily followed Sir Charles' footprints down the muddy lane. He must have stopped at a gate leading onto the moor, for I found a fresh pile of cigar ashes on the ground. But from the gate to the place where he fell the footprints changed. He appeared to have walked on his toes!

HOLMES: Were there signs of violence on his body?

MORTIMER: No, although his face was terribly distorted. I attributed his death to heart failure. Then I noticed something troubling not far from his body.

HOLMES: What was that?

MORTIMER: Some fresh, clear footprints.

HOLMES: A man's or a woman's?

MORTIMER: Mr. Holmes, they were the footprints of a gigantic hound!

WATSON: Good heavens!

HOLMES: Did anyone else see those footprints?

MORTIMER: No, and I wouldn't have given them a second thought if I hadn't known of the legend, and that Sir Charles believed in it and feared it. I also know that several farmers living near the Hall have reported seeing a large hound with glowing eyes and jaws. They now refuse to cross the moor at night!

HOLMES: What exactly do you want of me, Dr. Mortimer?

MORTIMER: First, your advice. Sir Charles' heir, Sir Henry Baskerville, arrives in London tonight.

HOLMES: Is Sir Henry the last of the Baskervilles?

MORTIMER: Yes. The only other Baskerville was Sir Charles' wicked brother, Rodger, the black sheep of the family. He died in disrepute in Central America, and had no children. You see, Mr. Holmes, every Baskerville who has lived at the Hall has met a tragic fate. *(Meaningfully)* I hesitate to take Sir Henry there.

HOLMES: Let me suggest that you meet Sir Henry and take him

to a hotel tonight. Bring him to see me tomorrow morning at ten o'clock. In the meantime, I will give this matter serious thought.

MORTIMER: I hope you will decide to investigate this case, Mr. Holmes. Thank you, and good day.

WATSON: Good day, sir. *(Pause)* What do you think, Holmes?

HOLMES: The change in Sir Charles' footprints indicates he suddenly ran in desperation until his heart burst.

WATSON: But what was he running from?

HOLMES: Something that terrified him out of his mind. He ran *away* from the house instead of toward it and safety! Sir Henry may be marked for a similar fate!

WATSON: The next morning Dr. Mortimer appeared with Sir Henry Baskerville, a handsome gentleman of thirty, wearing a well-worn brown tweed suit.

SIR HENRY: I'm very glad to meet both of you, gentlemen. I received an unusual message this morning. It's probably a joke, but I wonder if you would examine it, Mr. Holmes?

HOLMES: Certainly. *(After a pause)* It's on ordinary paper, and addressed to you at the Northumberland Hotel. Let me see . . . "As you value your life or your reason, keep away from the moor." Hmm. Who knew where you would be staying?

SIR HENRY: No one. Dr. Mortimer and I selected the hotel just last night.

HOLMES: Then someone must be following you! Watson, look out the window, will you?

WATSON: I don't see anything unusual . . . wait! There's a man with a black beard across the street, half hidden in a doorway. He appears to be watching this house.

HOLMES: Dr. Mortimer, do you know anyone with a black beard?

MORTIMER: Only Barrymore, the butler at Baskerville Hall.

HOLMES: See if you recognize him. . . . Careful, don't move the curtain.

MORTIMER: I can't be sure. He's wearing a hat pulled low over his face.

WATSON: Ah! He must have seen us. He's leaving.

HOLMES: Quick, Watson, after him!

WATSON: Too late! He's jumped into a cab and driven off!

HOLMES: That's unfortunate!

SIR HENRY: Dr. Mortimer told me about the footprints he found, and I've known the legend of the house since I was a boy; but I've never taken it seriously.

HOLMES: *Someone* is taking it seriously, Sir Henry. Whoever sent this message meant to warn you of possible danger. Has anything else unusual happened since you arrived in London?

SIR HENRY: Well, yes . . . I lost a boot. Last night I set a pair of boots outside my hotel room for the porter to clean. This morning I found only one.

HOLMES: Hm-m-m. It doesn't make sense for anyone to steal one boot.

MORTIMER: This message . . . that man who followed us . . . Sir Henry, do you think it's advisable for you to go on to Baskerville Hall?

SIR HENRY: It's obvious I must be on my guard, but nothing will prevent me from going to my ancestral home!

HOLMES: Very well, but someone should go along and stay with you for a while.

SIR HENRY: Yes, I would feel more comfortable with a companion. Could you come with me, Mr. Holmes?

HOLMES: No, I'm at work on another case, but I'm sure Dr. Watson can go.

WATSON: With pleasure!

HOLMES: Good. Report to me any facts you discover, Watson, and make the acquaintance of the neighbors.

WATSON: Who are the nearest neighbors, Dr. Mortimer?

MORTIMER: There is a naturalist, Jack Stapleton, and his sister, Beryl, who live in the house across the moor.

HOLMES: All right. Keep your revolver with you at all times, Watson. Sir Henry, you must never go anywhere alone, particularly on the moor at night!

SIR HENRY: I'll remember. Goodbye, Mr. Holmes, and thank you.

WATSON: Our journey to Devonshire was a pleasant one, and we soon arrived at the village near Baskerville Hall.

MORTIMER: I've ordered a carriage to take you to the Hall, Sir Henry.

SIR HENRY: Thank you. Why are all these police officers waiting around the station?

MORTIMER: An escaped convict is hiding on the moor.

WATSON: Oh? Who is it?

MORTIMER: Selden, the Notting Hill murderer.

WATSON: The throat slasher! Holmes once took an interest in that case.

SIR HENRY: I hope they'll catch him soon. Thank you for your help, Dr. Mortimer.

MORTIMER: I'll be at my home if you need me, Sir Henry. Goodbye!

WATSON: As our carriage rolled over the gray moor, a cold, whistling wind swept down upon us. Somewhere in that desolate place a killer lurked. I shuddered at the thought. Sir Henry wore a gloomy look. Soon we drove up the long, dark lane where Baskerville Hall glimmered like a ghost at the far end.

SIR HENRY: It's a frightening place, Dr. Watson, a place of death, but it is my home now. I won't turn back. Look—that must be Barrymore on the porch.

WATSON: Respectable-looking chap. I wish I could be certain he was the bearded man I saw watching Holmes's house.

BARRYMORE: Welcome, Sir Henry! Let me take your bags. You can warm yourselves by the fire in the library. My wife will serve dinner in just a few minutes.

SIR HENRY: Thank you, Barrymore. This is Dr. Watson, who'll be staying here as my guest for a while. Shall we get to that fire, Doctor? *(Pause)* Look at these lofty beams and oak-panelled walls! Impressive, isn't it? To think that Baskervilles have lived and died in this Hall for five hundred years!

WATSON: It's a dark and solemn residence, Sir Henry. I'll be glad to have some dinner and then retire early.

SIR HENRY: I agree. Perhaps things will appear more cheerful tomorrow.

WATSON: The next morning Sir Henry and I felt rested and in good spirits. After breakfast he had a number of papers to examine, so I took a walk onto the moor. It was rather a pleasant place in the bright sunlight. I hadn't gone far when I heard my name called, and saw a blond, lean-jawed man approaching with a tin box and a butterfly net.

STAPLETON *(Calling):* Dr. Watson! I'm Jack Stapleton. Dr. Mortimer told me of your arrival with Sir Henry.

WATSON: How do you do?

STAPLETON: We were afraid that after Sir Charles' death, Sir Henry would refuse to live here. Apparently he is not superstitious about the legendary hound.

WATSON: No, I believe not.

STAPLETON: I was very fond of Sir Charles. It's a tragedy that he allowed his imagination to get the better of him. But with his weak heart and jittery nerves, the sight of *any* dog at night might have alarmed him fatally.

WATSON: Do you believe it was a *dog* that frightened him to death?

STAPLETON: He believed in the legend completely. Have you a better explanation?

WATSON: I haven't come to any conclusion yet, Mr. Stapleton.

STAPLETON: Has Mr. Sherlock Holmes?

WATSON: I beg your pardon?

STAPLETON: Come, sir, I know who you are. And if *you* are here, Mr. Holmes must be concerned with this case. Will he be honoring us with a visit?

WATSON: No. He is working on a case in London.

STAPLETON: What a pity. But won't you come home with me and meet my sister Beryl?

WATSON: Thank you. I'd be delighted.

STAPLETON: The moor is a wonderful place, Dr. Watson, full of mysterious secrets.

WATSON: You must know it well.

STAPLETON: Yes, I do, although I've lived here only two years. As a naturalist, I've explored every inch of it. Do you see that bright green plain over there?

WATSON: It looks like a perfect place to ride a horse at full gallop.

STAPLETON *(With a harsh laugh):* It is the Great Grimpen Mire! One false step means death to man or beast. Only yesterday I saw a wild pony sucked to his death in that mud. But I've learned how to cross the mire safely.

WATSON: Suddenly a long, low moan swept over the moor. From a dull murmur it swelled into a deep roar, then slowly died away.

STAPLETON *(Casually):* Strange place, the moor!

WATSON: What *was* that? I've never heard anything like it!

STAPLETON: The farmers say it is the Hound of the Baskervilles calling for its next victim.

WATSON: Oh, come, sir, surely you don't believe such nonsense!

STAPLETON: The moor is full of unusual sounds and sights, Doctor. Look over there at those gray stone huts. They are thousands of years old. *(Suddenly)* Oh, excuse me, there goes a Cyclopides!

WATSON: A small moth fluttered across the path and Stapleton rushed after it, heading straight for the Grimpen Mire. I watched in amazement as he bounded from tuft to tuft over the treacherous bog. Then I noticed a beautiful young woman hurrying toward me.

BERYL *(Urgently):* Go back! Go back to London at once!

WATSON: I beg your pardon, madam?

BERYL *(Impatiently):* Please, go back to London and never set foot on this moor again!

WATSON: I'm afraid I don't understand you.

BERYL: You *must* do as I say! Oh! Here comes my brother. Say nothing about what I've said to you. Quickly, pick that orchid for me.

STAPLETON *(Sharply):* Beryl! I didn't expect to see you out here.

BERYL: I was looking for orchids, Jack. Sir Henry was kind enough to pick this one for me.

STAPLETON: Sir Henry? My dear sister, this is Dr. Watson, Sir Henry's guest.

BERYL *(Confused):* Oh! Please forgive me, Dr. Watson.

STAPLETON: I was just bringing Dr. Watson to meet you, Beryl. My sister shares my interests here, Doctor. We used to run a school in Yorkshire, but an epidemic forced us to close it. Fortunately, we discovered this place, where there are more than enough specimens for our collections. *(After a pause)* Do you think it would be convenient for us to call on Sir Henry this afternoon?

WATSON: I'm sure he would be delighted to see you.

STAPLETON: Beryl is especially eager to meet him. Our social life here is rather limited.

BERYL *(Quickly):* I hope we shall see you often, too, during your stay, Dr. Watson. Do visit us soon.

WATSON: The Stapletons walked on toward their house, and I hurried back to Sir Henry. The weird sound I had heard on the moor, and Beryl Stapleton's urgent warning filled me with great uneasiness. At the end of the first week I wrote a report to Holmes, adding that I believed Sir Henry was falling in love with his attractive neighbor, Beryl Stapleton.

SIR HENRY: She is a beautiful and intelligent young woman.

WATSON: May I ask if she returns your feelings, Sir Henry?

SIR HENRY: I believe she does, and yet, whenever her brother leaves us alone, she insists that I leave here at once.

WATSON: She knows the legend. Perhaps she fears for your life.

SIR HENRY: Nonsense! I'm beginning to think I have nothing to worry about. Nothing unusual has happened.

WATSON: I don't want to alarm you, Sir Henry, but for the past three nights I've heard someone in the passage outside my door.

SIR HENRY: So have I. It's only Barrymore, but perhaps we should follow him tonight and see what he's up to.

WATSON: It was past midnight when Sir Henry and I heard

Barrymore's step in the passage. We followed him to a room in the west wing and discovered him crouching at the window with a candle.

SIR HENRY *(Sharply)*: Barrymore! What are you doing?

BARRYMORE *(Startled)*: Sir Henry! I . . . I'm checking the window, sir, to be sure it's fastened.

SIR HENRY: Come, now, that won't do! Why were you moving that candle back and forth in front of the window?

BARRYMORE: Please, sir. I give you my word it has nothing to do with you.

WATSON: He might be signaling to someone outside.

SIR HENRY: Move the candle as Barrymore did, Doctor. Do you see anything on the moor?

WATSON: Yes! There's a light signaling back!

BARRYMORE *(Alarmed)*: No, no, sir! It's nothing!

SIR HENRY: Who's out there, Barrymore?

BARRYMORE: I can't tell you, sir.

SIR HENRY *(Angrily)*: Then you must leave my service at once!

MRS. BARRYMORE: Please, Sir Henry, this is all *my* doing.

SIR HENRY: Mrs. Barrymore! I didn't hear you come in. What does this mean?

MRS. BARRYMORE: My poor brother is starving out there on the moor, sir. Our light is a signal to him that food is ready, and he signals to show us where to bring it.

WATSON: Who is your brother, Mrs. Barrymore?

MRS. BARRYMORE: The escaped convict, Selden. Oh, I know you'll condemn me, but when he escaped from prison and came here, I couldn't let him starve.

SIR HENRY: Is this true, Barrymore?

BARRYMORE: Yes, sir. He's hiding on the moor until we can get him on a ship and away from England.

SIR HENRY: I see. Go to your room. We'll discuss this further tomorrow.

BARRYMORE: Yes, sir. Come, Eliza.

SIR HENRY: By thunder, Watson, I'm going after that murderer!

WATSON: I know Mrs. Barrymore means well, but she doesn't realize the danger her brother poses to everyone living near the moor. I'm coming with you.

SIR HENRY: Hurry! And bring your revolver!

WATSON: We were soon on the moor and closing in on the light, when suddenly out of the gloom that strange cry arose, first a long, deep mutter, then a rising howl that died away into a mournful moan. Sir Henry caught my sleeve, and I saw that his face was white.

SIR HENRY: Doctor! That . . . that was the cry of the hound! Can that legend really be true? That horrible howl has frozen my blood!

WATSON: Perhaps we'd better turn back.

SIR HENRY: No . . . no. Let's go on.

WATSON: Quietly now.

SIR HENRY: See there! Between those rocks!

WATSON: What a ghastly face! Those fierce eyes, that ragged beard!

SIR HENRY: Quick, before he gets away!

WATSON: We both leaped forward. Selden rose up and screamed a curse at us, then sprang away. Sir Henry and I rushed after him.

SIR HENRY (Gasping): We've lost him.

WATSON: I'm afraid so. Great Scott! Look up there!

SIR HENRY: Where?

WATSON: On that rock! I saw a man silhouetted against the moon. Now he's gone!

SIR HENRY: Was it Selden?

WATSON: Impossible. Selden ran in the other direction.

SIR HENRY: Doctor, my nerves are still quivering from that horrible cry we heard. Let's go back to the Hall.

WATSON: The next afternoon I was walking on the moor, puzzling over the previous night's happenings, when I noticed a boy carrying a bundle and looking around cautiously. My curiosity was aroused and I resolved to follow him. (Pauses)

The sun was setting when I saw the boy come out of a stone hut, then disappear onto the moor. Drawing my revolver, I approached the hut cautiously just as a man stepped out of it.

HOLMES: It's a lovely evening, my dear Watson. I believe I'll step outside and join you.

WATSON *(Surprised):* Holmes! I was never so glad to see anyone in my life!

HOLMES: Or more astonished, eh? I see you followed the lad I brought from London to be my messenger. I hope I didn't startle you too much last night.

WATSON: It was *you* I saw on the rock!

HOLMES: Yes. Too bad Selden got away. But I think we have a good grip on this case of the hound.

WATSON: You amaze me, Holmes. I thought you were in London, at work on another case.

HOLMES: That's what I wanted everyone to think. If I had come here with you and Sir Henry, our opponent would have been on guard.

WATSON: Who is our opponent?

HOLMES: Jack Stapleton!

WATSON: That butterfly collector? What's he up to?

HOLMES: Cold-blooded murder. But my nets are closing on him, even as his are closing on Sir Henry.

WATSON: What have you found out?

HOLMES: From your report that he used to run a school in Yorkshire, I made inquiries and learned that Stapleton is an assumed name, and Beryl is really his wife!

WATSON: His wife? But why does she pose as his sister?

HOLMES: To attract Sir Henry, so that he'll make frequent trips across the moor from Baskerville Hall to the Stapleton house. I need one more day to complete my case, Watson. Meanwhile, you must stay with Sir Henry every moment, and— *(Startled)* What's that?

WATSON: I hear a man screaming! And there's that savage howling again!

HOLMES: The hound! Quick, Watson, before we're too late!

WATSON: We rushed toward the sound of the terrible cries.

HOLMES: Down there, Watson, a man face down on the ground. He must have fallen. Careful, watch your footing.

WATSON: Oh, no! It's Sir Henry! I recognize the brown tweed suit!

HOLMES: He's dead. His skull is crushed!

WATSON: I'll never forgive myself for leaving him alone!

HOLMES: Stapleton will pay for this! He's using a hound to murder, and I'll prove it yet. But why was Sir Henry on the moor? He—(*Suddenly*) Watson! This man has a beard! This isn't Sir Henry. It's Selden, the convict!

WATSON: But the suit . . . oh, now I remember! Sir Henry gave his old tweed suit to Barrymore, and Barrymore must have given it to Selden to aid his escape.

HOLMES: Then the clothes were what attracted the hound.

WATSON: Is there *really* a hound in all this, Holmes?

HOLMES: Yes, Watson. Remember the boot Sir Henry lost in London? Stapleton must have taken it to give the hound Sir Henry's scent.

WATSON: But why was the hound loose tonight? Did Stapleton expect Sir Henry to be on the moor at this hour?

HOLMES: We may soon have an answer. Here comes Stapleton. Not a word to show our suspicions.

STAPLETON: Why, Dr. Watson, I hardly expected to see you out here. What's this? Is someone hurt? Don't tell me it's Sir Henry!

WATSON: See for yourself.

STAPLETON (*With a gasp*): Why, this isn't—(*Quickly*) Who is this?

WATSON: Selden, the escaped convict.

STAPLETON: Oh! How terrible. How did he die?

WATSON: He must have broken his neck falling over these rocks. My friend and I were out strolling when we heard a cry.

STAPLETON: Yes, I also heard a cry and came out to investigate. I was uneasy about Sir Henry.

WATSON: Oh? Why?

STAPLETON: I had invited him over for tea. When he didn't come, I became worried, especially when I heard the cry. I had no idea I'd find you and Mr. Sherlock Holmes on the scene.

HOLMES: You are quick to identify me, Mr. Stapleton.

STAPLETON: I've been expecting you ever since Dr. Watson arrived.

HOLMES: I'm afraid our acquaintance must be brief. I return to London tomorrow.

STAPLETON: So soon? Have you not been able to throw any light on this puzzling case of Sir Charles and the hound?

HOLMES: An investigator needs facts, not legends. I'm afraid there's nothing more I can do here.

STAPLETON: Well, even the finest detectives run upon a dead end now and then. Shall we just cover this poor fellow and call the police in the morning? Good night, gentlemen.

WATSON: Good night, Stapleton.

HOLMES: What nerve that fellow has! Did you see how quickly he recovered himself when he saw that the wrong man had fallen victim to his plot?

WATSON: The villain! Can't we arrest him now?

HOLMES: No. We have no proof. We haven't actually seen the hound, and we don't know why Stapleton is after the Baskervilles.

WATSON: Will you come in and see Sir Henry now?

HOLMES: Yes, but say nothing about the hound. Let him and the Barrymores think Selden died in the fall.

WATSON: Sir Henry was both pleased and surprised to see Holmes. We were eating a late supper when Holmes suddenly stared at the gallery of portraits.

HOLMES: Those are family portraits, aren't they, Sir Henry?

SIR HENRY: Yes, that's right.

HOLMES: Who is that in black velvet and lace?

SIR HENRY: Why, that is Hugo, the wicked man who started the legend of the Hound of the Baskervilles. Now, if you gentlemen will excuse me, I'm very tired. Good night.

HOLMES: Good night, Sir Henry. *(Pause)* Watson, bring the candle over here to Hugo's portrait. If I cover the hat and hair with my hand, whose face do you see?

WATSON: Good heavens! It looks just like Stapleton!

HOLMES: Yes. He is definitely a Baskerville, with the same ugly nature as his ancestor Hugo.

WATSON: Then he's after the estate and fortune.

HOLMES: Exactly. This portrait has supplied the missing link in the case. By tomorrow night Stapleton will be fluttering in our net, as helpless as one of his own butterflies!

WATSON: Early the next morning, Holmes began to set his trap.

HOLMES: Sir Henry, I understand you are dining with the Stapletons tonight.

SIR HENRY: Yes, and I'm sure they would be honored if you and Dr. Watson would join us.

HOLMES: I'm afraid we must decline. We are returning to London today.

SIR HENRY *(Anxiously):* But I thought you meant to stay until everything was settled.

HOLMES: Everything *will* be settled, my dear fellow, if you trust me and do exactly as I tell you.

SIR HENRY: What do you want me to do?

HOLMES: Tell the Stapletons that urgent business has called Watson and me to London, but we'll return in a day or two. Drive to the Stapleton house, then send your carriage home. Be sure to tell the Stapletons you intend to walk back.

SIR HENRY: What? Across the moor?

HOLMES: Yes.

SIR HENRY: But you've warned me not to!

HOLMES: *Now*, Sir Henry, it is absolutely necessary that you *do*!

SIR HENRY *(Sighing):* Very well, I'll do it, but I don't understand.

HOLMES: Trust me, Sir Henry, and don't worry.

WATSON: Holmes and I left Baskerville Hall after luncheon and drove to the railroad station, but we did not board a train.

HOLMES: Watson, we're staying here, but everyone, especially Stapleton, must believe we have left. As soon as it's dark, we'll go to the Stapleton house.

WATSON: It seemed ages before Holmes and I crossed the dark moor and hid behind a stone wall near the dining-room window at Stapleton's house.

HOLMES: Sir Henry and Stapleton are at the table, but I don't see Beryl.

WATSON: Sir Henry looks pale, poor fellow. You've asked a great deal of him to walk on the moor tonight. . . . There! Stapleton's leaving the room.

HOLMES: Watch closely, Watson. Sh! He's coming out the side door . . . crossing to that shed . . . unlocking the door and going in.

WATSON: What's that sound? Something growling?

HOLMES: Sh! He's coming out . . . locking the door . . . going into the house . . . and there, he's back with Sir Henry. It's strange that Beryl isn't with them.

WATSON *(Nervously):* Look at this fog, Holmes. It's getting thicker and drifting this way.

HOLMES: I hadn't counted on that. Sir Henry's life may depend on his starting home before that fog covers the path!

WATSON: Shall we move farther back, onto higher ground?

HOLMES: Yes, but not too far. We can't take a chance on having Sir Henry overtaken before he passes us. Blast this fog! I can hardly see my hand in front of my face!

WATSON: I hear footsteps on the path.

HOLMES: Be ready.

WATSON: It's Sir Henry.

HOLMES: Let him pass. There he goes. Now . . . what's that?

WATSON: A pattering sound . . . like an animal running. If I could only see through this fog—Great Scott! Holmes! What *is* it?

HOLMES: The most hideous hound I've ever seen! Look at the size of it!

WATSON *(In disbelief):* Fire in its mouth! Fire in its eyes! Is it real?

HOLMES: We'll soon find out, if I don't miss my aim.

WATSON: You hit it! I heard it yelp! But it's still running!

HOLMES: After it, Watson! It's mortal and can be killed. Hurry, before it reaches Sir Henry!

WATSON: That scream . . . it's Sir Henry! The hound's leaping at his throat! Shoot, Holmes! Shoot!

HOLMES: Stand ready to back me up. I have five shots left!

WATSON: I will never forget the sight of the appalling hound as five bullets struck its flanks! Yelping in pain, it leaped wildly into the air, snapped its glowing jaws, then fell heavily to the ground, thrashing and yowling until it finally went limp, and was silent.

HOLMES: It's dead! Is Sir Henry all right?

WATSON: He fainted, but he's coming round now.

SIR HENRY: What . . . what in heaven's name *was* that horrible thing?

WATSON: It looks like a cross between a bloodhound and a mastiff, as large as a young lion. But what makes its mouth and eyes glow?

HOLMES: Phosphorus paste. Very clever of Stapleton. I'm sorry we had to use you as bait, Sir Henry. I wasn't expecting this outlandish creature.

SIR HENRY: I'm all right now. *(Gratefully)* You saved my life!

HOLMES: Listen. Someone's coming!

BERYL *(Worried):* Sir Henry! Sir Henry! Are you all right?

WATSON: It's Beryl!

BERYL *(Breathless):* Oh, Dr. Watson! Is Sir Henry . . . Oh, there you are!

SIR HENRY: I'm fine, Beryl.

BERYL *(Relieved):* Thank goodness you're safe! But the hound . . .

WATSON: Dead, madam. Quite dead.

BERYL: At last! I no longer have to live a lie. When I learned

that Jack meant to set the hound after Sir Henry tonight, I
resolved to warn him, but Jack suspected me. He locked me in
a back room, and if one of the servants hadn't found me—

HOLMES: You are safe now. But where is Stapleton?

BERYL: When he heard the shots, he panicked. Just as I came
out of the house I saw him running wildly toward the Grimpen
Mire.

WATSON: But he couldn't possibly cross it in this fog!

BERYL *(Quietly):* No. He may find his way in, but he will never
come out again.

SIR HENRY *(Bewildered):* Why did Stapleton want to kill me?

HOLMES: I learned just this afternoon that he was your cousin
Rodger.

SIR HENRY *(Stunned):* My cousin! I thought I was the only
Baskerville left.

HOLMES: So did we. We were told that your uncle in Central
America had no offspring, but that proved to be untrue. He
had a son, as wicked as he, who was intent on getting the
Baskerville fortune. Only you stood in his way. That's why he
decided to move here and have that devilish hound kill you!

SIR HENRY: He would have succeeded if it hadn't been for you.
Mr. Holmes, Dr. Watson, I shall always be grateful to you.

HOLMES *(Heartily):* Good luck to you, Sir Henry! Come, Watson. If we hurry, we can just catch the midnight train to
London.

WATSON: Yes, Holmes. I believe this wraps up the case of the
Hound of the Baskervilles!

THE END

Cyrano de Bergerac

by Edmond Rostand

Characters

CYRANO DE BERGERAC, *poet and swordsman*
RAGUENEAU, *pastry cook*
COUNT DE GUICHE, *rich nobleman*
LE BRET, *Cyrano's friend*
CHRISTIAN DE NEUVILLETTE, *young soldier*
ROXANE, *young lady*
CAPTAIN OF THE GUARDS
TWO CADETS
MAN

TIME: *Mid-seventeenth century.*
SETTING: *Paris.*

RAGUENEAU: Fresh pastries! Custards! Hot rolls! Come to me, Ragueneau, for your cakes and confections. There is no finer cook in Paris! And while you devour my delicate delectables, I will tell you a story at no extra cost. A beautiful story that will bring tears to your eyes, laughter to your soul, and an irresistible urge to cheer for the hero. His name—Cyrano de Bergerac—an extraordinary man of extraordinary appearance. One of the greatest swordsmen in France. A brave soldier, proud and passionate poet, and stouthearted companion to all honest men. Perhaps you have heard of him? And the handsome young soldier, Christian de Neuvillette, and the lovely lady Roxane, whom they both loved to distraction? I assure you, their story is as rare as my chocolate cream puffs! It began fifteen years ago, in 1640, when a play was being presented at the Hotel de Bourgoyne in Paris. The actor Montfleury was performing, but Cyrano detested him and boldly interrupted him.

CYRANO: King of clowns, you are a blot on the beauty of art. Leave the stage at once!

RAGUENEAU: When Montfleury hesitated, Cyrano leaped to the stage, with his sword drawn.

CYRANO: Fly, you gaping goose! Shoo! Take to your wings before I pluck your plumes!

RAGUENEAU: Montfleury fled in terror and the audience rose to its feet in loud protest, but Cyrano faced them all. He was not afraid of anything or anyone.

CYRANO: Approach, young heroes! All who wish to die, raise your hands! This simpering sausage, this monarch of mountebanks who makes a mockery of acting, shall play here no more.

RAGUENEAU: No one dared approach Cyrano, but one man dared to speak. Such a fool he was!

MAN: Do you mean to take Montfleury's place, monsieur? Your clown's face will do very well.

RAGUENEAU: Certainly, this man had never heard of Cyrano's reputation with a sword. Cyrano turned to him and fixed him to his place with the fierce glare of a hawk.

CYRANO (Slowly, fiercely): Sir, are you by any chance referring to my nose?

MAN (Hesitantly): Well, monsieur, it can hardly be missed.

CYRANO (Shouting): Does it astonish you?

MAN (Nervously): No, monsieur, not at all. I merely—

CYRANO (Louder): Does it dangle like a trunk? Or is it as crooked as an owl's beak?

MAN (Becoming frightened): No, monsieur, of course not.

CYRANO: Do you find it just a bit large?

MAN (Very frightened): Oh, no, no, monsieur. It is very small.

CYRANO (Roaring): You imbecile! Don't lie to me! My nose is

huge. It is magnificent! A great nose indicates a great man, and I allow no one to insult me!

MAN *(Frantically):* Help! Let me out of here!

RAGUENEAU: The foolish man escaped out the door, but the Count de Guiche, a rich and powerful nobleman in the audience, was determined that Cyrano would not escape.

DE GUICHE: Sir, your nose is very large, indeed. Immense! An extremely unattractive appendage!

CYRANO: Ah! Sir, your rank is grand, but your speech is simple. Had you proper wit, you might have said in a friendly manner, "Sir, your nose is a rock! A crag! A peninsula!" Or in a sweet, kind voice, you might have inquired, "Sir, do little birds perch there when they come to sing to you?" Or, "Do be careful, sir. A weight like that might make you top-heavy." *(With rising fury)* You have not the intelligence to make a joke of me, and while I say these things lightly about myself, I allow no one else to make this feature of my countenance a theme for comedy.

DE GUICHE *(Angrily):* Bumpkin! Who are you?

CYRANO: Cyrano de Bergerac!

DE GUICHE: Buffoon! Poet! I have heard of you.

CYRANO: Then draw your sword, sir. As we joust, I will compose a rhyme just for you.

DE GUICHE *(Sneering):* You will never complete it.

RAGUENEAU: With all the ladies and gentlemen and common folk watching from every corner, Cyrano staged the finest performance I had ever seen in that theatre. With every thrust of his sword and line of his poem, he drove de Guiche to exasperation.

CYRANO:

Where shall I skewer you, peacock?
Here in your heart, or under your shawl?
Better for you to have shunned this brawl!
Hear how my steel rings musical!
Mark how my point floats light as foam,
Ready to drive you back to the wall!
Then, as I end the refrain, thrust home!

RAGUENEAU: Cyrano lunged, and de Guiche staggered, dropping his sword. He tumbled backward off the stage, and his friends rescued him and carried him out, sorely wounded and vowing revenge. How the audience cheered! Cyrano had won their admiration. But his comrade in arms, Le Bret, quickly drew him aside.

LE BRET: I am afraid you have made a dangerous enemy, Cyrano.

CYRANO: What do I care? de Guiche is a pompous fool. He insulted me and I gave him only half what he deserved!

LE BRET: He will not forget you, my friend. This wouldn't have happened if you hadn't broken up the play. Why do you hate Montfleury so?

CYRANO: He is a terrible actor, an insult to the theatre. And he dares to smile upon a beautiful lady like a great snail crawling over a rare, sweet flower!

LE BRET: Cyrano! Is it possible that you are in love?

CYRANO (*Reluctantly*): Yes, I am.

LE BRET: With whom? You have never mentioned anyone to me.

CYRANO: Le Bret, look at me. The plainest woman would despise me, with this nose of mine marching on before me by a quarter of an hour. Whom, then, should an ugly creature like me love? Why, only the most beautiful woman in the world. The most wise, most witty, most sensitive.

LE BRET: Your fair and gentle cousin?

CYRANO (*With a sigh*): Yes. Roxane.

LE BRET: Then go and tell her.

CYRANO: Impossible! How much hope have I with this nose?

LE BRET: You have your wit, your courage, your reputation as a swordsman. You must speak to her!

CYRANO: I cannot, Le Bret. She might laugh at me, and that is the one thing in this world I could not bear.

LE BRET: She would never laugh at you. She is too much a lady. . . . Ah! Here comes Ragueneau.

RAGUENEAU: Cyrano, I bring a message from the lady Roxane, your cousin.

CYRANO: What! From Roxane?

RAGUENEAU: Yes. She was in the balcony and witnessed your performance. She wishes to see you privately.

CYRANO *(Astonished):* She wishes to see *me?*

RAGUENEAU: She asks that you name a time and place.

CYRANO *(Overwhelmed):* Le Bret, she wishes to see me! Can you believe it? Where? I . . . I . . . your shop, Ragueneau! Tonight at seven!

RAGUENEAU: An excellent choice, sir. I will tell her at once.

CYRANO *(Excitedly):* Le Bret! She remembers that I exist!

LE BRET: Are you happier now?

CYRANO: Happy! I am a storm—a flame! I have ten hearts!

RAGUENEAU: That evening I welcomed Cyrano to my shop. While he waited for Roxane, I tried to persuade him to taste my succulent roast pheasant, but he wouldn't touch it. He seemed to be in a daze, and just sat down at a table with pen and paper before him.

CYRANO: I will write a letter to Roxane, unsigned, for I dare not speak such words of love to her. The letter I have written to her in my heart a thousand times, torn up, and written again—that is the one I will write now. "My dearest Roxane . . ."

RAGUENEAU: He wrote quickly until Mademoiselle Roxane appeared, whereupon he sprang to his feet and greeted her with a grand sweep of his plumed hat and a low, courtly bow.

CYRANO: Welcome, cousin. I am honored that you think of me.

ROXANE: Dear Cyrano, please sit down. I must know if you are still the same dear companion and friend that you were when we were children, playing by the pond in the garden at Bergerac.

CYRANO: Ah, Bergerac! How I miss it!

ROXANE: Yes. I remember how you used to make swords out of bulrushes.

CYRANO: And you made dolls out of dandelions.

ROXANE: We ate green plums.

CYRANO: And black mulberries.

ROXANE: And you did everything I asked you.

CYRANO: I could never refuse you. Nor can I now.

ROXANE: Then I will dare to tell you that I . . . I love someone!

CYRANO *(Breathlessly):* Yes?

ROXANE: Someone who does not know—at least, not yet.

CYRANO: Ah!

ROXANE: He loves me, too, but he is afraid and never says a word.

CYRANO *(Expectantly):* Yes?

ROXANE: He is a soldier in the Guards, in your regiment.

CYRANO: Yes?

ROXANE: And such a man! So proud!

CYRANO: Ah!

ROXANE: So brave!

CYRANO: Ah!

ROXANE: So handsome!

CYRANO: Ah! *(Suddenly, in dismay)* What? Handsome?

ROXANE: Though we have never spoken, our eyes have met and we both know that we love each other.

CYRANO *(Crushed):* I . . . I see. What is his name?

ROXANE: Christian de Neuvillette.

CYRANO: I don't know him. He must be a new recruit. Roxane, why do you tell me this?

ROXANE: Because he is a new soldier—young and impetuous— and I don't know what I would do if anything happened to him. You, Cyrano, are so brave, so invincible in a fight. I thought, perhaps, you might . . .

CYRANO: Protect him?

ROXANE: Yes! Will you, dear Cyrano, for me? For the sake of our long friendship?

CYRANO *(Hesitating):* I . . . I . . . yes, Roxane. Anything for you.

ROXANE: Will you be his friend, as well?

CYRANO *(After a pause):* I will be his friend.

ROXANE *(Delighted):* You are wonderful! Thank you, dear cousin. I must go now. Farewell.

CYRANO: Farewell. *(After a pause; in despair)* Oh, my Roxane! You will never know what torture you have just inflicted upon me! But my love for you will overcome it somehow.

RAGUENEAU: After Roxane left my shop, and before Cyrano could sufficiently recover, in came the Captain of the Guards, with several cadets from Cyrano's regiment. Le Bret had told them about Cyrano's performance at the theatre, and they had come to cheer him.

CAPTAIN: Here he is. Cyrano, you are a hero!

LE BRET: Cyrano, they want to hear all about it. *(Quietly)* But what is the matter with you? You look pale. Are you in pain?

CYRANO: Only in my heart, Le Bret. No one but you shall know.

1ST CADET: Come, Cyrano, tell us your story!

2ND CADET: Yes. Tell us how you skewered de Guiche! We have new men here who do not know your reputation.

CYRANO: It is simple to tell, my Gascons. After I chased that ridiculous bumbler, Montfleury, from the stage, one foolish spectator dared to stare at—

CHRISTIAN *(Interrupting):* Your nose, monsieur?

RAGUENEAU: From a far corner of the room came that bold remark. The cadets froze in place, unable to believe their ears. Cyrano stiffened, and his eyes flashed fire.

CYRANO *(Tensely):* Who said that?

CHRISTIAN: I did!

RAGUENEAU: A smiling young man, blond and extremely handsome, rose to his feet.

CYRANO *(Thundering):* I would know your name, sir, before you die!

CHRISTIAN: My name is Christian de Neuvillette, sir, and I assure you I am in the best of health.

CYRANO: Draw your sword, Christian de Neuvillette, and prepare to . . . to . . . *(Recognizing the name)* Christian de Neuvillette. Ah! It is you! *(To himself)* It *would* be he! *(Recovering, with difficulty)* Ah! Well! You are new. I will excuse your impertinence, your audacity on that account. *(In a calmer voice)* Now, as I was saying, this knave dared to stare

at me and I drove him from the theatre. Then I faced that
strutting peacock, de Guiche. He swung his sword and I
caught it fair on—

CHRISTIAN: Your nose!

CYRANO (*Roaring*): No more! Out of here, all of you! Leave me
alone with this Christian de Neuvillette!

1ST CADET: Cyrano will chop him into sausage!

2ND CADET: Mincemeat! There'll be nothing left of him!

RAGUENEAU: The cadets tumbled out of my shop and only
Cyrano and the bold recruit remained. To my astonishment,
Cyrano put away his sword and smiled at the young man.

CYRANO: Well, sir, you have courage. That pleases me. And you
are very handsome, which does not please me at all.

CHRISTIAN (*Perplexed*): Sir?

CYRANO: Come, put down your sword. I am Roxane's cousin,
and for her sake, you are spared.

CHRISTIAN (*Startled*): Her cousin! Sir, I am honored to meet
you. Please, forgive my rudeness. I only wished to show my
new comrades that I am not a coward.

CYRANO: A coward would not have spoken to me that way and
lived.

CHRISTIAN: If only I could win Roxane! I am dying of love for
her. Can you help me?

CYRANO (*With a sigh*): You might begin by sending her a love
letter.

CHRISTIAN: Oh, but I am a soldier, not a poet. When I am near
Roxane I am speechless! I could never find the words to speak
what is in my heart.

CYRANO: I have the words. Why not borrow them?

CHRISTIAN: What do you mean?

CYRANO: Take my poetic soul and let it speak to Roxane through
you.

CHRISTIAN: Sir! You would do this for me?

CYRANO: For *her!* And besides, it would be a poet's game.

CHRISTIAN: Very well, let us try the letter.

CYRANO: Here it is. I wrote it to an imaginary lady to amuse myself, but it will serve Roxane beautifully. Take it. It needs only your signature.

CHRISTIAN *(Gratefully):* Monsieur de Bergerac, you are a true and generous friend.

RAGUENEAU: Christian was such a happy young man! How was he to know that Cyrano was hiding his own aching heart behind the beautiful letters and speeches he wrote for Christian to send and speak to Roxane?

ROXANE: Cyrano, Christian is beautiful! Brilliant! He does not talk, he rhapsodizes!

CYRANO: And he writes well?

ROXANE: He is a master. The enchanting things he says are beyond description.

CYRANO *(To himself; sighing):* If only she knew!

RAGUENEAU: Every night for several weeks Christian came to Roxane's house to gaze at her on the balcony and speak to her as Cyrano had rehearsed him. But one night Christian wanted a change.

CHRISTIAN: Cyrano, I have taken my words and letters from you long enough. Now that Roxane loves me truly, I am not afraid to speak for myself.

CYRANO: Very well, if you insist.

CHRISTIAN: She is coming. *(In sudden panic)* Cyrano, don't leave! Step into the shadows so she won't see you.

ROXANE: Christian, I have been waiting for you. Speak to me in the pleasant twilight. No one will disturb us.

CHRISTIAN *(Fumbling):* I . . . I love you, Roxane!

ROXANE: Yes, Christian, speak to me of love.

CHRISTIAN *(Breathlessly):* I love you!

ROXANE *(Gently):* Yes, I know. Now be eloquent.

CHRISTIAN *(Nervously):* I . . . I love you . . . so!

ROXANE: Oh, do not jest with me! You must improvise. Rhapsodize!

CHRISTIAN: I . . . I would be so happy, if . . . if you love me, too.

ROXANE: Christian, tell me *how* you love me.

CHRISTIAN: How? Why . . . very much!

ROXANE *(Disappointed):* Is that all? *(Quickly)* You bore me tonight. Gather your dreams together into lovely words as you have before.

CHRISTIAN: I . . . I . . . I love . . .

ROXANE *(Sharply):* Christian! If that is all you can say, then good night!

CHRISTIAN *(Desperately):* Roxane! Wait, please! I will find the words!

RAGUENEAU: But the lady Roxane went inside and closed the window. Christian was devastated!

CHRISTIAN: Help me, Cyrano! I can't say what she wants to hear, and I shall die unless she loves me.

CYRANO: Very well. I'll stand here underneath the balcony and whisper what you must say to her. Call her.

CHRISTIAN: Thank you, Cyrano! *(Calling)* Roxane! Roxane!

ROXANE: What is it? Oh, you again? Go away! I don't think you love me any more.

CYRANO *(In a whisper):* No, not any more . . .

CHRISTIAN: No, not any more . . .

CYRANO *(In a whisper):* I love you ever more, and more and more.

CHRISTIAN: I love you ever more, and more and more!

ROXANE: Well, that's a little better. But why do you speak so haltingly? Has the evening air given you a cold?

CHRISTIAN: Why . . . yes, yes, I am a bit hoarse.

ROXANE: But still you can speak softly and I will hear you.

CYRANO: Christian, this is too difficult. You step here under that balcony and I will take your place. Give me your hat. I will imitate you with a slight cold. *(Louder)* Dearest Roxane, through the warm summer gloom my words grope in darkness toward the light of you.

ROXANE: But my words, well aimed, find you readily.

CYRANO: My heart is open wide and waits for them. But if you let a hard word fall upon me, you will crush me.

ROXANE: Never!

CYRANO: Night veils us both. You see the darkness of a long cloak in the gloom, and I see the whiteness of your summer gown. You are all light, I am all shadow. Hear that I love you, love beyond reason . . .

RAGUENEAU: Such beautiful words of love Cyrano spoke for Christian! So eloquent, because he was really speaking of his own passionate love for Roxane. Cyrano spoke until Christian climbed up to the balcony and claimed the kiss that Cyrano's words had won for him. Can you imagine the pain and jealousy in Cyrano's heart? Who knows how long he would have remained had not the Count de Guiche suddenly appeared at the gate.

DE GUICHE: Mademoiselle! What is this? Who is that with you?

CHRISTIAN: Sir, I am Christian de Neuvillette!

DE GUICHE: In the uniform of a Guard! Come down at once, you rogue! I'll have you put in irons!

CYRANO: You have no authority here! He is the lady's guest.

DE GUICHE: What! The buffoon de Bergerac! What are you doing here?

CYRANO: I have come to pay a call on my cousin, the lady Roxane. Perhaps Monsieur de Neuvillette and I should ask you why you are here at this late hour?

DE GUICHE *(Outraged):* How dare you question me!

ROXANE: I will answer for him, Cyrano. The Count de Guiche has been a suitor of mine.

CYRANO *(Shocked):* What?

ROXANE: But I never encouraged him, and he must now give way, for Christian is the only man I shall ever love.

DE GUICHE: So, you reject me for this peasant. Well, mademoiselle, say farewell to him! I have been made Colonel of the Guards. Tonight we leave for duty at Arras. *(Harshly)* Christian de Neuvillette, report to your regiment at once!

CHRISTIAN: Sir, I obey. *(Sadly)* Roxane, my love, I must go.

ROXANE: To fight with the Spanish?

DE GUICHE: Yes, to war! And Monsieur de Bergerac goes, too!

Say farewell, mademoiselle, for a long time. Perhaps forever!

ROXANE *(Desperately):* Cyrano, remember your promise to me! Take care of him!

CYRANO: I'll do my best.

ROXANE: Have him write to me faithfully.

CYRANO: I promise you will receive a letter every day.

RAGUENEAU: And so the young lovers were parted, and the company of Guards marched off to the siege of Arras. They fought bravely, but a famine struck and the Spanish proved to be stubborn fighters. The Gascon cadets suffered greatly.

1ST CADET: Who can sleep in this place? The firing never stops.

2ND CADET: There is not a crumb to eat. Not a drop to drink. How long can we survive?

CAPTAIN: Le Bret, where is Cyrano?

LE BRET: There, Captain, just coming in. The fool has been through the Spanish lines again.

CAPTAIN: Cyrano, are you all right?

CYRANO: Of course, Captain. They always miss me.

LE BRET: Why do you risk your life every morning to send a letter?

CYRANO: I promised Roxane that Christian would write every day. Poor lad, he is pale and weak.

CAPTAIN: We are all pale and weak! Starvation is one enemy we had not counted on.

LE BRET: A fine situation! While we besiege Arras, the Spanish besiege us! The men are losing their will to fight.

CAPTAIN: Cyrano, you know how to talk to them. Cheer them up!

CYRANO: Here comes de Guiche. Perhaps we will have a laugh at his expense.

DE GUICHE: Gentlemen, I have just had word that the Spanish will soon mount a major attack on this position.

CAPTAIN: Here! But we are outnumbered. Our supplies are low.

DE GUICHE: Captain, you and your Gascons must hold this position until reinforcements and supplies can reach you. Your orders are to engage the enemy and fight to the last man!

CYRANO: We know our duty, sir, and shall do it. You will be with us, of course!

DE GUICHE: I'm afraid not, Monsieur de Bergerac. I ride to meet the supply train, and leave you and your Gascons to lay down your lives for France.

LE BRET *(Bitterly):* The coward!

CYRANO: So de Guiche has a laugh at *our* expense! Well, my Gascons, tonight we die!

CHRISTIAN *(Miserably):* I'll never see Roxane again! Cyrano, you must send her one last letter—one that has my whole heart in it.

CYRANO: I already wrote a farewell for you, Christian—just in case.

CHRISTIAN: Why must it end like this?

CYRANO: It is nothing to die in battle. *(Reflectively)* But not to see her again is unbearable.

1ST CADET: Ho, Captain! A coach is coming this way!

CAPTAIN: Stand ready! It may be a trick.

RAGUENEAU: But it was no trick. A coach came rolling through the Spanish lines at top speed and stopped in the midst of the cadets. A dusty coachman leaped to the ground and opened the door for . . .

CYRANO: Roxane!

ROXANE: Good evening, gentlemen!

RAGUENEAU: The cadets were astonished to see a beautiful lady in their midst, smiling and calm, as if she hadn't just come through the enemy lines at great risk.

CHRISTIAN: Roxane, how did you get here?

ROXANE: My passport was a smile for every Spanish gentleman who stopped us, and I had only to say that my dearest love awaited me, and they let me pass! I do believe the Spanish are more romantic than the French.

CAPTAIN: Mademoiselle, it is dangerous for you to be here. There will soon be desperate fighting.

ROXANE *(Resolutely):* Captain, I will stay beside my dear Christian, and die with him if I must!

1ST CADET: Here is a brave lady. If only we had some refreshment to offer her.

ROXANE *(Lightly):* Some cold ham and chicken, some bread and fruit and white wine would be very nice.

2ND CADET: Alas, mademoiselle! We have nothing!

ROXANE: Don't be so sure of that. Look in the coach and see what you find. Don't you recognize my coachman?

LE BRET: It is Ragueneau!

1ST CADET: He has brought his cook shop to us!

2ND CADET: Bravo! A feast before we fight!

RAGUENEAU: The starving cadets crowded around the coach and the lady Roxane and I served them the finest repast they had known for days. Only Cyrano and Christian stood on one side, talking seriously to each other.

CYRANO: Christian, I must tell you that I have written to Roxane more often than you think. Every day, in fact.

CHRISTIAN *(Angrily):* Every day! But why?

ROXANE: Cyrano! Christian! Come, have something to eat.

CYRANO: Come, but say nothing to her about the letters.

CHRISTIAN: Roxane, this is so kind and generous of you. But tell me why you came here at such terrible risk.

ROXANE: Because I heard of your hardships and could not bear the thought of your suffering. And because of your letters, dear Christian! Each one was more wonderful than the last. I read them over and over, and each page was like a petal fallen from your soul, sweet and true. I had to come and be with you!

CHRISTIAN: But, Roxane—

ROXANE: Through your beautiful letters I found your true soul, and that is what I love the most.

LE BRET: Mademoiselle, come! The cadets wish to offer you a toast.

ROXANE: I'll only be a moment, Christian.

CHRISTIAN *(Miserably):* Cyrano, did you hear what she said? She doesn't love me any more. She loves you!

CYRANO: No! She doesn't know what she is saying.

CHRISTIAN: She loves only my soul, and my soul is *you!* And you love her! Don't deny it!

CYRANO: Yes . . . I love her. More than life itself!

CHRISTIAN *(Bitterly):* Then tell her, and let her choose between us.

CYRANO: She has already chosen you.

CHRISTIAN: No. I am tired of being my own rival. I want her love for myself, for what *I* am, or not at all. Go—tell her the truth.

RAGUENEAU: Christian walked quickly away from Cyrano who, after a moment of great torment, went to Roxane and drew her aside.

CYRANO: Roxane, Christian has doubts about what you just told him.

ROXANE: Oh, but he must believe me! His soul is so beautiful, that I should love him even if he were not young and handsome, even if he were unattractive . . . or even . . .

CYRANO *(With difficulty):* Or even . . . ugly?

ROXANE: Yes, even then I would love him. In fact, I should love him all the more!

CYRANO *(Brokenly):* Oh, how can I bear this happiness? Roxane, I have something to tell you.

RAGUENEAU: But at that moment the Spanish attacked and the cadets ran to their posts. For the next few terrible moments the roar of cannon fire and the cries of the wounded filled the air over the camp. Then came a lull in the shooting and Le Bret staggered through the smoke from the parapet.

LE BRET: Cyrano!

CYRANO: What is it?

LE BRET: Christian is shot! Mortally wounded.

CYRANO: Christian . . . dying! Then I can never tell Roxane the truth!

RAGUENEAU: Christian was brought down from the parapet and Cyrano was instantly at his side.

CYRANO: Christian, can you hear me?

CHRISTIAN *(Weakly):* Yes.

CYRANO: These words are for you alone. Roxane loves you!

CHRISTIAN: Then I die happy.

CYRANO *(Quietly):* And I die with you, in my heart.

RAGUENEAU: Moments later Christian was dead, with the lady Roxane weeping over his body, and Cyrano beside her.

CYRANO: He cannot hear you now. Come with me, Roxane.

ROXANE: There is a letter in his hand.

CYRANO *(Softly): My* letter.

ROXANE *(Weeping):* His last letter to me. Oh, Cyrano, he was a fine, gentle man, a poet with a heart deeper than we knew, a soul magnificently tender. And now he is gone!

CYRANO *(Softly):* My love mourns for me and does not know.

RAGUENEAU: At that moment a sound of trumpets rang through the noise and smoke over the parapet.

CAPTAIN: Our army comes! If we can hold on a little longer, we can win the battle! Cyrano, lead the charge! We will follow you!

CYRANO: I have two deaths to avenge now—Christian's and my own! Ho, Gascons! Forward!

RAGUENEAU: With Cyrano leading them, the cadets bravely charged the enemy and drove them back. The French were victorious, and that cowardly Count de Guiche never dared to interfere with Cyrano again. After the battle, the lady Roxane went to live in a convent in Paris, and Cyrano visited her faithfully every Saturday over the next fifteen years. Then, one Saturday I went to the convent to take some fresh bread to the lady Roxane, and found her weeping.

ROXANE: You are so kind to come, Ragueneau. Forgive my tears.

RAGUENEAU: My dear lady, why do you weep now?

ROXANE: I have just been reading over Christian's last letter. Our hearts still meet and his love flows all around me when I read it. But I must dry my eyes. Cyrano will come soon and I must be smiling for him.

RAGUENEAU: My poor old friend! He is so lonely and miserable, yet so proud! His poetry has made him many enemies, for he attacks almost everyone with his bitter rhymes.

ROXANE: It is his nature to speak out against injustice, and no one dares harm him. All fear his sword.

RAGUENEAU: Still, I have heard rumors in the streets that he may meet with some accident, and I worry about him.

CYRANO: Roxane!

ROXANE: Cyrano! You are late today. It is already twilight.

CYRANO: I was delayed.

RAGUENEAU: You look pale, my friend. Come, sit down.

CYRANO: I'm all right. I . . . oh-h-h!

ROXANE: Cyrano! What is the matter?

CYRANO: Nothing, nothing. Just my old wound from the battle at Arras.

ROXANE: Ragueneau, there is some wine in the kitchen. Would you bring it, please?

RAGUENEAU: Yes, of course.

ROXANE: Sit here, Cyrano. Will you take off your hat?

CYRANO *(Quickly):* No. There is a chill in the air.

ROXANE: We all have our old wounds. I have mine in this dear letter. It is so hard to read now, so torn and bloodstained.

CYRANO: Christian's letter? Roxane, you promised me that some day you would let me read it.

ROXANE: Yes, I did. Would you like to read it now?

CYRANO: Yes, I would.

ROXANE: The light is very dim.

CYRANO: I can see. *(After a pause)* "Farewell, Roxane, today I die."

ROXANE: It is kind of you to read it aloud.

CYRANO *(With great feeling, but growing gradually weaker):* "My heart is still so heavy with love I have not told. No more shall my eyes drink the sight of you like wine, never more follow the sweet grace of you, and my heart cries out, 'Farewell, my dearest, my own treasure, my love . . .'"

ROXANE: It is so dark. How can you see the words?

CYRANO: "I am never away from you. Even now I shall not leave you."

ROXANE: Cyrano!

CYRANO. "In another world I shall be the one who loves you beyond—"

ROXANE *(Stunned):* You are not reading the words, you *know* them! They are *yours!*

CYRANO *(Faltering):* No . . . no . . .

ROXANE: Now I understand everything. You spoke to me under the balcony, and you wrote the letters, all of them.

CYRANO: Roxane . . .

ROXANE: Why were you silent all these years? Why do you break the silence now?

RAGUENEAU: Cyrano, what recklessness! Le Bret has just come and told me everything!

ROXANE *(Alarmed):* What is it?

LE BRET: Cyrano was struck on the head in the street. A man dropped a heavy log of wood from a rooftop. I left him, unconscious and bleeding, and ran to get a doctor. But when I returned . . .

ROXANE *(Crying):* Cyrano!

CYRANO: I had to come, Roxane. I had to see you.

ROXANE: Your head . . . let me hold it.

CYRANO *(Rousing himself):* I should have been struck down by the sword of a hero, dying with laughter on my lips. What a jest! I was ambushed; my battlefield a gutter, my noble foe a knave with a log of wood!

ROXANE *(Miserably):* Oh, do not die! I love you! You are the only man I have ever really loved!

CYRANO: Roxane, do not mourn the less that good, brave, noble Christian, for he loved you truly. But perhaps the tears you let fall for him may for a little while be tears for me. My dearest love, farewell!

RAGUENEAU: And so my friend died bravely, mourned by his

love and his friends. Today I carry on my business as usual. I cook, I bake, and I tell his story so that it may live on even when I can no longer tell it. Cyrano de Bergerac! Roxane! Christian! There is no sweeter love story ever to be told.

THE END

20,000 Leagues Under the Sea

by Jules Verne

Characters

PROFESSOR PIERRE ARONNAX
CONSEIL, *his servant*
NEWSPAPER REPORTER
NED LAND, *famous harpooner*
CAPTAIN NEMO, *commander of the* Nautilus

ARONNAX: I am Pierre Aronnax, scientist and professor of the
mysteries of the ocean depths at the Paris Museum of Natural
History.
CONSEIL: My name is Conseil. I am servant and assistant to
Monsieur Aronnax.
NED: And I am Ned Land, harpooner, from Canada.
ARONNAX: The year is 1868, and we are among the few men who
have journeyed 20,000 leagues beneath the world's oceans.
CONSEIL: The events leading up to our adventure began two
years ago, when several ships in various seas around the world
sighted a mysterious, spindle-shaped object much larger than
a whale.
NED: It moved faster than any ship, emitted a strange light at
night, and spouted columns of water high into the air.
ARONNAX: This "monster," as it was called, intrigued scientists
throughout the world; but when it attacked two ships, pierc-

ing their iron-plated hulls with a powerful, unknown weapon, it became a threat to human lives. The public demanded that it be destroyed.

NEWSPAPER REPORTER: Monsieur Aronnax, will you tell the press your opinion of the monster?

ARONNAX: I believe it must be a narwhal, or sea unicorn, grown to excessive size. This creature's ivory tusk alone could slice into the hull of a ship.

REPORTER: Did you know, monsieur, that the United States is fitting out a high-speed ship, the *Abraham Lincoln,* to find and destroy the monster?

ARONNAX: Yes—as a matter of fact, I have just received a letter from the Secretary of the American Navy, asking me to join this expedition. Of course, I consider this a personal honor, as well as a great opportunity to represent my country in such a noble enterprise.

CONSEIL: Two hours later we were aboard the *Abraham Lincoln,* bound for the North Pacific, where the monster had last been seen.

ARONNAX: The ship was heavily armed, and among her passengers was a man known as the "Prince of Harpooners," Ned Land.

NED: Professor, how grateful I was for your company while we cruised the Pacific without sighting the monster!

ARONNAX: After four nerve-wracking months, we were about to give up the search when, on the evening of November 5th, we suddenly heard Ned shout.

NED *(Excitedly):* There it is! Look at that light under the water!

CONSEIL: I see it! Look, monsieur! It is coming toward us!

ARONNAX: As we stared in astonishment, the creature came after us at twice our speed! It circled us, rushed at us as if to attack, then stopped short and vanished into the darkness.

CONSEIL: At daybreak we spotted it again and gave chase, but the more we increased our speed, the faster it moved away.

NED: Confound the beast! It plays with us! Well, if we can't catch it, we'll blow it out of the water!

ARONNAX: The ship's cannon was fired twice.

NED *(Astonished):* I can't believe my eyes! The shots merely bounce off the creature into the sea!

CONSEIL: We refused to give up, and this maddening chase continued all day; but that night the monster rested and its brilliant light reappeared below the surface. Our ship stopped its engines and drifted quietly toward it.

NED: My harpoon is ready. We are almost there . . . now!

ARONNAX: Ned's harpoon shot out! We heard a deep, ringing tone as though he had struck a hard surface, and the dazzling light went out. Then two enormous jets of water swept over the ship's deck and carried me into the sea! The next thing I knew I was struggling frantically in the water.

CONSEIL: If you lean on my shoulder, monsieur, you will find it easier to swim.

ARONNAX *(Gasping):* Conseil! Thank goodness you are here. Where is the ship?

CONSEIL: It has drifted away from us, I'm afraid.

ARONNAX: My legs are numb, Conseil. I don't think I can swim much longer.

NED *(Calling):* Professor! Conseil! Over here!

ARONNAX *(Hopefully):* Is that Ned?

CONSEIL: Yes! I see him! He must have been swept overboard, too. Over there, monsieur. Just a little farther. . . .

NED: Give me your hand, and I'll pull you up!

ARONNAX *(Gasping):* You have saved us, Ned! But what is this thing we're standing on? It's hard . . . and smooth. . . . I've never seen anything like it.

NED: It is the creature, Professor, and it's made of iron!

ARONNAX: Iron! Then it is no creature at all, but a submarine!

NED: So I thought, too, but I cannot find an opening.

ARONNAX: Wait! What is that noise? We're . . . we're moving!

CONSEIL: Lie down, monsieur! Hold on to this mooring ring.

NED: As long as this thing moves on the surface, I've no objection. But if it dives, we are lost!

ARONNAX: We must contact whoever is inside. There has to be an opening somewhere.

NED: It's moving faster! If it keeps up this speed, we won't be able to hold on!

CONSEIL *(Frantically):* Monsieur! I believe we are starting to sink!

ARONNAX: Pound on the surface! *(Shouting)* Hello, inside! Stop the ship! Stop the ship!

NED *(Shouting):* Ahoy in there! Stop! Stop, or I'll kick a hole in your side!

ARONNAX: Kick harder, Ned! The water is up to our chins! Stop the ship! Stop the ship!

CONSEIL: It is stopping, monsieur. Look! Someone is opening the hatch.

ARONNAX: A man appeared from inside the ship, uttered a strange cry, then vanished. A few moments later eight strong men with masked faces dragged us down into the ship.

CONSEIL: In total darkness we were roughly pushed along a corridor.

ARONNAX *(Angrily):* See here, gentlemen, what is the meaning of this! We have done nothing! Who are you?

CONSEIL *(Bewildered):* Why don't you speak to us? What is the purpose of those masks you wear? Don't leave us here in this dank darkness!

NED *(Angrily):* What do they mean by this? Where are we? I can't see a thing!

ARONNAX: We seem to be in a small room . . . with iron-plated walls. I can pace off about ten feet . . . and here is a table.

CONSEIL: This silence is deafening! I hear nothing but our voices.

ARONNAX: The door is securely locked, and I can feel no other outlet. My friends, there is nothing for us to do but wait and be patient.

NED: Patient? How can we be patient when we are wet and freezing? And I'm starving! Whom are we dealing with here? Pirates? Cannibals? I thought surely that we would be saved, but now I believe our fates are worse than when we were drifting in the sea.

CONSEIL: Look! They have turned on a light!

ARONNAX: Someone is opening the door!

CONSEIL: A steward entered, laid some clothes and a tray of food on the table, then left without a word, locking the door behind him.

NED: Ah! Dry clothes! At least someone on this vessel is showing some kindness. What kind of meat is this? Filet of shark? Seadog steak?

ARONNAX: Whatever it is, it's delicious. These dishes are made of silver. We must be dealing with civilized people.

NED: What do these "civilized" undersea people intend to do with us?

CONSEIL: They do *not* intend to starve us, Monsieur Land— that's obvious. And those mats on the floor will make a comfortable bed. I think we are better off here than outside on the sea.

NED: Huh! That remains to be seen.

ARONNAX: The next morning our door opened suddenly and a tall, noble-looking man with piercing black eyes and a calm, proud manner appeared in the doorway. His commanding presence in our tiny quarters led us to the inevitable conclusion that this man must be the commander of this fascinating, yet terrifying vessel we found ourselves trapped in.

NEMO *(Brusquely):* So! You are the ones who have caused me and my crew such inconvenience.

ARONNAX *(Calmly):* I assume you are the captain of this vessel.

NEMO: You're very perceptive. I am Captain Nemo, and you are passengers on board my ship, the *Nautilus.* I confined you until I could learn who you are and how you came here. I also needed time to decide how I should deal with you. You have intruded on my existence.

ARONNAX *(Politely):* Without meaning to, sir.

NEMO *(Sharply):* Without meaning to? The *Abraham Lincoln* chased me and attacked me with cannon and harpoon, did it not?

ARONNAX: Sir, you must be unaware of the stir created by your strange craft. The *Abraham Lincoln* was sent to destroy a dangerous sea monster.

NEMO *(Heatedly):* Would it not have pursued and bombarded a submarine vessel as readily as a monster? I have every right to treat you as enemies. I could put you back on the platform of my ship, give the order to dive, and forget you ever existed!

ARONNAX: That would be the act of a savage, not a civilized man.

NEMO *(Thundering):* I am not what you call a civilized man! I have broken completely with society, and I do not obey its rules! I have no use for humanity, and I never will! *(Calmer)* However, I am not without some pity for shipwrecked men. Since fate has brought you here, you shall stay.

ARONNAX: What? Are we to give up all hope of seeing our homes and friends again?

NEMO: Yes! You have stumbled onto the secret of my existence. I can never send you back.

ARONNAX: In other words, we have the choice of life on this vessel, or death.

NED *(Angrily):* You have no right to keep us here against our will!

NEMO: You are angry, but Monsieur Aronnax will not complain that fate has linked his destiny with mine. Monsieur, I have studied your excellent books on the ocean depths. They are incomplete. I have seen and studied everything on the bottom of the sea, and I shall revisit it with you as my student. Our planet will reveal its amazing secrets to us!

ARONNAX: I admit that I am intrigued. If my interest in science can replace my desire for freedom, our association may offer some compensation.

NEMO: I'm glad to hear that. Come, gentlemen. Let us tour the *Nautilus*.

ARONNAX: How do you operate your craft, Captain?

NEMO *(Proudly):* Electricity! It provides our heat and light, and is the very soul of our mechanical equipment. The sea provides all our food, and materials for clothing and tools as well.

ARONNAX: Attached to the ship's hull was a rowboat used for excursions and fishing. The underwater glow we had seen was a huge searchlight, and air was stored in special tanks for use in emergencies. There were special diving suits and portable air tanks for underwater walks, and a formidable steel ram, easily capable of piercing another ship's hull. The *Nautilus* was truly a marvel, able to exist permanently on or under the sea.

NEMO: Tell me, Monsieur Aronnax, what do you think of the *Nautilus?*

ARONNAX: Captain, I am amazed at the scope of your vessel. Your library is certainly impressive—12,000 volumes!—and your museum, with masterpieces of nature, art, and sculpture, is one of the finest I have seen. And this organ is magnificent!

NEMO *(Proudly):* I love my *Nautilus!* She is an indestructible haven of peace. No man, ship or storm can touch her. I am her builder, her captain and her engineer.

ARONNAX: How did you build the *Nautilus* in secret?

NEMO: Its components were sent to me from different parts of the world, and my men and I built it on a small, deserted island.

ARONNAX: May I ask the cost of this undertaking?

NEMO: Five million francs, including the furnishings.

ARONNAX: Five million! You must be very rich, Captain.

NEMO: I am. The sea holds bountiful treasures upon which I draw freely.

ARONNAX: Before you decided to leave society, where. . . .

NEMO *(Harshly):* Enough! I warned you, Professor Aronnax, my life is none of your concern. Don't ever question me again!

ARONNAX: Nemo's outburst convinced me that I should respect his wishes. What a strange man he was! Engineer, scientist, and total mystery, all in one.

CONSEIL: Throughout the next two months, Captain Nemo took us underwater to the sea's most beautiful and unusual displays of plant and animal life. My master and I eagerly studied the magnificent creatures through the ship's glass wall panels. We were excited and amazed, and almost forgot that we were prisoners. Poor Monsieur Land, however, missed his active outdoor life, and was restless and irritable.

NED: Have you found out where we are going, Professor? How much longer will we be forced to stay on this ship?

ARONNAX: I don't know, Ned, but I wouldn't think of escape yet. This ship is a masterpiece of modern technology, and the sights we are seeing cannot be duplicated anywhere else! Let us enjoy the trip and learn as we go.

CONSEIL: On January 18th, the *Nautilus* floated on the surface in stormy waters. We found Captain Nemo on the outside platform looking through a spyglass. He seemed disturbed, and suddenly ordered the vessel to increase her speed. Intrigued by this, Monsieur Aronnax raised his spyglass, but the Captain violently snatched it from his hands.

NEMO: Put that down!

ARONNAX: But, Captain. . . .

NEMO *(Thundering):* I order you to put down that spyglass!

ARONNAX: Captain Nemo's eyes flashed with hate as he stared at a mysterious point on the horizon.

NEMO: Professor, you and your friends must be confined until I grant you your freedom again.

ARONNAX: We were instantly led to the cell where we had spent our first night.

NED *(Angrily):* What have we done to be locked up again?

ARONNAX: Captain Nemo is a man of violent moods. Something has seriously disturbed him, something we must not see or hear.

NED: It makes no sense to me! *(Calming)* But at least there is lunch on our table.

CONSEIL: We ate in silence, the dishes were removed, and then the light went out.

NED: In the dark again! I cannot bear this mystery. *(Yawning)* But, for some reason I feel sleepy . . .

CONSEIL: I, too, am suddenly very tired. My head feels strangely heavy. . . .

ARONNAX: As my two companions dropped into a heavy
slumber, I felt an irresistible drowsiness creeping over me. In
a flash I realized we had been drugged! *(Pauses)* When I
awoke the next morning, Captain Nemo stood before me,
looking tired and upset.

NEMO: You are a physician, are you not, Monsieur Aronnax?

ARONNAX: Yes, I am.

NEMO: Would you be kind enough to attend to one of my men?

ARONNAX: Of course, Captain.

NEMO: There was a collision last night, and he was injured.

ARONNAX: He led me to a cabin where a man with a deep head
wound lay moaning. I examined him carefully.

NEMO *(Worriedly):* What is his condition, Professor?

ARONNAX: I'm sorry—there's nothing I can do. He will die,
probably within two hours.

NEMO: Is there no hope for him?

ARONNAX: I shook my head. Captain Nemo clenched his fists
and then, to my amazement, tears appeared in his eyes. The
next day the dead man was buried in an underwater coral
cemetery.

NEMO: Our companion shall sleep quietly there beyond the reach
of sharks and . . . *(Savagely)* of men!

ARONNAX: How fierce was Nemo's defiance of human society!
The mysterious events surrounding our drugged confinement
and the dead crewman made me re-examine my thoughts. The
Nautilus must have collided with another ship on purpose!
Was the *Nautilus* satisfying Captain Nemo's desire for ven-
geance on the world?

CONSEIL: On January 24th we passed the coast of India.

NED: There are railways and fellow countrymen in India. Don't
you think we should bid Captain Nemo farewell? I long to be
on land again!

ARONNAX: I think it will be a long time before our feet touch
land, Ned. We three know the secrets of the *Nautilus* now,

and I doubt that Captain Nemo will set us free to reveal them to the world.

NED: Then what will happen to us?

ARONNAX: I don't know. I have learned enough on this voyage to write a new book, but I can't publish it unless we escape. However, if our first attempt fails, the Captain will never allow us another chance.

NED: I have it! The next time we cruise on the surface within sight of land, we'll seize the rowboat and try to get away!

ARONNAX: The voyage under the ocean continued. Near Ceylon the Captain and I braved the danger of sharks and dived to the famous pearl fisheries. But in the Mediterranean's well-traveled sea lanes, he kept the *Nautilus* submerged or far from shore.

NED: Can Captain Nemo have guessed we are planning to escape?

ARONNAX: Perhaps. We must be extremely careful.

CONSEIL: Off the coast of Spain, we explored the sunken Spanish treasure galleons that littered the sea floor. This was how Captain Nemo had made himself a billionaire.

ARONNAX: I was the Captain's guest on a thrilling excursion to the great submerged city of Atlantis, and then the *Nautilus* struck a southerly course toward the polar regions.

NED: Confound it! What chance of escape do we have now?

CONSEIL: I can only advise you to be patient until we cruise near land again, my friend.

NED *(Storming):* I do not know how to be patient! I am not a scientist! I cannot sit for hours poring over notes and specimens as you do! I want my freedom! If I do not get off this ship soon I will take desperate measures.

ARONNAX: Wait, Ned! See? We have crossed the Antarctic Circle!

NED: But the great ice shelf is impassable! Captain Nemo may be a superman, but he's not stronger than nature. He'll have to turn back!

CONSEIL: My master went to the Captain.

ARONNAX: I believe we are trapped, Captain Nemo. The *Nautilus* is icebound.

NEMO: Trapped? Not at all. We will continue on to the South Pole!

ARONNAX *(Incredulous):* The South Pole!

NEMO: Yes. We will discover that unknown region together and set foot where man has never been before.

ARONNAX: But how do we proceed?

NEMO: *Under* the ice shelf!

ARONNAX: The *Nautilus* was dug free, then dived to begin its awesome cruise under the ice.

NED *(Bitterly):* We are going to the South Pole, but we'll never come back!

CONSEIL: After three anxious days beneath the ice, we reached open sea again, and Captain Nemo took his bearings by the sun.

NEMO: The South Pole! I, Captain Nemo, take possession!

ARONNAX: Following this momentous conquest we began our return journey under the ice shelf. We had traveled a day when a violent shock suddenly threw us to the floor.

CONSEIL: For the first time we saw an anxious look on Nemo's face.

ARONNAX: What happened, Captain?

NEMO: An accident caused by a trick of nature, Professor. An enormous iceberg has overturned and struck the *Nautilus*. We are caught between the ice shelf and the capsized iceberg.

NED *(Alarmed):* We are trapped! There is scarcely 60 feet of water between the ice and us! What will we do?

NEMO: Gentlemen, unless we free ourselves, we may be crushed between the ice walls, or we may suffocate, since our air tanks have only two days' supply of oxygen. We will dock on the iceberg and attempt to cut through it.

ARONNAX: Soundings revealed that 30 feet of solid ice had to be cut to free the ship.

CONSEIL: The men began at once, using the diving suits and

portable air tanks. After twelve hours, six hundred and fifty cubic yards of ice had been removed.

NEMO: If we can cut as much every twelve hours, it will take four days and five nights to finish the task.

ARONNAX: But we have only two days' supply of fresh air!

NED *(Frantically):* Even if we get out of here, we are still under the ice shelf and cut off from the open sea!

ARONNAX: The situation seemed desperate. The next day the air could no longer be renewed inside the *Nautilus*.

CONSEIL: How can we describe our desperate struggle for air? The tortures of gasping for breath, hour after hour, day after day, cannot be put into words.

NEMO *(Slowly):* Gentlemen, it is the sixth day. We must use the *Nautilus* to break through the remaining ice . . . or we shall die.

CONSEIL: The valves were opened wide and water poured in to increase the weight of the ship.

NED *(Alarmed):* We are sinking!

CONSEIL: The ice is cracking! Do you hear it?

ARONNAX: We are breaking through!

NED: Suddenly the *Nautilus* dropped through the ice like a cannonball! With propeller turning at full speed, she raced northward with her suffocating passengers.

ARONNAX: For what seemed an eternity I lay on my bed, struggling desperately for breath. I could no longer see or hear. My body seemed paralyzed. I felt I would die at any moment.

CONSEIL *(Faintly):* I cannot last, I'm so weak. . . .

ARONNAX: And then, when I thought I would never draw another breath, the *Nautilus* burst through the ice into the open sea!

CONSEIL: The hatches were thrown open and waves of fresh air flooded in to save us! We experienced incredible elation as we breathed in the life-saving oxygen.

ARONNAX: As the *Nautilus* moved north toward the Americas, we realized we had been on board for six months.

NED: We have travelled 17,000 leagues! *(Anxiously)* Professor, before Captain Nemo leads us into another death trap, I want to leave this ship!

ARONNAX: I agree with you, Ned. He has carried this too far. We must seize the first opportunity to escape.

CONSEIL: We passed the West Indies and then cruised near the Bahamas.

ARONNAX: The underwater caves near the Bahamas are often inhabited by giant squids twenty feet long.

CONSEIL: Oh? Are their heads crowned with eight wriggling tentacles that look like a nest of snakes?

ARONNAX: That's correct.

NED: Do they have huge green eyes set near the tops of their ugly heads?

ARONNAX: Exactly.

CONSEIL: And are their mouths like enormous parrots' beaks?

ARONNAX: Precisely. *(Puzzled)* But how do you both know so much about giant squids?

CONSEIL: Monsieur Land and I are looking at some at this moment.

ARONNAX: Why, they're all around us! I count at least seven. What horrible monsters!

NED: Wait! What happened? The propeller has stopped. We are floating, but not moving.

NEMO: Gentlemen, one of the squids has caught our propeller and stopped our progress. We will have to surface and destroy these monsters.

ARONNAX: Destroy them? How?

NEMO: With axes.

NED *(Eagerly):* And my harpoon! I'm ready for some action!

CONSEIL: The bolts had hardly been unscrewed when the hatch shot up and a long tentacle snaked through the opening. It grabbed a crewman and pulled him upward with irresistible force.

ARONNAX: We tried frantically to rescue the man, but he died in the squid's unbreakable grip. How furiously then we attacked those hideous, wriggling creatures!

CONSEIL *(Gasping):* These tentacles seem to grow back as fast as we cut them off!

ARONNAX: This black ink they throw out . . . I can't see!

NED: There are more of them now! They're all over the ship!

NEMO *(Thundering):* Let none of these murderous vermin escape! They are the most despicable monsters in the sea!

ARONNAX: The horrid battle raged on for a quarter of an hour—then finally the mass of squirming arms and formidable jaws gave way. What was left of the mutilated squids vanished beneath the waves.

CONSEIL *(Exhausted):* We have won the battle, but I feel no pride in victory.

NEMO: We can have no pride when the life of one of my crewmen has been lost.

ARONNAX: With that the Captain withdrew to his cabin. As we continued north into the Gulf Stream, neither Captain Nemo nor any of his crew appeared. We were left to ourselves.

CONSEIL: On May 18th we sailed off Long Island, only a few miles from New York Harbor. We were ready to try our escape, but again a storm broke and drove us away from land.

NED: Professor, I am nearing the end of my patience! In a few days we will pass Nova Scotia, not far from my home in Quebec! This would be the perfect time to escape!

ARONNAX: For many days we cruised aimlessly in the Atlantic and saw no sign of the Captain. Then the *Nautilus* drew near the southernmost tip of England. As we surfaced I went outside and noticed a ship outlined against the horizon. Ned and Conseil soon joined me.

NED *(Excitedly):* A ship! Rescue is at hand! Do you see a flag?

CONSEIL: No. I cannot tell her nationality. But look there! It's a warship! She is firing at us!

NED: We must signal to them that we are prisoners. Then they may try to rescue us.

CONSEIL: Monsieur Land was about to wave his handkerchief when he was struck down by a blow from Captain Nemo's iron fist.

NEMO *(Furiously):* You fool! Do you want me to fasten you to the prow of the *Nautilus* before it rams that ship? How dare you try to signal! Go below at once—all of you!

ARONNAX: Are you going to attack that ship, Captain?

NEMO: I am going to sink it!

ARONNAX: But . . . but, you can't do that!

NEMO *(Fiercely):* I shall do so! Do not judge me! We have been attacked and our answer will be terrible!

ARONNAX: Have you no mercy? What of the law?

NEMO: Professor, I am the law here! I am justice! I am the oppressed and the oppressor is in that ship! Through him all that I loved perished: My country, my wife and children, my father and mother. Everything I hate is in that ship! Speak to me no more! Go below!

ARONNAX: We obeyed, but I felt it would be better to sink with the warship than become accomplices to the Captain's vengeance.

COUNSEIL: Is there nothing we can do, monsieur?

ARONNAX: Before they close the hatches we must get out! Hurry!

CONSEIL: It is too late, monsieur! The hatches are closed and we are diving!

NED: We're increasing speed . . . gathering momentum for the attack!

ARONNAX: We were helpless, and speechless with shock as we felt the submarine's powerful steel ram tear through the body of the warship like a sailmaker's needle through canvas.

CONSEIL: We are at the mercy of a madman. There is no hope for us.

ARONNAX: The *Nautilus* left that place of desolation at tremendous speed. I crouched in my cabin, overcome by horror of Captain Nemo. Whatever he had suffered at the hands of men, he had no right to wreak such vengeance and make us witnesses to it!

CONSEIL: The *Nautilus* raced northward, seemingly without control. We saw neither Captain nor crew.

NED: My friends, we must escape tonight!

ARONNAX: If we only could, Ned! But how can we?

NED: I sighted land this morning, about 20 miles off. Captain Nemo seems to have abandoned us . . . it should not be difficult to take the rowboat and reach the coast. We'll meet at ten tonight. If anyone tries to stop us, we'll fight to the death!

ARONNAX: As ten o'clock approached I heard Captain Nemo playing wildly on the organ. He did not see me as I passed behind him, but I was struck by his tragic expression. He suddenly stopped playing and bent his head in his hands. Deep sobs wracked him.

NEMO (*Desperately*): Enough! Enough! I can bear no more!

ARONNAX: I rushed from the room and met Ned and Conseil at the rowboat. We began to unscrew the bolts that held it.

CONSEIL: Monsieur! I hear voices!

NED: If they find us, I'm ready to fight!

ARONNAX (*Urgently*): Listen! They keep repeating something.

CONSEIL: The maelstrom!

ARONNAX: No! It can't be! Surely we will not be dragged into that dreaded whirlpool at the very moment we are escaping!

CONSEIL: The *Nautilus* began to spin at breakneck speed! We were tossed about like a cork as the ship struggled in the fury of wind and water.

NED (*Shouting*): Hold on! Hold on! If we stay with the ship, we may be saved!

CONSEIL: But at that moment the bolts holding the rowboat broke loose and we were hurled into the whirlpool. I lost consciousness.

ARONNAX: When I regained my senses I was lying in a fisherman's hut on one of the Lofoten Islands off the coast of Norway. My two friends were safely beside me. How we escaped the whirlpool, I do not know.

CONSEIL: Did the *Nautilus* survive the maelstrom?

NED: Is Captain Nemo still alive?

ARONNAX: We don't know. But I hope that he and his beloved *Nautilus* escaped, and that someday I will learn his life story and the reason for his underwater isolation. I shall never forget those months aboard the *Nautilus*. How I wish all hatred would leave Captain Nemo's fierce heart, and that the scientist in him will rise up and continue the peaceful exploration of the seas for the benefit of all humanity.

THE END

Frankenstein

by Mary Shelley

Characters

CAPTAIN ROBERT WALTON
LIEUTENANT
DR. VICTOR FRANKENSTEIN
PROFESSOR
HENRY CLERVAL
FATHER
ELIZABETH
MONSTER
MAN
WOMAN
MR. KIRWIN

TO THE DIRECTOR

Generations of motion-picture and television viewers have seen Hollywood's versions of *Frankenstein*, but the popular movie and its offshoots actually differ greatly from the suspenseful, highly dramatic Victorian novel by Mary Shelley. In this script, the original words have been used whenever possible, and the events are also faithful to the book. By performing this adaptation, a new audience will learn the actual story of Frankenstein and may wish to read the book for the full account.

TIME: *Late 1700's.*

WALTON: I write this in the ship's log. One month has passed since my brave crew and I sailed from London on a journey to the North Pole, where man has never set foot. This morning we awoke to find our ship enclosed by ice on all sides. We were trapped! As we paced about considering what we might do, my lieutenant suddenly raised a shout.

LIEUTENANT: Captain Walton! Look over there! Something moving!

WALTON: Are you sure, Lieutenant? Ah, yes! I see it! It's a sled pulled by dogs!

LIEUTENANT: A man is driving it—a very tall man.

WALTON: A giant of a man, I'd say.

LIEUTENANT: He doesn't see us. He's going on past!

WALTON: Where can he be going? There's nothing but water and ice for hundreds of miles.

LIEUTENANT: He's gone! Captain, if you hadn't seen him, too, I'd swear I was dreaming.

WALTON: Scarcely two hours later, my lieutenant called me on deck again.

LIEUTENANT *(Urgently):* Captain, come quickly, sir! Another dogsled has come alongside the ship.

WALTON: I'll come on deck at once.

LIEUTENANT: Look, sir. There's only one dog alive in the traces, and the driver is exhausted. He said he won't leave the sled, but you must persuade him to come on board, sir, or he'll die.

WALTON: You're right. *(Calling)* Come aboard, sir, and let us help you! Can you hear me? Who are you?

FRANKENSTEIN: My name is Frankenstein. Dr. Victor Frankenstein. Captain, I will not board your vessel until you tell me where you are bound.

WALTON: We are on a voyage of discovery toward the North Pole.

FRANKENSTEIN: To the North? Then I will come aboard.

WALTON: Give me your hand. *(After a pause)* You are nearly

frozen, sir. What has brought you to this desolate place all alone?

FRANKENSTEIN: I seek one who flees from me.

LIEUTENANT: Does this person travel on a dogsled?

FRANKENSTEIN *(Eagerly):* Yes! Have you seen him?

WALTON: Yes. We saw him this morning.

FRANKENSTEIN *(Urgently):* Tell me which way he went. I must not lose his trail!

WALTON: Sir, you are exhausted. You have only one dog alive. You must stay with us.

FRANKENSTEIN *(Frantically):* No, no! Nothing must deter me! I must catch him! I . . . I . . .

WALTON: Hold him, Lieutenant! He's fainting.

LIEUTENANT: Here, sir, sit down.

FRANKENSTEIN *(Weakly):* I know you must think me mad. Let me tell you my horrible story. I have suffered great misfortunes and lost everything I ever loved. Now I wait for one event, and then I shall die in peace.

WALTON: Come, sir, you mustn't talk like that!

FRANKENSTEIN: Hear me, Captain, for I cannot die without telling my story. I swear to you that what I say is true.

WALTON: I am ready to hear you.

FRANKENSTEIN: I was born in Geneva, Switzerland, into a distinguished family. I passed a happy childhood, but as I grew older I burned with an insatiable desire to learn the secrets of heaven and earth, the inner spirit of nature, and the mysterious soul of man!

WALTON *(Good-naturedly):* So you aspired to learn chemistry and philosophy.

FRANKENSTEIN: Yes, but if only I had embarked on some other study! When I was seventeen, I went to the university. There I heard the lecture that decided my fatal course in life. My professor of chemistry said:

PROFESSOR: The ancient teachers of chemistry promised impossibilities and performed nothing! Modern masters promise very little, but they penetrate into the hiding places of nature and show how it works. They know how the blood circulates and how we breathe! They have acquired new and almost unlimited powers!

FRANKENSTEIN: Upon hearing those words, my mind was filled with one thought: I, Victor Frankenstein, would explore unknown powers and unfold to the world the deepest mysteries of creation! I read voraciously, attended numerous lectures, and cultivated the acquaintance of men of science. I spent endless hours in the laboratory—all in my great search for the secret of life.

WALTON: The secret of life! A bold search, Dr. Frankenstein!

FRANKENSTEIN: Yes, Captain. Too bold! I went on to study physiology and anatomy. I examined the change from life to death, and from death to life, and after months of incredible labor, I discovered how to bestow animation upon lifeless matter.

WALTON (Astounded): But that's impossible!

FRANKENSTEIN: No, Captain! What had been the study of the wisest men over the ages was within my grasp!

WALTON (Excitedly): If this is true, then you must share this wondrous knowledge with the world!

FRANKENSTEIN: No! Never! Never! Listen to me, Captain, and learn from my dreadful experience how dangerous certain knowledge may be. When I realized what power I held, I dared to put it to the test. I began the creation of a human being!

WALTON (Horrified): What? You didn't!

FRANKENSTEIN: Yes! A human being of gigantic stature—eight feet tall. I pursued my undertaking in secret. Can you conceive the horrors of my toil among graves and slaughter houses where I collected my materials? For nearly two years I worked in a laboratory at the top of my house. And then, one dreary November night, it was nearly finished. With the most painful anxiety I stood by the instruments that would infuse a spark of being into the lifeless human form I had made. And then—it happened

WALTON *(Tensely):* What happened?

FRANKENSTEIN: The dull yellow eye of my creature opened! He breathed! His arms and legs moved! He sat up—his gigantic form towering over me! I had intended that he be handsome, but how horrible he was! His yellow skin scarcely covered the work of muscles and arteries beneath. His hair was a lustrous black, his teeth pearly white, but these were a horrid contrast to his watery eyes, his wrinkled face and straight black lips. I was filled with horror and disgust. A mummy brought to life could not have been as hideous.

WALTON *(Shaken):* Doctor, you are upset. Rest a while before you make yourself ill again.

FRANKENSTEIN *(Agitated):* I cannot rest, Captain. From the moment I gave life to that creature, I have known no rest! I saw his innocent eyes fixed on me and heard the inarticulate sounds he uttered, then I screamed and fled from the room. I would have left town for good had I not met a dear friend in the street. He had come from Geneva to visit me.

CLERVAL *(Warmly):* My dear Victor! How glad I am to see you!

FRANKENSTEIN *(Uneasily):* Henry! What a surprise. What brings you here?

CLERVAL: Your family is worried because they have not heard from you in nearly a year. Elizabeth is especially concerned.

FRANKENSTEIN: I . . . I've been very busy, Henry.

CLERVAL *(Worriedly):* You look ill, Victor. So thin and pale. You cannot have slept in several nights.

FRANKENSTEIN: I have been deeply engaged in an experiment, but now it is over. You could not have come at a better time.

CLERVAL: Then let us go to your house. We have so much to talk about.

FRANKENSTEIN *(Quickly; panicky):* No, Henry, not my house. Not tonight! He might be there! *(Frightened)* I can't look at him again! I can't! I can't! I can't!

CLERVAL (*Alarmed*): Victor! What's the matter? Are you ill?

FRANKENSTEIN: I fainted, and then I fell into a nervous fever that confined me to bed for several months. Henry was my constant companion. How good a friend he was! And yet while my body recovered, my mind retained the horror of the Monster I had made. It had disappeared. I wondered what had happened to it and if I would ever see it again.

CLERVAL: Victor, you must come home with me now. Your family will welcome you, and I believe a change will do you good.

FRANKENSTEIN: Henry was right. I could no longer endure the sight of my instruments and books. He arranged for our journey home, but on the day we were to leave, I received a shocking letter from my father.

CLERVAL: My dear friend, what has happened?

FRANKENSTEIN (*Brokenly*): My little brother . . . William! He's dead! Murdered!

CLERVAL (*Horrified*): No! That cannot be!

FRANKENSTEIN: Yes. He was strangled . . . in a wood near our house.

CLERVAL: That dear child! Who could have done such a brutal thing? My poor friend, what consolation can I offer?

FRANKENSTEIN: No one could console me. I returned home to my grieving father and stepsister, Elizabeth. Then one day I went to the lonely wood where my dear little brother had died. I knelt down and wept, but suddenly, I felt I was not alone. I sprang up, and saw before me the hideous towering form of the demon I had made!

WALTON: What? He was there in Geneva?

FRANKENSTEIN: Yes, Captain, after all those months! I shrank back at the sight of him! And then a horrible thought struck me. Had *he* murdered my brother? I stood frozen with anguish. No one else could have murdered that beautiful, innocent child! Suddenly the Monster moved closer, stretching out his great arms to me, and then, to my eternal amazement, he spoke to me.

MONSTER: Frankenstein! My creator!

FRANKENSTEIN: Devil! How dare you approach me!

MONSTER: So you also hate me, even as all men I have encountered hate and despise me.

FRANKENSTEIN (*Savagely*): Yes. If only I could, by ending your miserable existence, restore my brother whom you have so diabolically murdered!

MONSTER: I meant to be his friend, but he cruelly rejected me! I acted out of the deepest anger!

FRANKENSTEIN (*Enraged*): Fiend! Monster! How I wish that I had never given you life!

MONSTER: But you did! Why did you hate and reject me? My soul burned with love, yet you deserted me! (*Miserably*) For all these many months I have wandered alone. I have sought human company, and observed men and women, learning to copy their ways, and to imitate their speech. Yet wherever I go, women and children scream in terror at the sight of me, and all men seek to destroy me.

FRANKENSTEIN: His words had a strange effect on me. What had I done in deserting him? He had been like a child, left alone to fend for himself in a world that could never accept him. What terrible loneliness and pain he must have suffered!

MONSTER: I have sworn eternal revenge upon you for my suffering! You can save your life, though, by granting my most urgent request.

FRANKENSTEIN: What do you dare ask of me?

MONSTER: You must make a companion for me! A female formed as I am, that I may never be lonely again.

FRANKENSTEIN (*Furiously*): What? Create another like you to join you in your fiendish wickedness? Never!

MONSTER: Listen to me! Give me a companion and my frustrations and anger will vanish in the sympathy and care of my companion. We shall live peacefully and harm no one. Frankenstein, you cannot refuse me!

FRANKENSTEIN: Perhaps I have no right to withhold from you the small portion of happiness that is in my power to bestow. I consent to your demand, on your solemn oath to leave the habitations of man forever!

MONSTER: Once I have my companion, I swear that no man shall ever see us again. Begin your labor at once! I shall watch your progress with great anxiety, and I shall follow you wherever you go—remember that! When you have finished, I shall appear to you again.

FRANKENSTEIN: He left me, and I went home with slow and heavy steps. My agony was unbearable, but what could I do? My brother was dead. I feared for the safety of my loved ones. My only choice was to do as the Monster said. I prepared to leave home and return to my laboratory. My father was terribly concerned about my state of mind.

FATHER: My son, perhaps I can suggest something to soothe and calm you. I have always looked forward to your marriage to Elizabeth. She has been like your loving sister since childhood, and yet she is not your kin by blood. She loves you dearly. Perhaps now is the time for your marriage, that you may comfort each other and find a new life together.

FRANKENSTEIN: Father, I love Elizabeth with all my heart, but there is something I must do before we can be married. I must study and work in England for a few months, but I promise you, Elizabeth and I shall be married upon my return.

FATHER: Very well, Victor. Travel and restore your spirits. Take Henry Clerval as your companion. It will ease my mind to know you are not alone.

FRANKENSTEIN: And so I bade Elizabeth farewell.

ELIZABETH: Hurry home again, Victor. While you are gone, take comfort in Henry's companionship, and think often of me.

FRANKENSTEIN: You shall always be in my thoughts, Elizabeth. I cannot explain to you the work I must do, but trust me, I cannot leave it undone. Take care of my father while I am gone.

ELIZABETH: Yes, Victor, I will. Write often, for you cannot imagine how lonely it will be here without you.

FRANKENSTEIN: And so Henry and I departed for England. For

a few weeks we traveled about that lovely country, and then to Scotland. But my torment soon drove me to a parting with my friend.

CLERVAL: Why do you wish to go on alone, Victor?

FRANKENSTEIN: The work I have to do would only bore you, Henry. I'll join you again in a month or two.

CLERVAL: As you wish, Victor. But write to me, or I shall become worried and come searching for you.

FRANKENSTEIN: I left Henry in a bustling sea town and went on alone to one of the remote Orkney Islands. There, in a wretched hut, with only a few poverty-stricken neighbors, I began my dreadful work. I toiled day and night with enthusiastic frenzy that blinded me to the horror of my task. But dreadful thoughts plagued me. What if this female creature should be as wicked as her mate? What if she chose not to isolate herself? What if they had children who might spread over the earth and terrorize man for ages to come? Had I the right to inflict this curse upon unborn generations? I trembled! My heart seemed to fail me! And then I looked up and saw the Monster in the window, a ghastly grin wrinkling his lips!

MONSTER: I have come to claim my bride, Frankenstein! Give her to me!

FRANKENSTEIN: No! No! I can never bring to life another like you!

MONSTER: Stop! Don't! What are you doing? Stop!

FRANKENSTEIN: In a passionate rage, I tore the female creature to pieces, and the Monster howled in despair.

MONSTER: Frankenstein, do you dare break your promise, destroy my hopes?

FRANKENSTEIN: Yes! I dare!

MONSTER: I have the power to make your life wretched beyond imagination! You are my creator, but I am your master! Do as I command you!

FRANKENSTEIN: No! I defy you!

MONSTER: I shall never allow you to be happy while I suffer!

Beware of my revenge, Frankenstein! Your hours from this night on shall pass in dread and misery. I leave you now, but I shall be with you on your wedding night!

FRANKENSTEIN: I sprang at him, but he eluded me and fled from the hut. I saw him leap into a boat and head for the mainland. Frantically, I threw the remains of the female form into a large basket, along with several heavy stones. This I placed aboard my small boat and then sailed out about four miles from shore. When the moon was briefly covered by a cloud, I cast the basket into the sea and watched it sink from sight. Then I fell into an exhausted sleep. I don't know how long I slept, but when I awoke, the sun was high and I was drifting near a village on the mainland. When I landed, an angry crowd of people came to meet me, and one man, who seemed in authority, spoke harshly to me.

MAN: Sir, you will follow me at once to Mr. Kirwin's to give an account of yourself.

FRANKENSTEIN (Puzzled): Why am I to give an account of myself? Who is Mr. Kirwin?

MAN: A magistrate. You will tell him what you know about the murder of a young man here last night.

FRANKENSTEIN: I know nothing. I was not here last night.

MAN: We'll see about that. Come this way!

FRANKENSTEIN: I was brought to hear the testimony of several witnesses.

MAN: I found the body, Mr. Kirwin. He was a handsome young fellow, and he had been brutally strangled.

WOMAN: Terrible!

KIRWIN: Tell me, my good woman, have you seen this man before?

WOMAN: Oh, yes, Mr. Kirwin. He was drifting in his boat, just off the shore where they found the poor lad dead.

KIRWIN: Come into the next room, sir, and view the corpse.

FRANKENSTEIN: Very well, if you insist. (After a pause; grief-stricken) It's Henry! My dearest friend! He has been destroyed too by my ghastly mistake. (Moans)

KIRWIN: He's fainted. Come, take him into the cell.

FRANKENSTEIN: I knew nothing more until I awoke in prison, with Mr. Kirwin standing over me.

KIRWIN: Are you better now?

FRANKENSTEIN (Weakly): I believe I am. How long have I been here?

KIRWIN: Two months. Ill of a fever and near death many a time.

FRANKENSTEIN: I wish I were dead! I am the most miserable of men!

KIRWIN: I hope you can soon procure evidence to free yourself from the criminal charge placed against you.

FRANKENSTEIN: You are kind to say so, but tortured and persecuted as I am, how can I fear death?

KIRWIN: I know how you have suffered, being seized and charged with murder. And then the tragic sight of your friend, murdered in so unaccountable a manner and placed, as if by some fiend, across your path.

FRANKENSTEIN (Perplexed): How do you know all this?

KIRWIN: I examined the papers you carried with you that night. I found a letter to your father, and I wrote to Geneva.

FRANKENSTEIN: Good heavens! What new scene of death has been acted? Whose murder am I to lament now?

KIRWIN: Be calm, sir. Your family is perfectly well, and your father has come to see you.

FRANKENSTEIN: My father! Let him come to me!

KIRWIN: He is here.

FATHER: Victor! My son!

FRANKENSTEIN (Joyfully): Father, you are safe! And Elizabeth?

FATHER: Safe and well. My poor child! My son! You traveled to seek happiness, but a fatality seems to pursue you.

FRANKENSTEIN: Father, a horrible destiny hangs over me, and though I have prayed for death, I know now that I must live to fulfill that destiny.

FATHER: Do not talk so! Only get well, Victor. You will be cleared of this charge and I will take you home.

FRANKENSTEIN: In another month witnesses testified that I had been on Orkney Island at the hour Henry Clerval's body was found. I was freed from prison. But the cup of life was poisoned for me. I saw nothing but a frightful darkness through which two watery, clouded eyes glared fiercely at me!

WALTON: Did you return to Geneva with your father?

FRANKENSTEIN: Yes, I went home to my beloved Elizabeth. I longed to be happy with her, but I could not forget the creature's threat.

MONSTER (Ominously): I shall be with you on your wedding night!

FRANKENSTEIN: Such was my sentence! The Monster meant to destroy me, but if I should defeat him, then I might yet find happiness with my dear Elizabeth. I knew I could not delay my destiny any longer. Elizabeth and I were married, and after the marriage ceremony, my bride and I traveled to a country inn. I took every precaution to defend myself in case the Monster attacked me, but as night fell with a raging storm, a thousand fears arose in my mind. Every sound terrified me, yet, I resolved that I would not shrink from the conflict I knew was soon to come. Try as I might, I could not hide my agitation from Elizabeth.

ELIZABETH (Worried): What is it that upsets you, my dear Victor? What is it you fear?

FRANKENSTEIN: Don't worry, my love. After tonight all will be safe. Go on upstairs. I will check through the house once more, and then I will join you.

ELIZABETH: As you wish. I love you so much, I cannot bear to see you so worn and anxious.

FRANKENSTEIN: I kissed her, and she left me. I searched every passage and corner of the inn, but discovered no trace of the Monster. I was beginning to think that some fortunate chance had prevented his coming, when I heard a shrill, piercing scream! In an instant the horrible truth rushed into my mind! Elizabeth screamed again. I dashed to our room, and flung myself through the door—but too late! (Sobbing) Elizabeth!

My beloved Elizabeth lay lifeless on the bed. And in the window, the hideous fiend stood grinning!

MONSTER: My revenge is complete, Frankenstein! Now you are as miserable as I!

FRANKENSTEIN: I drew my pistol and leaped at him, firing a shot. But he sprang to the ground and was lost in the darkness. My grief and rage were uncontrollable. I was determined to destroy him, or die! I have followed his trail for many months, Captain. He has cunningly lured me on, leaving his tracks for me to follow, and his messages carved in trees, on rocks and ice—all to rekindle my fury!

MONSTER: Follow me, Frankenstein! I seek the everlasting ice of the North, where you will feel the misery of cold and frost. But you have made me immune to these discomforts. Only you shall suffer in this place! Come, my enemy! Follow me!

FRANKENSTEIN: If my dogs had lived, I might have caught him. We might have had our final combat—but it is not to be. Captain Walton, I have told you all. *(Groans)* In a fit of ambitious madness I made this creature, but I forsook him because my duties toward my fellow man had greater importance. In response this demon destroyed my family and friends, and I know not when his thirst for vengeance will end. He *must* be destroyed!

WALTON: Doctor, speak no more. You will do yourself great harm.

FRANKENSTEIN: My body has failed me, Captain. I shall not see another sunrise. You must swear to me that if the Monster appears here after my death, you will thrust your sword into his heart! *(Urgently)* Swear to me!

WALTON *(Alarmed):* Doctor Frankenstein! Lieutenant, he's fainted again.

LIEUTENANT: Shall I bring the surgeon, sir?

WALTON: I'm afraid it's too late. The poor man has breathed his last. May his tortured soul find peace.

LIEUTENANT *(Suddenly):* Captain . . . there is someone in the passage.

WALTON: Bar the door. Let this man rest undisturbed.

MONSTER *(Howling):* Frankenstein!

LIEUTENANT: Captain, it's the Monster!

WALTON: Stand firm, Lieutenant! We have swords, and he is unarmed.

LIEUTENANT *(In awe):* But look at the size of him! His face! *(Terrified)* This is a nightmare!

WALTON: Steady, Lieutenant! *(Calling)* Creature! What do you want?

MONSTER: Do not try to keep me from my master! *(Miserably)* Frankenstein! Frankenstein! *(Weeping)* I have destroyed you by destroying everything you loved. I would beg your forgiveness, but now you cannot answer me! In destroying your hopes, I did not satisfy my greatest desire for love. I am still alone and utterly miserable!

WALTON *(Angrily):* Wretch! If he still lived, he would yet be the object of your vengeance! Your evil must be stopped!

MONSTER: Stay your hand! This very night I shall die by my own hand. Farewell, Frankenstein! My misery was greater than yours, but soon my pain will be ended on the funeral pyre I shall light around my hideous form. Farewell!

LIEUTENANT *(Shaken):* This was no nightmare. Captain, have we seen the last of him?

WALTON: I believe so. Without his creator, he has nothing to live for. Frankenstein was a man of genius, but he suffered greatly because of it. When we return to England, I shall share this incredible story with whoever desires to hear it. I shall never forget Frankenstein—or the sight of his creation, the lonely, haunted Monster.

THE END